E N C O U N T E R I N G

GOD

ENCOUNTERING

GOD

A Spiritual Journey from Bozeman to Banaras

Diana L. Eck

BEACON PRESS / BOSTON

BEACON PRESS
Boston, Massachusetts
www.beacon.org

Beacon Press books are published under the auspices of
the Unitarian Universalist Association of Congregations.

20 19 18 17 16   15 14 13 12 11 10

This book is printed on acid-free paper that meets the uncoated
paper ANSI/NISO specifications for permanence as revised in 1992.

Text design by David Bullen
Composition by Wilsted & Taylor

Library of Congress Cataloging-in-Publication Data
Eck, Diana L.
Encountering God : a spiritual journey from
Bozeman to Banaras / Diana L. Eck.
p. cm.
Originally published: Boston : Beacon Press, c1993. With new pref.
Includes bibliographical references and index.
ISBN 978-0-8070-7301-8 (alk. paper)
1. Christianity and other religions. 2. Eck, Diana L. I. Title.
BR127.E25 2003
291.1'72—dc21
2002036114

This book is dedicated to my mother, Dorothy Eck,
and to the memory
of my father, Hugo Eck,
and my brother, Laurence Eck

Contents

Preface 2003

In the ten years since the publication of *Encountering God* in 1993, issues of religious difference have been front-page news all over the world. People of every religious tradition have exhibited the wares of religious chauvinism and violence, using religious language and symbolism to stake out political territory. Others in those same traditions have opposed the belligerence of their co-religionists and have put the energies of their faith to the transformative work of bridge-building and peace-making.

In the past decade we have also begun to talk about "globalization"—the transnational currents of a shrinking world. With all its positive and negative connotations, globalization has opened our eyes to the ways in which our economies, our political boundaries, our communication systems, and our conflicts are inextricably linked. The recognition of our deep interdependence should go hand in hand with globalization. Often, however, it does not, and globalization then leads to what is effectively a new regime of colonial domination. The expansion of terrorism and the attacks of September 11, 2001, make clear the vulnerability, even of the powerful, in a world in which boundaries are dotted lines, at most.

Religious communities are participants in the globalization of world systems. Even as ethnic, cultural, and religious "identity" movements resist the homogenizing powers of globalization, they employ its systems of communications and technology. At one end of the spectrum, our global systems create channels of interfaith dialogue across cultures and religions; they create networks of environmental activists and new coalitions of religious leaders. At the other extreme, these same systems distribute the energies of a new tribalism and religious extremism. Are we now at the beginning of an era that will see the bridging of civilizations, indeed a creative dialogue of civilizations? Or will the decades ahead be marked by rigid and rivalrous adherence to religious, cultural, and national identities? The future of the "blue planet" so poignantly visible from space depends very much on the choices we make as all of us envision the future. Developing a refined awareness of our interdependence is a challenging intellectual and spiritual task. The critical question is whether "we" humans can come to understand and perhaps even appreciate our religious differences, while recognizing that we are deeply related and dependent upon one another for our survival.

Broad demographic changes are also part of our new global reality. Massive movements of refugees and economic migrants have created a new geo-religious and geo-cultural reality. In the United States, the trends in immigration since 1965 have brought the religious traditions of the world to our doorstep and have made American religious life more complex. Newcomers have brought with them not only their luggage and economic aspirations, but their Qur'ans and Bhagavad Gitas, their images of Krishna, the Bodhisattva Kuan Yin, and the Virgin of Guadalupe. Some come fleeing religious fanaticism and cherish the freedom not to be religious at all. In short, the world of "east is east and west is west" has been superceded by a new demographic reality. It is precisely the interpenetration and proximity of great civilizations and cultures—east and west, north and south—that will be the hallmark of the twenty-first century. Each part of the world is marbled with the colors and currents of the whole. We are majorities here or minorities there, but we live and worship in each other's presence.

My own work, in the course of this past decade, has taken me on a return journey from India to America, from Banaras back to Boston, investigating with my students and colleagues the dimensions and challenges of these profound changes in America's religious landscape. The Pluralism Project (www.pluralism.org), which I launched in 1991, has produced an educational multimedia CD-ROM, *On Common Ground: World Religions in America,* and I have written another book, *A New Religious America: How a "Christian Country" Has Become the World's Most Religiously Diverse Nation.* That book explores the question of religious difference in the context of America's civic life.

Encountering God deals more with religious difference in a theological perspective, bearing in mind that our theological questions are not quite the same as our civic questions. Our civic question is how "we" as citizens can build creative multireligious societies in which our differences can increasingly become the very source of our strength and creativity. Our theological question is how "we" as Christians or Jews or Muslims will think about our own faith anew in relation to the faith of our neighbors. It is true, however, that our increasing engagement with one another in civil society may well provide the context for new and transformative theological thinking.

When *Encountering God* was first published, the Parliament of the World's Religions was convening in Chicago. It was a centennial observance of the 1893 World's Parliament of Religions, which I discuss in Chapter 2. By 1993, a gathering of religious leaders from around the world was not so extraordinary. But what *was* extraordinary was the public display of America's own religious diversity. In 1893, thousands of invitations were sent out by the Chicago coordinating committee, which was largely Protestant Christian. By 1993, the tables were turned and the guests were now the hosts. Chicago's religious communities formed fourteen host-committees to invite and sponsor their co-religionists. The Hindu host-committee included planners from two enormous new Chicago temples. The Buddhist Council of the Midwest brought together Asian-American Buddhists from across the spectrum of Asia—immigrants from Thailand, Cambodia, Vietnam, and Korea—as well as first-generation Euro-American Buddhists. The Muslim community of greater Chicago included dozens of mosques and nearly half a million Muslims. Jain participants had built a new temple in Bartlett, Sikhs had constructed a modern *gurdwara* in Palatine, and Zoroastrians had a new center in Hinsdale—all in suburban Chicago.

How will we understand and interpret one another as people of faith, living virtually next door, working together in the workplace, sending our children to the same school, involved in the concerns of the same neighborhood? Equally important, how will we understand *ourselves* as people of faith in a world in which it is simply impossible to deny the vibrancy of communities of faith different from our own? Here in America, our encounter with one another is no longer through ideas, texts, and media representation alone, but through the immediacy of coffee-shop conversations, dorm-room discussions, and civic coalitions against homelessness. Our fears and suspicions are no longer abstract either. People of every faith experience the erosion of trust in their neighbors with each volley of religious violence and with each incident of racial or religious prejudice.

The questions raised in this book are likely to be with us for some time, as people of different religious traditions struggle to achieve a respectful and appreciative understanding of one another. What is it about religious difference that causes so much trouble? Must our differences be so divisive, or can they be steered toward creative relationships, rather than competitive rivalries? Can our encounter with people of other faiths enrich our understanding and experience of the one we call "God"?

As we respond to these questions, our religious traditions require the energies of a new reformation and transformation. Rabbi Jonathan Sacks of Britain speaks of the need to appropriate "the dignity of difference" in a world of many faiths.[*] The Iranian Muslim philosopher Abdolkarim Soroush wants to distinguish between an Islam overly concerned with "identity," guarding borders and boundaries, and an Islam that flourishes amid plurality in a climate of freedom and democracy.[†] The South African Muslim Farid Esack finds his commitment as a "witness bearer for Allah in an unjust world" strengthened by his work alongside Christians in the struggle for justice.[‡] Feminist thinkers such as Fatima Mernissi, Judith Plaskow, and Rosemary Ruether continue to push their own religious traditions to a deeper analysis of gender difference and its relation to the wider questions of religious difference.

As a Christian, I can attest to the yearning for new theological thinking that moves beyond the patrolling of our Christian borders. In the past decade, I have received countless letters from Christians who have suffered under the theological abuse of fundamentalism and have left the church behind. And I have heard from dozens of church groups using *Encountering God* as a text for weeks of honest and searching discussion. It is clear that many people are ready to look afresh at those few biblical verses that, for too long, have led Christians to a simple, unreflective belief that people of other faiths are outside the saving

---

[*] Jonathan Sacks, *The Dignity of Difference: How to Avoid the Clash of Civilizations* (London: Continuum, 2002).

[†] Abdolkarim Soroush, *Reason, Freedom, and Democracy in Islam* (Oxford: Oxford University Press, 2000).

[‡] Farid Esack, *On Being a Muslim: Finding a Religious Path in the World Today* (Oxford: One World, 1999).

grace of God: "I am the way, the truth, and the life. No one comes to the Father but through me" (John 14.6) and "There is salvation in no one else, for there is no other name under heaven given among men by which we may be saved" (Acts 4.12). Do such verses really give us self-evident, adequate guidance for thinking about the faith of our neighbors? I don't think so, and for ten years now I have heard from Christians who are grateful to read these passages in a new light and to look again at Jesus' insistent love for both neighbors and strangers in the gospels. Christian faith is not premised on diminishing or dismissing the faith of our neighbors. We, too, yearn to claim the "dignity of difference."

The past decade has seen the flowering of a grassroots interfaith movement in the United States, as people of many faiths come together in their own communities. In Columbia, South Carolina, Partners in Dialogue brings people of different faiths together to talk about common life experiences. The Mall of America Religious Council in Minnesota provides a space for interreligious learning in America's largest retail mall. On Thanksgiving Eve in 2000, Christian and Muslim communities in Milwaukee came together in a covenant service, pledging to know one another better as people of faith. While there was a wave of hate crimes targeting Muslims and Sikhs in the aftermath of the September 11, 2001, catastrophe, there was a far stronger surge of interfaith outreach and cooperation. As the Pluralism Project documented the range of responses, it became clear that each hate crime generated its own counter-force of determined outreach, reconciliation, and repair. Following an attack on a mosque in Toledo, for example, two thousand people circled the mosque, holding hands in a ring of protection and prayer. Following the shooting death of a turbaned Sikh in Mesa, Arizona, thousands came to the civic center to express their sorrow and support his family. Many new interfaith initiatives sprung up during the months following September 11, 2001, including one in my hometown, in Bozeman, Montana.

Such initiatives, of course, will often meet resistance, especially as we move toward a Christian reformation in our relations with people of other faiths. Bozeman's Christian clergy association was divided as it wrestled with the question of whether to join with representatives of local Jewish, Muslim, Baha'i, Buddhist, and Unitarian communities. The interfaith coalition that emerged left behind an opposition group of Christian clergy. Across the country, one need only tune in to certain Christian television and radio programs to hear the ada-

mant views of those for whom relationship with people of other faiths is seen as
a dangerous betrayal of the Gospel.

Both the hopeful new reality of interfaith efforts and the resistance to them
became a national story in the United States in the weeks following September
11, 2001. Many of the large public memorial services were interfaith services and
none attracted as much national attention as the service in New York's Yankee
Stadium for the families of September 11 victims. Catholic, Protestant, Jewish,
Muslim, Sikh, and Hindu representatives offered prayers from their respective
traditions. In a world of religious strife, the event displayed the hopeful possibility of harmony, but the conservative Missouri Synod Lutheran Church did not
see it that way. It suspended the leader of its Atlantic district for participating in
the service and demanded that he apologize "to the Lord and to all Christians"
for praying on the same platform with "pagans." In their view, the event wrongly
signaled that all religions pray to the same God and put Christians on an equal
footing with people of other faiths.

This incident is instructive, for it gives us a sense of the intense feeling and the
deep theological confusion that "encountering God" in the prayers, presence,
and faith of the "other" might precipitate. Especially among exclusivist Christians there has been an unprecedented tantrum of theological pronouncements.
Prominent Southern Baptist clergy have asserted that the God Muslims worship
is not the same God known to Christians and Jews. A leader of the denomination
insisted that "Allah is not God," although he later said he had no time to learn
anything about Islam. A prominent cabinet officer and member of the Assemblies of God church insisted that "Islam is a religion where you send your son to
die for God, but Christianity is a faith where God sends his son to die for you."
There are many things Christians should find disturbing about such statements,
and I know they leave many a Christian longing for a deeper and more helpful
understanding of God in a world of many faiths. Although our religious neighbors are closer than ever before, our sheer ignorance of one another is all too evident. Allah is, after all, the Arabic word for God, and it is the same term Arab
Christians use in their prayers and praises.

In February of 2000, I participated in large conference organized by the biblical scholar Marcus Borg on "God at 2000." The Muslim theologian and historian of science Seyyed Hossein Nasr reminded us, "All that we can say of God is
nothing compared to what we cannot say." Rabbi Harold Kushner said, "Building our faith on questions, rather than answers, increases the likelihood of won-

derment in the face of God." I began my own reflections saying that the one we Christians call "God" is not "ours" but transcends our imagining and is more mysterious than everything we think we mean. Every religious tradition evokes the mystery in one way or another. Those of us who are Christians speak of the complexity of God as Creator, as Christ, and as Holy Spirit. Jews do not write out the word God, the Holy One, the "I am" who spoke to Moses in a burning bush. Muslims do not image God in any human form, indeed in any form at all, and Hindus speak of 330 million gods, which amounts to the same thing. The sage of Ecclesiastes suggests the irony of our dilemma when he writes, "God has put eternity into our minds—but so that we cannot find out what God has done from the beginning to the end" (3.11).

Yet each of our religious traditions has its dogmatic and dissonant voices that proclaim angry and possessive ideas of God. Some such folks in the Christian camp were picketing the "God at 2000" conference, Bibles in one hand and placards of protest in the other. They condemned us all in the name of Jesus Christ, with expansive, nearly exhaustive lists of who would meet the fires of God's wrath: "Warning! Buddhists, Hindus, Psychologists, Fornicators, Hare Krishnas, Liars, Catholics, Gays, Lesbians, Mormons, Muslims, Liberals, Unsubmissive Wives! God's Judgement!"

To see God as our special ally in judgment is a dangerous move. It is too easy to call such a God into the service of our own projects. Our possessive ideas of God may become graven images of ourselves as we raise the sacred canopy of our religion over the most self-serving of worldviews. Extremist Christians read God's apocalyptic confrontation with evil into the latest world events, Muslim suicide bombers trigger their bombs crying "God is Great," Jewish settlers patrol their God-given territory with rifles, and Hindu nationalists salute a muscular Lord Rama drawing back his bow against the enemy. But do we really believe the God of all creation sides with us in war and helps us win? That God gives land and prosperity to our tribe alone? That God blesses America above all others? Can we continue to cling to ideas of God that are essentially provincial, imagining, even now in the twenty-first century, that God is primarily, if not exclusively, concerned with us and our tribe? I can sing "Give me that old-time religion! It's good enough for me!" with as much gusto as anyone. But I know that the old-time religion will only be "good enough" if we are able to grapple honestly and faithfully with the new questions and challenges that come of living in the multi-religious world of today.

The Buddhist poet and philosopher Thich Nhat Hanh once wrote, "Discussing God is not the best use of our energy." * Given our tendency to stake out the mystery for ourselves, we can readily see his point. For the most part, Buddhists do not use the language of "God" at all, but speak only of the "far shore," the Reality which we cannot grasp, but to which we may awaken. The Dalai Lama, certainly one of the great religious leaders of our time, speaks powerfully to the deepest spiritual challenges confronting our world today without employing the word "God" at all. But as long as those of us in theistic traditions continue to speak about God in personal terms, as I do, we are responsible for our use and abuse of this language. We are responsible when our God-talk becomes idolatrous.

All of our God-talk comes with images and ideas of who God is and how God relates to us—as shepherd and king, father and mother, savior and friend, lover and judge. The world's religious communities propose many theisms, and there are many theisms even within Christianity. There are also many monotheisms, many ways of seeing God as one and universal. Christianity and Judaism, Islam and Hinduism are all monotheistic, but in quite different ways. Each monotheism casts a different constellation of poetry, for we are treading in the realm where human imagination stretches into the vast cosmos and beyond.

Our God-language, like the rest of our language, constitutes the very pattern of speech and thought in which we live. Our encounter with people of other faiths gives us the precious opportunity to become theologically bilingual, to understand the God-language of another community, and to understand our own more clearly in the process. Only in the give-and-take of dialogue will we come to see just how our languages are very different and how they are alike. Encountering God in all God's fullness enables us to see how rich and profound our many theisms really are. Encountering God in this way, we can perhaps move from competitive theism and the strife it has produced to dialogical theism, a deep and searching dialogue in which we all learn from and challenge one another in our understandings of the one we call God.

* Thich Nhat Hanh, *Living Buddha, Living Christ* (New York: Riverhead Books, 1995), p. 21.

Preface 1993

This is a book about faith and the challenge religious diversity poses to people of faith in every religious tradition. It is a book that begins with the premise that our religious traditions are more like rivers than monuments. They are not static and they are not over. They are still rolling—with forks and confluences, rapids and waterfalls. Where those rivers of faith flow depends upon who we are and who we become. I write as a Christian, so this book is specifically about being a Christian in a world of many faiths, about God and the meanings of Christian God language to a seeker like myself who has traveled the path with Hindus and Buddhists, Muslims and Jews, Jains, Sikhs, and Native Americans. It is a book about how my encounters with people of other faiths have challenged, changed, and deepened my own faith.

I am a student, scholar, and teacher of the comparative study of religion. My academic specialization is the Hindu tradition and the multiple religious traditions of India, where I have lived and worked. For fifteen years I have taught about India and the comparative study of religion to undergraduates and graduate students at Harvard University. I am also a Christian, involved in the Harvard-Epworth United Methodist Church in Cambridge and in the interfaith dialogue work of the World Council of Churches, based in Geneva, Switzerland. For fifteen years I was on the WCC Working Group on Dialogue with People of Living Faiths and for eight of those years chaired that group as moderator. Our work was both regional and global—facilitating the engagement of Christians in dialogue with people of other faiths and enabling the churches to think about the implications and meanings of that dialogue.

Both my academic work and my work in interfaith dialogue have brought me into relation with people of many religious traditions, including Muslim, Christian, and Hindu thinkers who struggle very directly with the question of religious diversity. Some are activists concerned with militarism, the degradation of the environment, and racism. They see clearly that global interdependence is the great fact and challenge of our time, the implications of which we must discern quickly, and that interreligious dialogue is a necessity for working together on issues none of us can solve alone. Others are theologians and philosophers trying to articulate from the standpoint of their own tradition, whether Christian or Buddhist or Muslim, how they might understand the diversity of religions in light of their own particular heritage. On the whole, however, most of the people I have met are ordinary people in all walks of life, not necessarily out to change the world or to save it, but simply to live in it with a greater understanding of their neighbors of other faiths.

My work in the World Council of Churches has also enabled me to meet a wide range of Christians. The WCC is an "ecumenical," movement, from the Greek word *oikos*, which means "the whole inhabited earth." Over three hundred churches in every continent participate—Protestant and Orthodox, African and Asian, ancient churches dating back to the first century and churches only a few decades old. Among those with whom I have worked are some of the most vigorous proponents of interreligious dialogue—church people from Asia, Africa, and the Middle East for whom dialogue is an urgent life and death matter. As a rabbi friend in Britain once put it, "It is dialogue or die."

I have also met a great many people in Christian churches throughout the world who are, quite frankly, suspicious of interreligious dialogue. They see it as detracting from a vigorous Christian mission, as the abandonment of Christian commitment to "the way, the truth, and the life" in Christ. They see it as an unaffordable luxury in areas where the church is challenged aggressively by Muslim revivalism as in parts of Africa or overwhelmed numerically by Buddhist or Hindu cultures as in Thailand or India. I have also learned a great deal from the discipline of dialogue with these people, Christians in my own tradition who are critical of some of my deepest commitments and concerns. Because of them, I have had to think more deeply and honestly about my own faith. I have had to respond to questions no one at Harvard would ever think to ask me. I remember an especially heated and difficult discussion on dialogue and mission and the "destiny of the unevangelized" at a worldwide meeting of the Commission on World Mission and Evangelism held in San Antonio, Texas, in the spring of

1989. After the session, a reporter from the German radio network asked for an interview. Her first question was "Give me a quick yes or no: Is Christ the only way to salvation?" After a long pause, I told her audience that I was only a professor at Harvard; I would have to leave the question of salvation up to God. It is often the case that the most difficult dialogue is within our own tradition.

My work as a teacher, however, is not at all removed from these issues of interreligious relations. My students now include Muslims, Hindus, Buddhists, and Sikhs as well as Christians and Jews. My colleagues on the faculty are Buddhist, Muslim, Confucian, and Jewish. When I think about the practical meanings of interreligious dialogue, the theological meaning of religious diversity, or about what some in the churches still speak of as the "destiny of the unevangelized," I am thinking not about a faceless crowd of people I do not know, but about students, colleagues, dear friends, and teachers—in India, at Harvard, and around the world—whose faces I know like the faces of my own family. This is the kind of world in which all of us increasingly live.

Toward the end of my term of work with the WCC, in January of 1990, we called a meeting of Christian theologians who had been working on the question of what is sometimes called the "theology of religions." How do Christians understand, theologically, the great diversity of human religious traditions? The meeting included Catholic thinkers such as the late Pietro Rossano, the bishop who had long led the Vatican's Secretariat on Non-Christians, the Reverend Jaques Dupuis of the Gregorian University, and Dr. Paul Knitter of Xavier University; Orthodox theologians such as Bishop Anastasios Yannoulatos of Athens and Kenya, Metropolitan George Khodr and Dr. Tariq Mitri of Lebanon; and Protestant theologians such as Dean Robert Neville of Boston University School of Theology, Dr. Itumelang Mosala of the University of Cape Town, the Reverend Cracknell of Wesley College, Cambridge University, Professor Françoise Smyth-Florentin of Paris, and Dr. Judo Poerwowidagdo of Indonesia. Like so many week-long marathon meetings, it involved days of hard work, late nights, drafting, discussing, worshiping, and then repeating it all again.

That January there was a new current in the river of the Christian tradition, a current in which the voices and testimonies of Christians who had lived their lives in dialogue with people of other faiths could be felt with force. "It is our Christian faith in God which challenges us to take seriously the whole realm of religious plurality. We see this not so much as an obstacle to be overcome, but rather as an opportunity for deepening our encounter with God and with our neighbors," we wrote in our official closing statement. "We find ourselves recognizing a need to move beyond a theology which confines salvation to the explicit personal commitment to Jesus Christ." We spoke with complete honesty and with one voice to "affirm unequivocally that God the Holy Spirit has been at work in the life and traditions of peoples of other living faiths." Together we were able and willing to say a good deal more than I had wanted to venture to the woman from German radio: "Our recognition of the mystery of salvation in men and women of other religious traditions shapes the concrete attitudes with which we Christians must approach them in interreligious dialogue." We went on to insist that interreligious dialogue must transform the way in which we do theology, becoming a source and basis of theological work. If we are to speak of God today, we must include in our reflections what we have learned in dialogue with people of other faiths.

The Indian philosopher Krishnamurti has said, "Relationship is the mirror in which we see ourselves as we really are." This is especially true in our relationships with people of other religious traditions. In the give and take of dialogue, understanding one another leads to mutual self-understanding and finally to mutual transformation. My encounter with Hindus has enabled me to understand my own faith more clearly and has required that I understand my own faith differently. It would only be honest to say that my faith as a Christian has been shaped by several religious traditions. This book is an attempt to articulate the ways in which this has been so. While I use my own experience as illustrative, I am convinced that there are a great many people, Christians and others, who have similar experience and who share these concerns—in their own ways, in their own key, and in their own lives.

In the first chapter of this book, I write of my own journey as a Christian from Bozeman, Montana, where I grew up as a teenager active in the Methodist church, to Banaras, India, where I experienced a real challenge to my own faith as a Christian. I encountered a multitude of gods in Banaras and I met dedicated, socially concerned, spiritually alive Hindus who worshiped them. In this chapter, I address the ways in which theological questions—questions about God, about life, death, and meaning—are shaped by this kind of encounter and need to be addressed in the light of it.

In the second chapter, I turn to the common journey of American culture over the past one hundred years since the World's Parliament of Religions in 1893, contrasting the experience of European immigrants such as my own grandparents and great-grandparents from Sweden and the experience of immigrants from Asia. The landscape of America now includes Buddhist, Muslim, and Hindu Americans. As our human interrelatedness has grown, so has the urgency of asking new questions about religious diversity and difference.

In Chapters 3 to 5, I address three classic topics of Christian thinking: the ultimacy of God, the accessibility of the incarnation in Jesus, and the mystery of the Holy Spirit. I address these in dialogue with the challenging questions posed by people of other faiths and in each case try to ask how my own understanding has been transformed and enlarged because of that encounter. Chapter 6 then raises the question of "spirituality" or spiritual discipline. Why is there such a hunger for spiritual renewal these days and what does it mean to be a Christian who has "crossed over" into the spiritual discipline of another tradition to learn the practice of meditation from a Hindu or a Buddhist teacher?

Chapter 7 outlines three responses to the challenge of religious diversity—the exclusivist, the inclusivist, and the pluralist response. The exclusivist insists upon the exclusive and sole truth of one's own religious tradition, excluding all others. The inclusivist sees one's own religious tradition as including the others, interpreting the other's faith in one's own terms. The pluralist accepts the fact that many voices will speak in the exploration of religious truth, each in its own terms, trusting the encounter of real dialogue to reach a deeper understanding of one another's faith and of our own.

Finally, in Chapter 8, I explore the importance of interreligious dialogue not only for mutual understanding and transformation, but for the transformation of the world in which we live and for which we all have responsibility. The term *interdependence* increasingly describes the global nature of ecological, political, and economic issues. Might we also begin to speak of religious interdependence?

Because this is a book that emerges from dialogue, I should say that there is almost nothing in this book that is wholly my own. It has come from study with Hindu teachers, dialogue with Hindu, Muslim, and Jewish friends, sitting with Buddhist meditation groups, and visiting Jain temples and Sikh *gurudwaras*. It has come from working and worshiping with Christian communities—in Montana, in Cambridge, and throughout the world. Through my work with the World Council of Churches, I have also had the opportunity to participate in interreligious meetings of the International Council of Christians and Jews, the International Jewish Committee on Interreligious Consultations, the International Association for Religious Freedom, the World Conference on Religion and Peace, and the Vatican's Pontifical Council for Interreligious Dialogue. Here at home, I have always had the opportunity for enriching discussions of these matters with members of the congregation at Harvard-Epworth United Methodist Church.

I am especially indebted to the many friends and colleagues with whom I have shared active and rewarding years on the WCC Working Group on Dialogue with People of Living Faiths. Colleagues from India, Bangladesh, Thailand, Russia, the West Bank, the Cameroons, and Argentina, representing the whole spectrum of Christian confessions, have taught me a great deal about the diversity and richness of perspectives within the Christian community. As someone who never had a formal theological education, I am especially indebted to the theological tutors I had in this work: Wesley Ariarajah, a Sri Lankan Methodist minister and the director of the Sub-unit on Dialogue with People of Living Faiths of the WCC; Krister Stendahl, former dean of Harvard Divinity School and bishop of Stockholm; Kenneth Cracknell, former director of the Council on Relations with People of Other Faiths of the British Council of Churches and now dean of Wesley Seminary at Cambridge University; and Stanley Samartha, the first director of the Dialogue Sub-unit and a pioneer in this work in the WCC. Underlying it all is the inspiration of my mentor at Harvard, Wilfred Cantwell Smith, who was addressing these topics thirty years ago with insight that is still provocative and prophetic.

These chapters began as talks and lectures. In 1988, United Methodist Bishop Melvin Talbert, then of Seattle, invited me to deliver the Everett W. Palmer Lectures at the University of Puget Sound; these form the core of three of the chapters here. Others were prepared in early form for the Katherine Fraser Mackay Lecture at St. Lawrence University in 1985, a symposium at Harvard University's 350th anniversary celebration in 1986, the inaugural meeting of the North American Interfaith Network in 1988, the Iliff Week of Lectures at the Iliff School of Theology in Denver in 1989, and the Price Lecture Series at Trinity Church in Boston in 1989.

Finally, I would like to thank those friends who helped and encouraged me along the way by reading chapters and assuring me that it really was worthwhile for a lay theologian to venture into these subjects—my friend and colleague Melanie May, my cousin Kathy Dodds Miller, my office staff, Carole Bundy and Nancy Colbert, my colleagues John B. Carman and Mike Fonner here at Harvard, my friend and colleague on the Working Group, Jean Zaru, my friend and fellow pilgrim, Kathryn Walker, and the resident elder of our extended house-hold, Joan Erikson. I would like to thank my editor, Lauren Bryant, and my copy editor, Chris Kochansky, for their painstaking work on the manuscript. Above all, I would like to thank my mother, Dorothy Eck, who has supported me through these years from Bozeman to Banaras, and my dear friend and most cherished critic, Dorothy Austin, who has shared in so much of this journey.

CHAPTER I

Bozeman to Banaras

Questions from the Passage to India

I GREW UP in Bozeman, Montana, in the Gallatin Valley, one of the most beautiful mountain valleys in the Rockies. The Gallatin River cuts through a spectacular canyon to the south, then flows like a stream of crystal through the fertile farmlands of the valley. I had three horses stabled on our land by the Gallatin and spent hours every week riding along the river. By the time I was twenty, I had made my way "back East," as we called it, to Smith College, and then much further east to India, to the Hindu sacred city of Banaras, set on the banks of another river, the Ganges. Banaras was the first real city I ever lived in. It was a city in the time of the Buddha, twenty-six hundred years ago, and the guidebooks called it "older than history." Bozeman had been settled for scarcely one hundred years.

As a twenty-year-old, I found Banaras to be about as far from Bozeman as any place on earth. The smoke of the cremation pyres rose night and day from the "burning ghats" along the river. The Ganges is a much bigger river than the Gallatin; it is a powerful river that seemed to flow with authority and peace as it slid along the ghats, the great stone steps of the city, where Hindus bathed by the thousands at dawn. Today these two places, Bozeman and Banaras, both convey the spiritual meaning of the word *home* to me. And these two rivers, the Gallatin and the Ganges, both flow with living waters I would call holy. Worlds apart, they carry currents of life and meaning whose confluence is in me, deep in my own spiritual life. All of us have such rivers deep within us, bearing the waters of joining streams.

This book is an exploration of the encounter of Bozeman and Banaras, a religious encounter that raises at the very deepest levels the question of difference, the inescapable question of our world today. The issues of race and culture, language and gender, take us into the question of difference in complex and multiple ways, but deeper still, I believe, are the issues of worldview, of religion, and of religious difference. For me, the question has its particular angularities, as it must for each of us. What does it mean, now, to be a Christian, having come to see with my own eyes the religious life of Hindu, Buddhist, and Muslim friends with whom I have lived in professional and personal relationships for many years? How has my own Christian faith been challenged and reformulated by taking seriously what I have learned in this encounter?

I begin this exploration with my own experience, not because my experience is so special but because it illustrates the kinds of personal, social, and theological encounters that are increasingly the reality of our common world. Today people of every faith meet one another, develop deep personal or professional friendships, perhaps even marry one another. Our experience with people of other faiths may be difficult or rewarding, or both. In any case, our "interfaith dialogue" does not usually begin with philosophy or theory, but with experience and relationships. Individually and collectively, our experience has now begun to challenge traditional religious thinking and to contribute decisively to the reformulation of our theologies.

For many people religion is a rigid concept, somewhat like a stone that is passed from generation to generation. We don't add to it, change it, or challenge it; we just pass it along. But even the most cursory study of the history of religions would undermine such a view. Religious traditions are far more like rivers than stones. Like the Ganges or the Gallatin, they are flowing and changing. Sometimes they dry up in arid land; sometimes they radically change course and move out to water new territory. All of us contribute to the river of our traditions. We do not know how we will change the river or be changed as we experience its currents. My task here is to articulate the questions that I know are not mine alone. As John A. T. Robinson put it in another context, that of rising secularism, some thirty years ago, "All I can do is to try to be honest—honest to God and about God—and to follow the argument wherever it leads."[1]

When W. W. Alderson first saw the Gallatin Valley in July of 1864, just two months after Montana became a U. S. territory, he wrote:

> The valley and the stream looked so pleasant and inviting that we con-
> cluded to lay over and look around. . . . The grass was tall everywhere, and
> as it was just heading out, the valley looked like an immense field of grain
> waving gracefully before the gentle breeze. . . . We had come to dig for
> gold and make a fortune in a year or two, but . . . the fever abating, we con-
> cluded to locate right here and engage in farming.[2]

Today Bozeman is a thriving city with shopping malls and sprawling suburbs, but in my childhood it was a small college town of twelve thousand, a grid of tree-lined streets with Main Street running right down the middle. It was named for John Bozeman, a pioneer trail guide who, along with Alderson and two other members of the Bozeman Claim Association, had laid out the town in August of 1864. As a Girl Scout I earned a merit badge by writing the history of Bozeman's pioneer heritage: the sagebrush and gophers, the wooden sidewalks and muddy streets, the first cabins built in the summer of 1864, the Laclede Ho-tel on the site where the Montgomery Ward was later built. By the 1890s there was a train depot, an opera house with a ladies' parlor, and Cy Mount's Palace Sa-loon, with its gambling rooms lined with fine and intricately inlaid wood. And there were fine brick houses, one of which, I found, had retained its red color be-cause the bricks had been soaked in stale beer before they were laid. There was one black man in town, Sam Lewis, who ran the barber shop. And there was an alleyway between Main and Mendenhall that was called Chinatown, with a laundry business and a restaurant.

The church I grew up in, the First Methodist Church on South Willson, was the oldest Methodist church building in the state. The foundation stone had been laid in 1873 by the first minister, the Reverend T. C. Iliff, in the days when Bozeman was still a frontier town with dirt streets and Saturday night shoot-outs. Mary Iliff, in her memoirs of life on the frontier as a young minister's wife, recalled her utter astonishment when she was presented with six Sioux scalps by a Nez Perce medicine man named Amos, in gratitude for a kindness she had shown in boiling a sack of eggs for him. With trembling hands she thanked him for his gift.[3]

T. C. Iliff, along with W. W. Van Orsdel, whom we knew as the legendary Brother Van, were the charismatic circuit riders who set the stage for Montana

Methodism—preaching and singing with such charisma they were called the Heavenly Twins. Brother Van had answered an appeal in the *Christian Advocate* of St. Louis at a time when there were only ninety-five Methodists in all of Montana: "Are there not half a dozen young men in our theological schools who are ready to band together and, taking their lives in their hands, emigrate to this new country and assist in giving the privilege of the gospel to its people?"[4] Brother Van and T. C. Iliff rode horseback from town to town, tending to their congregations. Iliff eventually became the field secretary for the Methodist church and the namesake of the Iliff School of Theology in Denver. Brother Van worked for forty-seven years as a Montana preacher and was said to be the "best-loved man in Montana" when he died. The anthem of Montana Methodism was and still is "Brother Van's Song," a beautiful, rousing hymn about the faith of those who plant and sow not knowing if they will live to see the harvest. The refrain soars with the words "The tears of the sower and the songs of the reaper shall mingle together in joy, by and by." It is a song of frontier farmers, who regularly lived with the risk of losing their crops, and frontier preachers who labored in faith not knowing if the harvest would come.

Montana is a big state with a strong sense of identity. From the windows of our house just at the edge of that grid of tree-lined streets, I could look out over a field of cattle to Bear Mountain. I learned the names of all the mountains that circle the valley—the Bridger Range, the Spanish Peaks, the Madison Range, the Tobacco Roots. And the rivers, too—the Gallatin, the Madison, and the Jefferson, all given their names by Lewis and Clark, who came through the valley in 1805 and 1806 with their Shoshone guide, Sacajewea. At Three Forks, just thirty miles up the valley from Bozeman, the three rivers join to form the Missouri. It is spectacular landscape, its size and vastness somehow made comprehensible by the act of naming and the mastery of those names. I gradually learned the names of mountains and rivers all over the state, for as teenagers my friends and I thought nothing of driving four hundred miles for a weekend basketball tournament or a Methodist youth rally. I learned another Montana reality as well: that this vast landscape included lands set apart as reservations for the native peoples who had lived here and whose homeland this was long before John Bozeman or any of the settlers had come—the Crow and the Northern Cheyenne in the southeast, the Blackfoot in the north, the Flathead and the Kootenay in the west. There were invisible borders and multiple cultures.

Our Methodist church camps were summer meeting places where I got my first taste of a wide and vibrant sense of the church. Various churches built their own cabins in Luccock Park, the camp in the hills above the Paradise Valley near Livingston. Those log cabins, named for our towns "Bozeman," "Livingston," "Billings," and "Big Timber," nestled like miniatures below the towering mountains we called Faith, Hope, and Charity. There in our summer camps we teenagers in the Methodist Youth Fellowship, the M.Y.F., enacted the rites of bonding and commitment that are so formative in the adolescent experience of religion: confessing our secrets and dreams, singing round the campfire at night, sitting in silence and prayer as the fire began to die down, holding crossed hands in a circle of commitment around the glowing embers. When I became the state M.Y.F. president, I also went to the Flathead Lake camp, nearly four hundred miles away in the northwest part of the state. There the cabins were called "Kalispell," "Missoula," and "Great Falls," and there we sat on logs in the outdoor chapel at Inspiration Point for what we called "morning watch," looking out at daybreak past the wooden cross, over Flathead Lake toward the Mission Range.

I did a lot of building as a teenager in the Montana M.Y.F.—roofing, mixing cement, pounding and pulling nails. There were work camps every summer. We built a dining hall at Luccock Park under the supervision of my father, an architect and builder. We built a church at a little settlement called Babb on the Blackfoot Reservation in the grassy, windy prairie land east of Glacier National Park. We lived for a month in two spacious tepees, talking late into the night, sleeping in sleeping bags around the fire, and rising early for morning watch on the hilltop just above our campsite. We took an old schoolbus to Mexico, again with my father and mother, and built a silo on a rural-development farm near Patzcuaro. Our workdays included drilling holes for dynamite, blasting, and mixing cement for the master masons from the little village of Huecorio to use in raising the stone walls of what had to be the most elegant and durable silo in all of Mexico. There our days began with morning watch on the rooftop terrace, where the twenty of us studied the Bible and sang hymns looking out over the farmlands toward Lake Patzcuaro with its island village of Janitzio.

The most durable product of these teenage summers, at least for me, was a sturdy faith in God, a very portable sense of what constitutes the church, and a commitment to the work of the church in the world. I arrived at Smith College in the fall of 1963 straight from the March on Washington, where I had been with the national M.Y.F. delegation. I joined these friends again during the spring vacation of my freshman year to lobby in Washington, D.C., for the Civil Rights Bill. Civil rights and Vietnam War, racism and militarism, were the is-

sues that shaped the whole context of college in the sixties, during the years I
was at Smith. They came together in complex ways. One of my first summer
jobs was a short stint working for the Montana Board of Health on the Northern
Cheyenne Reservation out of Lame Deer in southeastern Montana. I saw at first
hand the racism of my own state, where I had rarely met an African American,
but had also rarely seen the real conditions in which most of the Native American peoples lived. After two weeks in Lame Deer, I was invited to an all-night
prayer meeting of the Native American church. As we settled into a circle
around the fire in the tepee, my host told me that the service was to pray for the
Cheyenne boys who were serving in Vietnam. There were six from the tiny
town of Lame Deer alone. The night was unforgettable: rounds of peyote,
chanting, prayer, drumming. It was a form of worship I had never seen, among
people who were virtual neighbors and yet virtual strangers to me in Montana,
people whose sons and brothers were disproportionately drafted for service in
Vietnam.

It was in this context of the Vietnam War that I first went to India. The move
had only an indirect logic to it, a logic animated by the concern and yet the inadequacy so many American college students felt about the U.S. war in Asia. As a
sophomore in college, I was aimed toward the study of Latin America. But when
I saw the announcement of the University of Wisconsin's College Year in India
program posted on the bulletin board in Wright Hall during midyear exams, I
was immediately drawn to the possibility. Nothing and no one in my past had
prepared me for an encounter with that part of the world. I knew nothing of
Asia. In fact, the Vietnam War seemed a tragic testimony to how little most of us
in America knew about Asia. The boys from Lame Deer were there. A few
friends from my high school were there. My friends from Amherst thought of
nothing but how to avoid going there. So I applied to go to India. It was Asia.
Close enough. Maybe I would learn something. I took a spring term course
taught by a visiting professor from Poona on the thought of two of India's most
important twentieth-century thinkers, Gandhi and Aurobindo. That summer—which was for some a Mississippi summer, for some a Vietnam summer—I spent in the language labs at the University of Wisconsin learning
Hindi.

In September of 1965, with a new group of friends from the summer of language study in Madison, I arrived in India. There was not much in Bozeman or
Northampton, or even in Patzcuaro, that could have prepared me for Banaras, a
vibrant, congested city sitting high on the banks of the River Ganges. Its inten-

sity was overwhelming. I had been in Banaras only a few days when I wrote home, "Wandering half-scared through the side-walk narrow streets near the Chowk market today was an exhausting experience, exhausting because it was as if I had walked through all of India, seen, felt, tasted, smelled it all in three hours. There were too many people, too many faces, too many cows, too many catacomb streets and dead ends, too little air. The utter concentration of life, work, misery, odor, and filth in this area of the city was staggering."

Despite my feelings of claustrophobia and bewilderment, I was immediately impressed by the religiousness of Banaras. There religion was surely *the* most important observable fact of daily life. The whole city seemed to revolve on a ritual axis. There were temples everywhere, large and small, inhabited by images of gods and goddesses whose names I did not know, whose multi-armed forms I could not even distinguish one from the other, and whose significance was totally beyond my grasp. The bathing ghats along the Ganges were the scene of morning rituals for pilgrims. We had not been there more than a day or two when we rose before dawn and took rickshaws to the riverfront to see the sights for which Banaras is so famous. Thousands of Hindus were there at Dasashwamedh Ghat, bobbing in the water, standing waist deep their hands folded in prayer, chanting to a crescendo of bells as the sun rose over the river. Perhaps the one piece of my Montana past that I brought with me to the comprehension of that first dawn on the Ganges was "morning watch." For two miles along the ghats, Hindus bathed in the Ganges and worshiped as the sun broke the horizon. The city pulsed with the life of faith as vibrant as any I had known, and as different.

That year I came to know, for the first time, people of faith from a tradition not my own. I did not know any Jews, let alone Hindus or Muslims, when I set off from Montana for Smith College. I knew little of the faith of others, but at that point in life I was quite clear about the center of my own Christian faith: love, justice, human dignity, and the steady sense of being linked in kinship to Christ and to the Christian community. It was a faith nourished, as all faith finally is, by people—energetic, loving, committed, visionary people. The only people of that sort I knew—and I had the good fortune of knowing quite a few of them as a teenager—were Christians.

It was in Banaras that I experienced the first real challenge to my faith. Not surprisingly, it did not come in the form of ideas, even though I was enrolled in a course in Advaita Vedanta philosophy at the Banaras Hindu University. It came in the form of people—Hindus whose lives were a powerful witness to their faith. I had conceived a completely naive fieldwork project on "Hinduism and the Indian Intellectual." Knowing little about Hinduism myself, I concocted a set of questions about the gods, the meaning of *karma*, the meaning of reincarnation, and so forth, and set out on my bicycle to meet scholars, poets, and professionals in Banaras and to ask what they believed. It was not a very good project, but I couldn't have found a more interesting introduction to India.

One of those I met was Achyut Patwardhan, a former freedom fighter who had spent his share of years in prison in the service of the nonviolent movement for India's independence. He was a man of simple, self-giving love. Like the civil rights leaders I had admired at home, he had put his life on the line in the service of justice. "You see suffering," he said to me, "and you don't debate about it or make yourself act. Those who love simply act, respond naturally with the spontaneous good that is human. Perhaps all you can do is take another person's hand. This, then, is sufficient." Patwardhan was, to me as a twenty-year-old, a man of God and a great spiritual friend at a time of my life when questions were tumbling through my mind. He was a man whose life was a witness to love and justice. He was very much like the people I had most loved and admired as a teenager. But he was not a Christian. He did not find an example and a companion in Christ, as I did. To my surprise, it did not seem to me that he somehow ought to be a Christian. What did this mean about some of the biblical claims of my own tradition?

In November I met J. Krishnamurti, a man who did not fit any category at all. He was giving a series of daily talks at Rajghat in Banaras. Not only was he not a Christian, he was not a Hindu, not a Buddhist. That was just his point. "Truth is a pathless land," he said. "You cannot approach it by any path whatsoever, by any religion, by any sect."[5] He did not say, Follow me. On the contrary, he said, "I desire those who seek to understand me to be free, not to follow me, not to make out of me a cage which will become a religion, a sect."[6] He did not care for the labels of any religion. Indeed, he observed the way in which we fearfully, anxiously, shape our whole lives by religious, political, cultural, and personal labels and names—all of which function as a buffer zone of security between ourselves and the experience of life.

Krishnamurti posed my first real encounter with the "otherness" of a worldview. No one in my world had ever asked about the value of labeling, judging, discriminating, and categorizing experience or suggested that by doing so we distance ourselves from experience. We call it a beautiful sunrise on the Ganges and don't ever really see it because we have dispensed with it by giving it a name and label. Perhaps we write a poem about it to capture it in words or take a photograph of it and feel satisfied that we "got it." We name so-and-so as a friend or an enemy. The next time we encounter that person, the pigeonhole is ready. Are not our minds perpetually busy in these maneuvers? I must admit, at twenty it had never occurred to me to ask such questions. And what about religion? Is it really just a name? I had to ask myself about being a Christian. Did the name matter? Did the label provide me with a shelter or barrier to shield me from real encounter and questioning? What did I have invested in this name? Everywhere I turned I saw question marks.

It is possible, however, that Krishnamurti's ideas would have meant little to me had not Krishnamurti himself been so arresting. Never had I experienced the quality of presence—I suppose now I would say "spiritual presence"—that he brought into a room. It is what I then called his "existentialism," for want of a better word. He spoke without notes, simply, directly, and he continually named and challenged the nature of our attention to him. Were we taking down notes? Why? Were we hoping to seize what he had to say? Were we comparing his ideas to those of Teilhard de Chardin or Zen Buddhism? Were we judging his thoughts with our likes and dislikes? Why couldn't we just listen? Is simple presence and attention so impossible? The questions Krishnamurti asked were not about the world and its injustices, they were questions about me and my habits of apprehending the world. Though I had read some of Paul Tillich's work the year before and had especially liked *The Shaking of the Foundations*, this was the real shaking of the foundations for me.

Krishnamurti and Patwardhan were important to me precisely because they were what Christians might call "witnesses" to their faith; they somehow embodied their faith in their lives. In retrospect, it is somewhat embarrassing to articulate this as a discovery, but as a twenty-year-old it came as news to me: Christians did not have a corner on love, wisdom, and justice. Christians were not the only ones nourished by faith and empowered by their faith to work to change the world. I knew nothing of the Hindu devotional traditions of *bhakti* then, but I met people—like Krishnamurti and Patwardhan—whose very lives were a message of God-grounded love. These people, unbeknownst to them, pushed me into a life of work and inquiry, spiritual and intellectual. I became a student of comparative religion and focused my work on Hinduism and the traditions of India. And as a Christian I began to realize that to speak of Christ and the meaning of incarnation might just mean being radically open to the possibility that God really encounters us in the lives of people of other faiths.

That first year in Banaras changed the course of my life. I have been back and forth to India a dozen times now. I did doctoral work in comparative religion and wrote my thesis and then my first book on the city of Banaras—which Hindus call Kashi, the City of Light. It is a study of what the city, the Ganges, and the gods mean to Hindus. When I returned for research on my doctoral thesis, eight years after that first year in Banaras, I learned the names of all those gods, their stories, their powers. I visited as many of the city's thousand temples as any Hindu. I went up and down the ghats of the riverfront, learning their hidden shrines by heart. I circled the city on my bicycle and visited its protective guardians. I spoke to teachers and priests, scholars and pilgrims. Perhaps my teenage fieldwork along Main Street in the saloons and churches of old Bozeman had whetted my appetite for taking on one of the world's oldest and most complicated cities.

When I had finished the book on Banaras, I began a study of the Hindu temples and shrines that link the whole of India in interwoven networks of pilgrimage places. I traveled up and down the sacred rivers of India, visiting the headwaters of the Ganges in the Himalayas, the Narmada in the highlands of Madhya Pradesh, the Godavari in the hills of Maharashtra, and the Kaveri in the Coorg hills of the south. I went to major temples and wayside shrines and visited the four *dhams*, the divine abodes at the four corners of India—Badrinath in the northern Himalayas, Rameshvaram at the tip of southern India, Puri on the Bay of Bengal in the east, and Dvaraka on the Arabian Sea in the west. As a scholar and professor of religion, this kind of intellectual work is no small challenge—to glimpse the world of meaning in which people of another faith live their lives and die their deaths. But it is another question—equally important but very different—which I am pursuing here: What does all this mean to me, as a Christian?

Theology in the Encounter of Worlds

The meeting of Banaras and Bozeman, "East and West," can be duplicated in a hundred keys and a hundred languages. The encounter of worlds and worldviews is the shared experience of our times. We see it in the great movements of modern history, in colonialism and the rejection of colonialism, in the late-twentieth-century "politics of identity"—ethnic, racial, and religious. We experience our own personal versions of this encounter, all of us, whether Christian, Hindu, Jewish, or Muslim; whether Buddhist, Apache, or Kikuyu; whether religious, secular, or atheist. What do we make of the encounter with a different world, a different worldview? How will we think about the heterogeneity of our immediate world and our wider world? This is our question, our human question, at the end of the twentieth century.

My own versions of this question are How can those of us who are Christians articulate our own faith fully aware of the depth and breadth of the faith of others? How do we affirm our own holy ground even as we sojourn in the holy lands of other faith traditions, even as we find ourselves to be more than sojourners, to be at home there? How is Christian faith, or a "Christian worldview," challenged and changed when we take seriously the fact that we are not alone as religious people, when we recognize as truly religious the traditions, the lives, and the pilgrimages of our neighbors of other faiths?

Not everyone has encountered the gods of India, but in the 1990s most people have encountered something of a religion not their own and have found questions welling up, expressed or unexpressed, about the meaning of this encounter for their own faith. For Christians, it might be a Passover seder or a Sabbath meal shared with Jewish friends; it might be the Ramadan fasting of a Muslim colleague here in North America, or time spent living or traveling in an Islamic society, where prayer is so visible and natural a part of daily life. Many Christians have taken up Buddhist or Hindu meditation practices, and have wondered about the relation of these disciplines of meditation to their own faith. Many have seen the film *Gandhi* or have read Gandhi's autobiography and felt the religious challenge of the Sermon on the Mount presented more clearly in the life of this twentieth-century Hindu than in that of any contemporary Christian. Many have sensed the holiness of the Dalai Lama and asked what such holiness has to do with the things they call holy in their own tradition. Many have read the scriptures of other traditions of faith, like the Bhagavad Gita, and have wondered what the insights they have gained might have to do with their own faith.

The questions that rise from experience to challenge the real meaning of our faith are basic theological questions. They are theological because they have to do with ultimate meaning, with the one we call God, with articulating our faith in a way that makes sense both of our tradition and the world in which we live. What is Banaras to a Christian? Who is Krishna? When Muslims pray to Allah do they pray to the God Christians know in Christ? Is there one God whom we all know by different names? Are there different gods? False gods? These are questions that academics and theologians find awkward to address, or want to address only by raising hermeneutical, or interpretive, considerations, backpedaling quickly away from the questions themselves. Yet to be honest as persons of faith who encounter the religious life of other faiths and are both challenged and enriched by that encounter requires that we ask such questions. They emerge out of the very heart of our experience. And they are not theoretical questions with no relevance to the lived-in world. Our answers fundamentally shape the way in which we think of the cultures and the peoples with whom we share that world.

Questions such as these are raised, of course, within each community of faith—by Jews, Christians, Muslims, Hindus, Buddhists, and others. How do Muslims think about Christians and Hindus? How are Buddhists challenged by the strong language of ethical monotheism as articulated by Jews, Christians, and Muslims? Today people of all faiths are more or less aware of one another, and those who articulate the meaning of faith for today must do so in the complicated context of religious plurality. I am keenly interested in what people of other faiths are saying as they work to interpret the world anew in the light of their experience, but they must speak for themselves. I speak only as a Christian, convinced that those of us who are Christians cannot close our eyes to the diverse world of human religiousness, affirming our faith as if others, with their claims and questions, did not exist. Jesus engaged fully and openly with the people of his world and his time, regardless of tradition, culture, ethnicity, or social status. Our Christian faith requires no less of us.

Morning in Chiang Mai

It was nearly twenty years after those daybreak mornings at Inspiration Point on Flathead Lake, and more than ten years after my first glimpse of dawn on the Ganges, that I led a morning worship service in Chiang Mai, Thailand, and found that I had moved farther toward the frontiers of Christian faith than I had realized. As a lecturer at Harvard, I had been invited by the World Council of Churches to a theological consultation on interfaith dialogue. People representing the whole spectrum of Christian views on mission and dialogue were there in Chiang Mai, a quiet city where the Buddhist tradition suffused daily life and where saffron-robed monks could be seen walking silently past our hotel in the morning, stopping at homes and shops to receive in their begging bowls the food given as alms by the laity.

I was asked to be responsible for morning worship on one of the eight days of the consultation. Since we had all come together to discuss theological issues in Christian relations to other faiths, I thought it would be appropriate to include a responsive reading from another religious tradition. I chose a passage from the fourth chapter of the Bhagavad Gita, where Lord Krishna teaches the struggling Arjuna that whenever righteousness decays and unrighteousness is on the rise, He, the Lord, comes into being in age after age. When we came to the responsive reading, I read my part and was astonished to find that perhaps only a third of those present seemed to be joining in the response. The rest sat in silence. I had not anticipated for a moment that it would be troublesome to this group of theologians to meditate upon the scripture of another tradition in this worship context, but I learned a great deal that day about my own tradition. I had unwittingly unleashed a major controversy. What I had done was discussed—indeed hotly debated—right down to the issue of whether or not the incident should be mentioned in the report of the consultation, and if so, at what point.

The most extreme opponents to the responsive reading from the Gita were those who objected to what the passage had to say—it spoke of many divine incarnations and of rebirth. Furthermore, they objected to the fact that they had been asked to take these words upon their lips in a worship context. Others were opposed because, they said, responsive reading is not a form of study but of prayer, and they could not be asked to pray in the words of another tradition. Some appreciated including a Hindu scripture in Christian worship and saw it as a way of taking seriously the spiritual challenges of the Bhagavad Gita. I am sure, however, that the majority of those there—both those who took the controversial words of the Gita upon their lips and those who did not—were simply uncertain. What did the passage mean? What would it mean for a Christian to speak these words?

In 1938, when Christians of the International Missionary Council gathered in Tambaram at Madras Christian College to discuss "The Christian Message in a Non-Christian World," D. G. Moses, an Indian Christian professor of philosophy at Nagpur University, rose in the midst of the debate and said, "Time was when each thought his own religion superior. . . . But with the ever-increasing means of communication and transportation and the growing study of comparative religion, the old attitude has been made impossible. We know too much of the religions of the world today to assume naively the unquestioned superiority of one's own faith."[7] For some, the point Professor Moses made was obvious. At the Tambaram conference were Asian Christians as well as Western missionaries who had spent their lives in Asia and who had come to know intimately and appreciatively the religious lives of devout Hindus, Muslims, or Confucians. For many others at Tambaram, however, to see Christianity as one tradition of faith among others equally ancient and resonant was to crack open the door of relativism.   .

What Moses expressed at Tambaram resounds even more profoundly in our world today. The tremendous growth in the study and understanding of religion, the translation of the sacred texts of Hindus, Buddhists, and Muslims, the deeper understanding of their traditions of faith, *has* made the old attitude impossible. Those of us who are Christians speak of the uniqueness and centrality of Christ, and yet at the same time we know that our Muslim brothers and sisters affirm the uniqueness and centrality, indeed the finality, of God's revelation in the Holy Qur'an. And we know that when Buddhists speak of insight into the nature of life, death, and suffering, they are not speaking of a narrow truth that is peculiar to Buddhists, but are making a claim to universal truth which they invite all of us to see for ourselves.

People of many religious traditions bear witness to the truth, the transcendence, the universality, the uniqueness, and the distinctive beauty of what they have known and seen. To recognize this plurality of religious claims as a profoundly important fact of our world does not constitute a betrayal of one's own faith. It is simply a fact among the many facts that emerge from the historical and comparative study of religion. What we make of that fact from our different perspectives of faith is one of the most important challenges of our time. This challenge cannot be addressed by academic scholars of religion alone, for it is not solely a matter of understanding the religiousness of others, though that alone is an enormous task. It is a matter of interpreting our own religious world and faith in the light of that understanding. In other words, how does the understanding of others, which is the aim of the scholar of comparative religion, reshape our self-understanding? We know from human experience that the reformulation of our self-understanding happens constantly in interpersonal relations, but how does it happen in interfaith relations?

4 *The Sceptics, the Seekers, the Saved*

This book addresses theological questions, but it is not a book *about* theology, to make a fine distinction. There has been a flood of books about theology and religious pluralism in the past ten years. They are for the most part schematic books that line up Christian alternatives to this "problem" of pluralism. They are important books, but there is a once-removed quality to them. They are written primarily in the tribal language of theologians, for theologians, about theological problems. For the most part, the authors do not engage in rethinking their own faith, but rather theoretically ponder how one might do so if one were to try. But theological questions are not merely theoretical; they are the life and death questions of real people attempting to live with intellectual and personal honesty in a world too complex for simplistic answers. Here I have tried to write for ordinary people who do not think of themselves as theologians, but who struggle with real questions of faith in the world in which we live.

For some who will read these pages, Christianity is a problem. They may not understand how a person like me, a scholar and professor in a large secular research university, could be a Christian at all. They have perhaps long since given up on religion and find the public image of Christianity narrow, fanatical, or simply irrelevant. I don't blame them. I too sometimes find the public image of the Christian tradition disturbing and even repelling. While my own experience of the church, from Montana Methodism to the World Council of Churches, has been life-giving and has helped me to grow, I know that many people have very different experiences in churches that are stagnant, irrelevant to their lives, or even destructive. It is no wonder that they have turned away. No religion is without ugliness, perversion, and distortion, for religious traditions, especially religious institutions, are not dropped from heaven, but are our human creations as we struggle to respond to our sense of the Transcendent. Many of the people who have dropped out of churches in disgust or boredom are truly interested in religious questions and intrigued to discover that some people like myself, who call themselves Christians, wrestle with the implications of Hindu philosophy, practice "Buddhist" meditation, and think that Christianity is not over, but still in the process of becoming.

There are others for whom it is not Christianity, but the interaction with other religious traditions that poses the problem. These people are very much part of the river of the Christian tradition, but they are not sure what to make of the traditions of faith that have watered different lands and nurtured other civilizations. They do not have a feel for what it would be like to be anything but a Christian. Some are actively hostile to the presupposed truths of other religious traditions and insist that they are not truth at all, but falsehood; they would not speak the words of the Bhagavad Gita because they believe these words are simply untrue, blasphemy. They have very clearly articulated theologies; they know just what they believe and why. Most Christians do not live with such certainties, however. They may be cautious about other faiths, or they may be quite open and yet feel they do not know enough about any other faith to be engaged with its claims to truth.

One thing is certain. In thinking about other faiths, most churchgoing Christians have imprinted upon their minds a few lone fragments of scripture. There is John 14:6: "I am the way, and the truth and the life; no one comes to the Father but by me." There is Acts 4:12: "And there is salvation in no one else, for there is no other name under heaven given among men by which we must be saved." This is all the theological equipment they have to grapple with a new world of many faiths. And when they travel to India and see the mind-boggling variety of the Hindu tradition, or when they meet Muslims across the street in Leeds or Lexington, or when their colleague at the office heads for the Buddhist meditation center after work, or when their daughter dates and marries a wonderful young man who is Muslim or Jewish, these fragments of scripture are simply not enough to make sense of the world and their experience in it.

This book, then, is a theology with people in it. They are the people I have encountered in my studies of the history of religion, in my fieldwork in India, and in my travels throughout the world. I cannot think about Christianity and about my own faith without hearing their voices, so it makes sense to give them narrative space in my theological thinking. What questions do they ask of me? What questions do I ask of them? This mutual questioning and listening is what is meant by "interfaith dialogue." While dialogue may be pursued at carefully arranged meetings and consultations, like the many I have participated in through working with the World Council of Churches, the most compelling and important dialogue is that which arises in the communities and contexts of our daily lived experience, what some would call "the dialogue of life." Interfaith dialogue, whether the intentional and formal dialogue of the interfaith movement or the informal daily conversation at the street corner, is the very context out of which Christians must seek a new understanding of faith today.

Feminism, Liberation, and Pluralism

For me, this task is doubly complex because I hear not only the voices of Hindu or Buddhist friends and teachers as I write, but also the voices of women within my own tradition who have never been given much narrative space in the history and theology of Christianity. Indeed, the voices of women have not been fully heard in Hinduism, Buddhism, Islam, or Judaism either. Our voices have been suppressed in the texts and in the leadership of most of the world's religious traditions, though it is clear that women have done much to sustain the vibrance and vigor of these very traditions. So it is always with a profound sense of dissonance that I view the formalities of many world interfaith events, where the colorful male panoply of swamis, rabbis, bishops and metropolitans, monks and ministers line up together for a photograph of interfaith fellowship. They are portraits of a fading world, for women's hands and voices are reshaping all of our traditions.

The emergence of women's voices is worldwide—as priests and pastors in the Christian tradition, as rabbis and theologians in the Reform and Conservative Jewish tradition, as feminists in the Orthodox Jewish community, as Gandhian activists and scholars in India, as Muslim feminists insisting on their right to the radical justice and equality of the Qur'an. As the Buddhist tradition grows in new soil in the West, many of its finest teachers are women. As the Catholic church experiences the turmoil of our century, many of its leaders, ordained or not, are women. Even where women's voices are not yet fully heard, they sound the beginnings of real religious revolutions. In every tradition, these are revolutions happening before our very eyes.

Liberation theology, feminist theology, and pluralist theology are all major currents in the Christian tradition today. All three are about the redefinition of the *we* in theological thinking and the renegotiation of the *we* in our common political and cultural life. They are all attempts to reconstruct more inclusive and more relevant forms of Christian thinking and Christian engagement. Liberation theologians articulate the Gospel as understood by the poor, the marginalized, those who speak the word of truth outside the houses of privilege and comfort and who insist that our priorities be set, not by the interests of the mighty, but by the priorities of the poor. Feminist theologians give voice to the concerns of both women and men who insist on the presence and perspective of women in Christian leadership, teaching, and interpretation. Pluralist theologians insist that Christians must also listen to the voices of people of other faiths and not pretend that we can do our theological and ethical thinking in a vacuum, without engaging in energetic interreligious exchange.

Unfortunately, there has not as yet been much interrelation between these three currents of theological thinking. Many Christians who speak of the "preferential option for the poor" seem not to recognize that most of the world's poor are not Christians who will speak the Gospel in a new prophetic voice—they are Muslim poor or Hindu poor. To hear their voices necessitates interreligious dialogue. Many of those who want to listen to the voices of Buddhists and Hindus pay scarcely any attention to the voices of women and reinforce in their interreligious dialogue the patriarchies of all the traditions; many who want to give voice to the perspectives of women within the Christian tradition don't think for a moment about Hindus and Buddhists. Everyone is busy on his or her own front. In a sense this is not a criticism, for feminist and womanist theologians, liberation theologians, and pluralist theologians have all, in their own ways, unleashed their respective revolutions in Christian thinking today. I believe, however, that we all must begin to think of these issues together, for I am convinced that they belong together as part of our effort to rebuild a sense of community that does not make difference divisive and exclusive.

When I first went to India in 1965, I had not heard the word *feminism* or connected gender issues with theological thinking. While I was in India, Betty Friedan came to the Smith College campus to speak about *The Feminine Mystique*. Mary Daly was probably still at her typewriter working on *The Church and the Second Sex*, which was published in 1968. Her book *Beyond God the Father*, which so shaped the intellectual world of graduate studies in the seventies, was still years away. But there in India, living and studying in Banaras, I encountered a multitude of gods and goddesses imaged in poetry, song, and stone. In India, through the rich theological imagination of Hindus, my understanding of God the Father was challenged by the language of God the Mother, God the Dancer, God the Lover, and God the Androgyne. In India I encountered the problem and the limits of my own religious language several years before I felt it surface through the currents of feminist writing in the Christian church. When I said, "Our Father, . . . "—which I still do—there began to be footnotes at the bottom of my mind, mental reservations about just what Father means and does not mean. And the list has become longer through the years.

Dialogue in which we listen as well as speak may seem so commonsensical it is scarcely worth making a fuss over. And yet dialogue, whether between women and men, black and white, Christian and Hindu, has not been our common practice as an approach to bridging differences with understanding. Power and prestige make some voices louder, give some more airtime, and give the powerful the privilege of setting the terms for communication. We have had a long history of monologues. Much of the Christian missionary movement has been based on a one-way discourse of preaching and proclamation, with little thought to listening and little space for it. The Christian mission movement moved, for the most part, in the wake of European empires and in the company of the politically and economically powerful. The church did not have to listen—in India, in East Asia, in Africa, or in South America.

Mutual Transformation

Today the language of dialogue has come to express the kind of two-way discourse that is essential to relationship, not domination. One might call it mutual witness: Christians have not only a witness to bear, but also a witness to hear. In the process of mutual testimony and mutual questioning, we not only come to understand one another, we come to understand ourselves more deeply as well. It leads to what John Cobb calls "mutual transformation."[8] Dialogue does not mean that we will agree, but only that we will understand more clearly and that we will begin to replace ignorance, stereotype, even prejudice, with relationship. It is the language of mutuality, not of power.

During the years in Banaras I worked and studied with two teachers, both men in their eighties, whose equanimity and patience, love of learning, love of God, and love of the Ganga, the River Ganges, were luminous. They became family to me, and I to them. In my study of the Hindu tradition, I asked many questions of them. But I was not the only one with questions. They had questions, too. "Why do you pour yogurt on the gods?" I would ask, astonished. "Is it true that Christians in the West wear their shoes right into churches?" they would ask, equally astonished. When I asked about the worship of Shiva and Krishna, I was also asked about Christ.

I could hear them sizing me up, interpreting me in their own world of meaning. Who was this woman who had come from so far away, who asked so many questions about temples and gods, who studied Sanskrit and made so many mistakes? My friends in Bozeman may have wondered, as I have myself, how it was

that a young woman who grew up in the high valleys and fresh air of the Rocky
Mountains was so drawn to the city of Banaras, studying temples in its crowded
alleyways and breathing the air of the cremation grounds. But this posed no
problem to my teachers and friends in Banaras. "You must have been a Hindu in
your last lifetime," said one. "You lived here in Banaras in a former life, which is
why you have such a feeling for this city," said another. "You were part of our
family, which is why you have come to be among us now," said another. One of
my teachers, Kuber Nath Sukul, insisted, "You are my granddaughter, because
your mother was born just about the time my only daughter died. Welcome
home."

In our relationship, I surely was a witness to my own faith as a Christian. They
knew I was a Christian, that I was a Protestant, and that even so I went to the little Catholic church that met in an apartment building called Vishnu Bhavan at
the end of Lanka Street. But I was not the only one to bear witness to my faith. So
did my teacher Ambika Datta Upadhyaya, whom I addressed with the reveren-
tial and affectionate title Pandit-ji, when he spoke with quiet confidence about
the meaning of death, even his own death. So did his wife, whom I called Mata-
ji, in her observances of fasting and prayer. So did my friend Shanti and her family, poor as they were, with so many children and but one buffalo to count as
wealth, when they offered me a tumbler of sweetened milk at each and every
visit.

The give and take of dialogue among people of religious faith must inevitably
raise questions for our own faith. These are the questions that should shape our
theological thinking. When I read the Bhagavad Gita, I cannot isolate the understandings and questions that have emerged from that scripture in a separate
file of my mind and go about my spiritual business as a Christian as if I had never
read it. If I have been touched, challenged, or changed by the Bhagavad Gita, I
must deal with that remarkable fact. If I find the Gita to be a comfort in moments
of loss or grief or difficult ethical choices, which I do, I must make sense of that
fact when I think about my Christian faith.

Just as I cannot isolate what I have learned from the Bhagavad Gita, so I
cannot bracket the life I have shared with Hindus when I wrestle with what it
means for me to be a Christian today. I cannot put aside the bonds of respect
and affection that link me to these people, and place them, even gently, outside
the Kingdom. A. G. Hogg, who was the principal of Madras Christian College
at Tambaram for nearly three decades, put it very well when he spoke of discovering real faith among the Hindu students with whom he worked for so

many years. In the presence of such faith, he wrote, we should feel not merely respect, but religious reverence. At the International Missionary Council in 1938,
he asked rhetorically of his fellow missionaries,

> Is there any such thing as a religious faith which in quality or texture is
> definitely not Christian, but in the approach to which one ought to put the
> shoes off the feet, recognizing that one is on the holy ground of a two-sided
> commerce between God and man? In non-Christian faith may we meet
> with something that is not merely a seeking but in real measure a finding,
> and a finding by contact with which a Christian may be helped to make
> fresh discoveries in his own finding of God in Christ?[8]

Among Hogg's students at Madras Christian College was the young Radhakrishnan, who was to become one of modern India's finest Hindu philosophers.
It is no wonder the British educator felt the challenge of a genuine faith and a
compelling, but very different, theological vision. There are many Christians
who have had the experience described by Hogg, sensing in the presence of true
faith, whether Hindu or Muslim or Buddhist, that we should take off our shoes,
for the ground on which we are standing is holy ground. It is holy not only because it is sacred for the Hindu, Muslim, or Buddhist. It is holy ground where we
ourselves may be challenged to deeper faith.

CHAPTER 2

Frontiers of Encounter

The Meeting of East and West in America since

the 1893 World's Parliament of Religions

ALL OF my ancestors were immigrants from Småland and Varmland in Sweden. On my father's side, they came to Minnesota and then Montana. On my mother's side, they came to Illinois, moved on to Iowa, and finally ended up in the Pacific Northwest. They were among the 1.3 million Swedish immigrants who came to America between 1840 and 1930. They were all Swedish Lutherans. I was sharply confronted with their heritage and my own not long ago when I spent the morning at the annual Paryushana rites at the Jain Center of Greater Boston, which is in the town of Norwood on a quiet residential street called Cedar Street, in a church that had formerly been a Swedish Lutheran Church.

The Jains, a community of Gujarati immigrants from India with religious roots going back at least to the sixth century B.C.E., have owned the building for ten years now. The cut-crystal chandeliers reminded me of those in the church in Šunne, where Grandma Eck grew up. Nothing else in the sanctuary, however, would have been familiar to her. The pews had been removed and the entire room carpeted. On the raised altar area were tables bearing fine marble images of the Jain saints called *tirthankaras*, "those who have made the crossing" from this life of birth and death to the utter freedom of the far shore. At the altar, Jain laity, their mouths and noses covered with a white band of cloth so as not to inadvertently injure microscopic life-forms, were making traditional offerings of flowers, incense, and water to the *tirthankaras*. The sanctuary was crowded with people and filled with song and incense.

Paryushana is the holy day marking the end of the annual period of austerity and fasting, so everyone was in an ebullient mood. A feast was to follow in the back yard, where a huge yellow and white striped tent, America's version of the Gujarati *shamayana*, had been erected. The Jain community of the Boston area, an unusually high percentage of them in the computer industry, turned out by the hundreds for the occasion. As Gujarati families poured out of the church and toward the feast, the women wearing bright saris and shawls, I strolled up Cedar Street to take perspective on the colorful scene. A few doors up I met one of the neighbors, a Catholic woman who had never been into the temple, but who waved her hand with satisfaction toward the old Swedish church and its new congregation and said, "This is what makes America!"

In 1893 the World's Parliament of Religions convened in Chicago in connection with the World's Fair which celebrated the four hundredth anniversary of Columbus' arrival in the Americas. For most Americans this two-week assembly was their first encounter on this continent with people of the great religious traditions of Asia. One hundred years ago most of the 150,000 American visitors who attended one or more sessions of the Parliament had never before heard the voice of a Buddhist, a Hindu, or a Muslim; one could probably count the number of Hindus in North America on the fingers of one hand. In the 1890s T. C. Iliff and Brother Van still wrapped their leather reins around the hitching posts in downtown Bozeman. Contemplating the centennial of this Parliament, this one-hundred-year span seems a very long time indeed. The world has turned over and over again with social, political, and cultural revolution. The "New World," built on the backs of ancient native cultures, has grown quickly, energetically, and, for some, ruthlessly.

What was a fair and a somewhat artificial parliament in 1893 is today the reality of Chicago. The metropolitan yellow pages list dozens of entries under the headings "Churches: Buddhist" or "Churches: Islamic." There are said to be seventy mosques in Chicago today and almost half a million Muslims. The suburbs of the city boast two sizable and elaborate Hindu temples, to say nothing of the dozen smaller places of Hindu worship. There are at least twenty Buddhist temples and meditation halls—from those of the Japanese Zen tradition to those of the Cambodian, Vietnamese, and Laotian Buddhist refugee communities. There is a Zoroastrian fire temple. There are Baha'is and Jains,

Sikhs and Afro-Caribbean Voodoo practitioners. The Chicago planning committee convened nearly fifty cosponsoring religious groups to organize the centennial of the Parliament in 1993. This local committee, called the Council for a Parliament of the World's Religions, was more representative of the world's religions than the Parliament itself had been.

Much has happened to the United States in the one hundred years since the Parliament. One hundred years ago, my own great-grandparents were just getting settled in what to them was a new world. They were among the millions of immigrants who came from Sweden, Ireland, Poland, and Italy—Protestant, Catholic, and Jewish. America became a nation of immigrants, though not without prejudices and bigotry and exclusion. Beginning in the 1880s, the U.S. Congress passed a series of Asian exclusion acts that attempted to limit and even eliminate immigration from Asia. Such an immigration policy remained substantially in effect through the 1950s. John F. Kennedy was writing on the history of immigration and the need for the liberalization and reform of American immigration law at the time of his assassination: "To know America . . . it is necessary to know why over 42 million people gave up their settled lives to start anew in a strange land. We must know how they met the new land and how it met them, and, most important, we must know what these things mean for our present and for our future."[1] When the immigration act proposed by President Kennedy was finally passed and signed into law in 1965, a new era of immigration began, bringing people from all over Asia to the United States. The Jain temple on Cedar Street in Norwood, with its Swedish cut-glass chandeliers, stands as a symbol of the changes over these one hundred years. The Roman Catholic neighbor down the street expressed what Kennedy would surely have wanted to say as well—"This is what makes America."

The World's Parliament of Religions

The World's Parliament of Religions convened for more than two weeks in September of 1893. It was not really a world event except in intention and vision. It was planned by American Christians, mostly Protestants, and it could as easily be seen as one of the opening events of the modern Christian ecumenical movement as the first act in the modern interreligious movement. There were relatively few Asians present, and the sole Muslim speaker was a New Englander who had converted to Islam. Even so, the vision of the Parliament was lofty and it set forth questions of interreligious relations that are as vivid today as they were in 1893. In convening the Parliament, chairman John Henry Barrows proclaimed, "Our meeting this morning has become a new, great fact in the historic evolution of the race which will not be obliterated."[2]

There were some for whom this "new, great fact" was questionable and even objectionable. The Archbishop of Canterbury had declined to come because "the Christian religion is the one religion." He went on to say, "I do not understand how that religion can be regarded as a member of a Parliament of Religions without assuming the equality of the other intended members and the parity of their positions and claims."[3] Apparently the Sultan of Turkey also objected to the Parliament, and as a result, representatives of the Arab Muslim world did not attend. The General Assembly of the Presbyterian Church, meeting in Portland, Oregon, in 1892, expressed its disapproval. The monks of the Engaku-ji Buddhist monastery in Kamakura, Japan, were likewise sceptical and sought to dissuade their abbott, Soyen Shaku, from going; they thought it would be "improper for a Zen priest to set foot in such an uncivilized country."[4] Despite their apprehensions, Soyen Shaku insisted on going and the young monk who drafted his letter of acceptance in English was D. T. Suzuki, who later became the preeminent cultural translator of the Zen Buddhist tradition from Japan to North America.

When the Parliament opened, a replica of the Liberty Bell tolled ten times, once for each of the great religions represented. Charles Carroll Bonney, the president of the Parliament and one of its first visionaries, began his address, "Worshippers of God and Lovers of Man, let us rejoice that we have lived to see this glorious day!" He saw the Parliament as evidence that "the finite can never fully comprehend the infinite," and declared, "Each must see God with the eyes of his own soul. Each must behold him through the colored glasses of his own nature. Each one must receive him according to his own capacity of reception. The fraternal union of the religions of the world will come when each seeks truly to know how God has revealed himself in the other."[5] John Henry Barrows then welcomed the delegates and confessed, "When, a few days ago, I met for the first time the delegates who have come to us from Japan, and shortly after the delegates who have come to us from India, I felt that the arms of human brotherhood had reached almost around the globe. But there is something stronger than human love and fellowship, and what gives us the most hope and happiness today is our confidence that 'the whole round world is every way bound by gold chains about the feet of God.' " He described the days which lay ahead as "the first school of comparative religions, wherein devout men of all faiths may speak for themselves without hindrance, without criticism, and without compromise, and tell what they believe and why they believe it."[6] And so they did.

One of the most vibrant and dramatic of the Parliament participants was Swami Vivekananda, who was among those who spoke for the Hindu tradition. His challenge was that of a widely pluralistic worldview. In addressing his "sisters and brothers of America," he declared that he was proud "to belong to a religion that has taught the world both tolerance and universal acceptance." The Archbishop of Canterbury would indeed have been uncomfortable hearing Vivekananda proclaim so forcefully, "It is the same light coming through different colors. . . . But in the heart of everything the same truth reigns; the Lord has declared to the Hindu in his incarnation as Krishna, 'I am in every religion as the thread through a string of pearls. And wherever thou seest extraordinary holiness and extraordinary power raising and purifying humanity, know ye that I am there.' "[7]

Among the Buddhists at the Parliament was the Sri Lankan Buddhist reformer Dharmapala, who asked the audience in a large lecture hall, "How many of you have read the life of the Buddha?" When only five raised hands, he scolded, "Five only! Four hundred and seventy-five millions of people accept our religion of love and hope. You call yourselves a nation—a great nation—and yet you do not know the history of this great teacher. How dare you judge us!"[8] One of the Buddhists from Japan was equally challenging, pointing explicitly to the anti-Japanese feeling in America and deploring the signs that read "No Japanese is allowed to enter here." "If such be the Christian ethics—well, we are perfectly satisfied to be heathen," he said. The Japanese are not so concerned, he said, whether someone is called a Buddhist, a Shintoist, or a Christian, "the consistency of doctrine and conduct is the point on which we put the greatest importance."[9]

There was little Muslim participation at the Parliament. Islam was represented by the American convert Mohammed Webb, who spoke directly to the prejudices and images of Islam in the West. "There is not a Muslim on earth who does not believe that ultimately Islam will be the universal faith." But he went on, "I have not returned to the United States to make you all Mussulmans [Muslims] in spite of yourselves. . . . I do not propose to take a sword in one hand and the Koran in the other and go through the world killing every man who does not say 'There is no God but one and Mohammed is the prophet of God.' But I have faith in the American intellect . . . and in the American love of fair play, and will defy any intelligent man to understand Islam and not love it."[10]

Among the scholars who sent messages to the Parliament was J. Estlin Carpenter from Oxford University, who made it clear that the comparative study of religion had opened up the concept of revelation to what he called the "Bible of humanity." "Philology has put the key of language into our hands," said Carpenter. "Shrine after shrine in the world's great temple has been entered; the songs of praise, the commands of law, the litanies of penitence, have been fetched from the tombs of the Nile, or the mounds of Mesopotamia, or the sanctuaries of the Ganges. The Bible of humanity has been recorded. What will it teach us? I desire to suggest to this Congress that it brings home the need of a conception of revelation unconfined to any particular religion, but capable of application in diverse modes to all."[11]

Despite such visions of a much wider conception of revelation, the Parliament was dominated, on the whole, by Christian participants with a universalist fulfillment theology—the view that Christianity represents the flower and fulfillment of the religious hopes and aspirations present in other faiths. One eloquent expression of such a view was that of the Reverend Joseph Cook of Boston: "Old man and blind, Michael Angelo in the Vatican used to go to the Torso, so-called—a fragment of the art of antiquity—and he would feel along the marvelous lines chiseled in by-gone ages, and tell his pupils that thus and thus the outline should be completed. I turn to every faith on earth except Christianity, and I find every such faith a Torso. But if its lines were completed it would be a full statue corresponding in expression with Christianity."[12] Even Mr. P. C. Mozoomdar of the reformist Brahmo Samaj movement in India said in the course of the Parliament, "I regard Christ as an essential factor in the future of India. . . . The Parliament of Religions opens up the gate of a golden era, an era which shall purge off all the un-Christian elements of the different faiths, both Christian and non-Christian, and unite them all in Christ."[13] Professor Goodspeed, a historian of religion at the University of Chicago, foresaw at the Parliament a universal ethical religion for the future. "That religion," he said, "is not so much Christianity as Christ. Such was the deepest voice of the Parliament."[14]

As for the relation of Christianity to other faiths, the Parliament was very cautious. In his summary report, chairman Barrows was careful to state that "there was no suggestion on the part of Christian speakers that Christianity was to be thought of as on the same level with other religions."[15] For the most part,

Christians claimed universality for Christianity, while listening with earnestness to the witness of Muslims, Buddhists, and Hindus. It was with satisfaction that Barrows recalled how all the representatives of the great historic religions prayed together daily the Lord's Prayer. "The Christian spirit pervaded the conference from the first day to the last. Christ's prayer was used daily. His name was always spoken with reverence. His doctrine was preached by a hundred Christians and by lips other than Christian. The Parliament ended at Calvary."[16]

Apparently not everyone felt that the Parliament pointed unequivocally to the manifest destiny of Christianity. Barrows allowed in his report that "it was felt by many that to claim everything for Christianity and deny any good in other religions is not Christian, and is an impeachment of that Divine goodness which is not confined to geographical limits and which sends its favors upon the just and upon the unjust. Christians came to rejoice with an increased hopefulness as they perceived that religion, however imperfect, is, after all, the best there is in man, and that God is not confined in his mercy and benefactions to any favored race or people."[17] He added these lines of verse:

> So many roads lead up to God
> T'were strange if any soul should miss them all.

Despite the dominance of Christian discourse, the spirit of the Parliament was really something quite new. In his summary statement, Barrows wrote, "It was a novel sight that orthodox Christians should greet with cordial words the representatives of alien faiths which they were endeavoring to bring into the light of the Christian Gospel; but it was felt to be wise and advantageous that the religions of the world, which are competing at so many points in all the continents, should be brought together, not for contention but for loving conference, in one room."[18] The atmosphere was described as one of "mutual tolerance, extraordinary courtesy, and unabated good will."[19] In closing, Vivekananda thanked the "noble souls whose large hearts and love of truth first dreamed this wonderful dream, and then realized it," and proclaimed, "The Parliament of Religions has proved to the world that holiness, purity, and charity are not the exclusive possessions of any church in the world."[20] At the final session, Rabbi Emil Hirsch of Chicago announced, "The day of national religions is past. The God of the universe speaks to all mankind."[21]

In the overall composition of the Parliament there were many omissions. Of the major speakers only two were African-Americans. Commenting on the World's Fair as a whole, the president of Haiti, Frederick Douglas, called the

"White City" created for the event a "whitened sepulchre" for blacks.[22] Fannie Barrier Williams, one of the two African-Americans to address the Parliament, declared, "It is a monstrous thing that nearly one-half of the so-called evangelical churches of this country repudiate and haughtily deny fellowship to every Christian lady and gentleman happening to be of African descent. . . . The hope of the negro and other dark races in America depends upon how far the white Christians can assimilate their own religion."[23]

About ten percent of the participants in the Parliament were women. Theirs were some of the clearest and most powerful voices. Julia Ward Howe spoke with a certain scepticism about the noble ideals of all the religious traditions and asked provocatively "why the practice of all nations, our own as well as any other, is so much at variance with these noble precepts?" She continued, "I think nothing is religion which puts one individual absolutely above another, and surely nothing is religion which puts one sex above another."[24] Elizabeth Cady Stanton, who was then working on *The Woman's Bible* (published in 1895), addressed the Parliament, insisting that attention to the poor is the only way to salvation. She quoted the scriptural passages "God is no respecter of persons" and "He has made of one blood all the nations of the earth." And she challenged the assembly by declaring, "When the pulpits in our land shall preach from these texts and enforce these lessons, the religious conscience of the people will take new forms of expression, and those who in very truth accept the teachings of Jesus will make it their first duty to look after the lowest stratum of humanity."[25] The Reverend Antoinette Brown Blackwell, one of the few ordained women to speak, seemed to confirm Stanton's vision: "Women are needed in the pulpit as imperatively and for the same reason that they are needed in the world—because they are women. Women have become—or when the ingrained habit of unconscious imitation has been superseded, they will become—indispensable to the religious evolution of the human race."[26]

Finally, despite the overflowing sentiments of universal fellowship expressed at the Parliament, there were no Native Americans there. Indeed, one of the shocking facts of the Chicago World's Fair was the display of American Indians on the midway as curiosities. For many from the "Old World," they were as exotic as Vivekananda. No native elder or chief, however, spoke at the Parliament, and as far as I know no Parliament participant spoke to regret the absence of this religious perspective. Native American religiousness was clearly not seen as a religious perspective at all. Just three years earlier Chief Sitting Bull had been arrested and killed, the Ghost Dance had been suppressed, and 350 Sioux had been massacred at Wounded Knee Creek. On September 16, 1893, while the Parliament met, six and a half million acres of Cherokee, Pawnee, and Tonkawa reservation lands were opened for homesteader settlement and 50,000 settlers rushed to claim homestead lands on that day alone. Nothing of the trampling of native peoples was mentioned in the Parliament. No Black Elk, no Red Cloud, no White Calf was invited to speak of the vision of the native peoples of America. Not until eighty-five years later, with the American Indian Religious Freedom Act of 1978, was the integrity of Native American religiousness legally recognized. And even since then, native peoples have struggled constantly to prevent the degradation of sacred sites, to stop the display of sacred artifacts and bodily remains in museums, and to use ceremonial peyote in their rites.

A few months before the Parliament, in July of 1893, Frederick Jackson Turner delivered a much-discussed address to the American Historical Association in Chicago in which he asserted that the "frontier" was now closed: The 1890 census report had said, "The unsettled area has been so broken into by isolated bodies of settlement that there can hardly be said to be a frontier line." The movement toward the frontier line, beyond which lay what the American mythic imagination deemed "unsettled" territory, had been definitive for American consciousness. "Up to our own day American history has been in large degree the history of the colonization of the Great West. The existence of an area of free land, its continuous recession, and the advancement of American settlement westward, explain American development," said Turner. "And now . . . the frontier has gone, and with its going has closed the first period of American history."[27]

There in Chicago, in the summer of 1893, the western frontier was pronounced closed, and a new frontier of America's encounter with the East was about to open.

Swedes on the Frontier

In the summer of 1893, my great-grandmother Hilda Olson Fritz was picking blackberries for a living on the fire-scarred hillsides of the Olympic Mountains of Washington State, with a pistol on one hip and a baby on the other. The most precious cash commodity of these pioneers was blackberry jam, which they used in trade at the general store down on the bay. Hilda wrote of her long days, "I assure you, it was not easy to pick blackberries and carry a small child. When I set the baby down, I feared a cougar would bounce out, so my big revolver was always in the belt around my waist."[28]

Of all of the great-grandparents who were of Swedish immigrant stock, Hilda was the only one I knew when I was a child. I was four years old when I held her big pioneer hand and posed for a photograph with her on the front porch of the log cabin in the foothills of the Olympics. As Hilda told it, her father, Olaf Olson, left Sweden with "a great desire to come and aid Lincoln in the war for freedom from slavery." By the time he arrived, however, the war was over and Olaf had to settle for employment as a gardener in Des Moines. When he had earned some money he sent for his wife and children. Their decisions about where to settle—first in Rock Island, Illinois, and then in Stanton, Iowa—were motivated in part by the presence of a good Swedish Lutheran church. They were like so many European immigrants who settled in those decades in the Midwest; their farm life in Iowa, first in Stanton and then in Pocohontas County, was both rewarding and very difficult. There were blizzards, tornados, and crop failures. One year, Hilda wrote, "the grasshoppers left nothing. The turkeys ate so many grasshoppers they died, the hogs ate the dead turkeys and got the cholera."

After twenty years of struggle, the whole family moved further west, looking for the "free land" that pressed its imprint upon the imagination of these immigrant pioneers. Hilda and her husband-to-be, Olaf Edward Fritz—"Ed" for short—rode west with a cattle train. They made their way to the Pacific Northwest, where they settled in Port Townsend in 1889. The family leased a three-story building and started a hotel, where, as Hilda later put it, "no liquor was served and no Chinaman employed."

Further up the Olympic peninsula and inland, there was still homestead territory in the valley of the Dungeness River. Marian Taylor, the local historian of the Dungeness area, writes, "In 1891 four new families, three of them related, came as a group after having been told of the valley by an old prospector."[29] The three related families were Fritzes and Olsons, and the fourth would eventually be related too—the Hokansons, whose daughter Ida married Hilda and Ed's son Ike. When they all arrived in the summer of 1891, it was wild country. There were no roads from Port Townsend into the forests of the Olympic Mountains, so they took their supplies by boat up to Sequim Bay and hauled them on horseback up into the hills. It was a steep climb up from the bay. For five generations now our family has called the Fritz place by the name it must have had that first summer—Up in the Hills. Theirs was the life of real pioneers. Recalling their first cabin, Hilda wrote:

> The cabin was 12 by 14 feet. On the north side was the door, a large cedar slab hewed smooth. Also the fireplace and a wide cedar board to hold tin plates, tin cups, and other things. Under the window was a broad cedar log, very nice and smooth. That was our table. For seats we used small trees sawed off at the right heights. For beds we used fir branches that were woven together in a way that made them springy. I sewed gunny sacks together for two beds and found that the dry ferns made a good thin pad for the top of the fir-boughs. The branches from the fir trees, chopped fine, made a good covering for the floor and the smell of balsam was soothing.

Hilda made jam and bought their first pony with the proceeds. She planted a garden in what she called "the wilderness." She learned how to shoot and treed a wildcat. Her husband, Ed, got grouse and deer; she said if she had only one bear she could make it last through the whole winter. Toward evening on August 19, 1893, she built a fire for making jam, put the water on to boil, and headed out to the garden with her shotgun to get radishes and cabbage for supper and to see if she could shoot the rabbit that had been ravaging the garden. The sparks from the fire caught the cedar shakes on the roof and the cabin burned to the ground. "All that we had toiled so hard for through many years went up in smoke in less than an hour. But our courage, hope, and faith lived on and is still living."

Hilda was clearly a woman of faith. When I thumb through her old Swedish prayer book and her Evangelical hymnal, I wish I had really known her. I think about the similarities and the differences between her religious faith as a Swedish Lutheran and mine. In her journal she wrote a prayer that is, for me, a window into the religious sensibility of a woman who lived her adult life in relative isolation. "Grant us the peace of solitude. Give us the strength of the forest. Give us trust and faith that will stand by us in all tribulation. Help us to know that you, the Giver of joy and sorrow, are very near us and willing to help. For you know, O Lord, that we love not our fellow beings less, but nature more."

On September 11, 1893, Hilda would have been trying to keep house in a makeshift camp next to a burned-out cabin in the back hills of the Olympic Mountains as the World's Parliament of Religions opened in Chicago. By the winter, they had built the house of solid squared logs of Douglas fir where my grandfather Ike was born. Hilda may well have read something about the Parliament in the occasional copies of the *Seattle Times* that made their way "up in the hills," but I imagine she was preoccupied with building a new life in what was left of the frontier. The newspapers described the color and the spectacle of the Parliament—the eloquent turbaned Vivekananda, the scarlet robes of Cardinal Gibbon, the fiery Dharmapala from Ceylon swathed in white garments, the rainbow of pure silk worn by the delegates from China and Japan.

There were new worlds launched that September in Chicago and in the hills of the Olympics. Different as they were, they are both worlds that have come to be not only mine but ours as Americans. My great-grandparents and grandparents were at the last edge of the closing frontier in the West. The frontier of encounter with the East, the Orient, was just beginning.

At the time of the Parliament, the Swedes on the other side of the family, my father's side, were also beginning to come from the "old country" one at a time, Ecks and Nordquists. The Nordquists were a big clan, ten brothers and sisters in all. As soon as those who were here earned enough, they sent for the next in line. My grandmother Anna Nordquist was the last to come. She and her sister Signe and their mother, Louisa, sailed from Sweden to New York on the Lusitania in 1914. They traveled from coast to coast on the train. Both the newness and the caution they felt as Swedish women traveling alone across the whole stretch of this new world was conveyed by Grandma Anna's tale of buying a bagful of what they thought were apples in New York before getting on the train. When Anna tried one and found it soft, she spit it out and insisted they throw the whole bag away; only later did she discover that the rotten apples were peaches. Anna worked for a time as a maid in Portland, Oregon, before moving to Anaconda, Montana, where there was a large Swedish settlement. There she met my grandfather Theodore Eck, a carpenter and general contractor, at a big Swedish community picnic.

The world of my grandparents was the bipolar world of the "old country" and the new. Anaconda and Butte, Montana, dominated by the Anaconda Copper Company, were characterized by ethnic rivalries and mutual suspicion among the Swedes, Italians, Poles, and Irish. Asia did not figure in that world, despite the presence of a small Chinese population in Butte. Hindus, for the most part, lived in India, Muslims in the wide stretch from Indonesia to Morocco, and Buddhists in South and East Asia. My grandmother Anna Nordquist Eck had never met a Hindu or a Buddhist, or, very likely, anyone from Asia. In thinking through the meanings of life and death, she did not come in contact with the ideas of the Bhagavad Gita, or the Upanishads, or the Four Noble Truths. Though Hindu ideas had come gently into American literature through the writings of Emerson and Thoreau, Grandma Eck did not read the literature of American transcendentalism. In those days Americans encountered Asia, if at all, in the images gleaned from the relationships of mission. So vibrant was the idea of mission to Grandma Eck that when I returned from my first year in India she always introduced me proudly to her friends as "my granddaughter who is a missionary in India."

Asian Exclusion

The late nineteenth- and early twentieth-century image of America as a nation of immigrants simply did not include, in the American mythic imagination, immigrants from Asia. The torch-bearing arm of the Statue of Liberty was raised in New York harbor toward the Atlantic, not the Pacific. When Israel Zangwill, the nineteenth-century playwright, spoke of America as "God's melting pot"— melting, refining, and reshaping immigrant races and peoples into a new race— it was assumed that the peoples of the melting pot were European. A similar welcome was not extended westward toward Asia.

In 1882, the first Chinese exclusion act was passed. It specifically prohibited the entry of skilled and unskilled laborers from China into the U.S. and those who were already here were barred from eligibility for naturalization as citizens and their wives were made ineligible for entry. The debate in Congress over the bill was thick with anti-Chinese rhetoric. A member of the House of Representatives declared, "They do not wear our kind of clothes . . . and when they die, their bones are taken back to their native country."[30] The period of exclusion was reduced from twenty years to ten in the final bill. Only thirty-seven members of the House of Representatives opposed it, among them Congressman Joyce, who stated the case eloquently: "I would not vote for it if the time were reduced to one year or even one hour, because I believe that the total prohibition of these people from our shores for any length of time . . . is a cowardly repudiation . . . of a just and long established principle in our government."[31]

Chinese workers had come to Hawaii and then to the U.S. beginning in the 1840s as agricultural laborers and as miners. Chinese labor had built the railways across the West and up and down the Pacific coast. In Montana, Chinese had come to the gold and copper mines in Helena and Butte, where sizable

"Chinatowns" developed. An 1869 Helena newspaper article gives a glimpse of emerging Chinese culture: "Today is the (Chinese) annual Josh Day [*sic*], on which occasion their custom is to visit the burial places—as our China men and women have done, closing their ceremonies about 2 p.m.—burn incense and innumerable small wax candles about the head stones or boards of the graves, depositing a liberal lunch of choice eatables and drinkables, designed for the spirits of the departed; recite propitiatory prayers to their savior (Josh), and otherwise show themselves sacredly minded of the welfare of their dead."[32]

In 1870, when the first census of the Montana territory took place, the Chinese were 10 percent of the population. They contributed to the economy with Chinese businesses; there were two dozen Chinese-owned laundries in Helena alone. But Montana also experienced the rising xenophobia that led to the Chinese Exclusion Act. The Butte newspaper published articles filled with invective: "The Chinaman's life is not our life, his religion is not our religion. His habits, superstitions, and modes of life are disgusting. He is a parasite, floating across the Pacific and thence penetrating into the interior towns and cities, there to settle down for a brief space and absorb the substance of those with whom he comes into competition. His one object is to make all the money he can and return again to his native land, dead or alive. . . . Let him go hence. He belongs not in Butte."[33]

In 1892, the Geary Act extended the exclusion for another ten years. At the time of the World's Parliament of Religions, the Honorable Pung Kwwang Yu, a Chinese representative in Washington, D.C., spoke at the closing session of the pain of such prejudice: "I have a favor to ask of all the religious people of America, and that is that they will treat, hereafter, all my countrymen just as they have treated me."[34] In that same year, 1893, the Butte newspaper editorialized, "The Chinaman is no more a citizen than a coyote is a citizen, and never can be."[35] Montana historian Robert Swartout, Jr., looking back on this period, writes that anti-Chinese prejudice was "so pervasive that recognition of the Chinese role in the development of modern Montana would come only after most of the Chinese pioneers and their descendents had left the state."[36]

The exclusion that began with anti-Chinese legislation gradually dilated to include Filipinos, Japanese, Koreans, and other "Asiatics" as well, even "Hindoos" (meaning anyone from India). In the fall of 1907 my grandfather Ike would have been scarcely twelve in that cabin in the hills of the Olympics. That September, across Puget Sound in Bellingham, a mob of five hundred lumbermen attacked the simple homes of immigrant Hindu mill workers. Joan Jensen, who has documented the experience of Asian Indian immigrants in North America, tells the tale: "Battering down the doors, the mob threw belongings into the street, pocketed money and jewelry, and dragged Indians from their beds. The Indians fled, some injuring themselves by jumping from buildings in an attempt to escape. Those who did not move fast enough were beaten."[37] Hundreds of Indians were driven from town. The editor of the *Bellingham Herald* insisted, "The Hindu is not a good citizen. It would require centuries to assimilate him, and this country need not take the trouble. Our racial burdens are already heavy enough to bear. . . . Our cloak of brotherly love is not large enough to include him as a member of the body politic."[38] This perception of the Hindu must have held sway in Port Angeles, the lumber town on the Olympic peninsula. In 1913, the real estate brokers of Port Angeles and Clallam County pledged not to sell property to "Hindoos or to Negroes."[39]

The exclusion of Asians that had been launched with the anti-Chinese campaign of the 1880s was extended repeatedly by legislation pressed by an organization called the Asiatic Exclusion League. In 1924, the National Origins Act established permanent restrictions on immigration from outside the Western hemisphere, and prohibited the entry of aliens not eligible for U.S. citizenship, which included Asians. Severe restrictions on Asian immigration and naturalization lasted through World War II. During the war, anti-Japanese fear and suspicion spread to include hundreds of thousands of Japanese Americans who were citizens of the United States. The internment camps in which American citizens were placed during World War II recapitulated the sentiments that had generated the whole history of Asian exclusion.

Exclusion also meant, in some cases, denial of citizenship to those who were already here. In 1923, the Supreme Court of the United States ruled that "Hindus" could not be American citizens. The decisive case involved a certain Mr. Thind, a Sikh gentleman who had settled in California, married an American woman, and become a naturalized citizen. "Hindu" was understood as a racial, not a religious, group. Mr. Thind was now to be stripped of his citizenship because of his race. Hindus, the court reasoned, were not "free white men" and therefore did not qualify for American citizenship. Scholars apparently reminded the court that Indians and Europeans both came from the Indo-European language and racial family, but the judges ruled that such was not the perception of the "common man." "It may be true that the blond Scandinavian and the brown Hindu have a common ancestor in the dim reaches of antiquity, but the average man knows perfectly well that there are unmistakeable and profound differences today."[40]

A New "New World"

In 1965, a new immigration act initiated by John F. Kennedy was signed into law by Lyndon Johnson. Robert Kennedy, in supporting the act before the U.S. Congress, said, "Everywhere else in our national life, we have eliminated discrimination based on national origins. Yet, this system is still the foundation of our immigration law."[41] The new policy eliminated national origins quotas and opened the door again for immigration from Asia.

Gradually, in the course of the next two decades, the ethnic makeup of the United States came to include many more immigrants from Asia, the Pacific, and the Middle East. These new Americans have changed the religious landscape of the United States. Today there are Hindu and Buddhist temples and Muslim mosques in virtually every American city, most of them largely invisible because they are in homes and office buildings, or in former churches, Masonic lodges, and movie theaters. In the 1980s, however, evidence of the new religious reality began to become visible as majestic and imposing temples were consecrated, such as the Hindu Sri Meenakshi Temple in Houston and the Buddhist Hsi Lai Temple in Hacienda Heights, and as mosques were built, such as the one that rises from the cornfields outside Toledo or the one that occupies a whole city block at Third Avenue and Ninety-sixth Street in Manhattan. Immigrant America of the late nineteenth century often thought of itself as a new world when in fact it was the old world of Europe transplanted into a new environment. But the world of multireligious America in the late twentieth century is truly a new frontier.

One hundred years ago, Swami Vivekananda was a novelty and was treated like an exotic prophet in the parlors of Brattle Street in Cambridge and in the wealthy suburbs of Boston. Now there is a large South Asian minority population in Boston's wealthy suburbs. Hindus have consecrated a fine temple in Ashland, designed by a traditional Hindu temple architect from South India, built by a Wellesley engineering firm, and finished with religious images and ornamentation by a team of artisans trained in the workshops of Mahabalipuram. An adjacent residential compound houses three full-time priests. The Ganesha temple in Flushing, New York, and the Sri Venkateshwara Temple in Pittsburgh were the first full-scale Hindu temples in the United States, both built in the late 1970s. Now there are large Hindu temples with their elaborate towers in virtually every major metropolitan area—in Aurora outside Chicago, in the hills of Malibu near Los Angeles, in Lanham, Maryland, outside Washington, D.C. There are temples in Flint, Michigan; Allentown, Pennsylvania; Whittier,

California; Beavercreek, Ohio; Smyrna, Georgia; Kenner, Louisiana. There are summer camps for Hindu young people. Were he to tour the United States today, Swami Vivekananda would be greeted at Bengali summer picnics and Hindu heritage family camps.

A century ago, Dharmapala denounced America's ignorance of the life and teachings of the Buddha. Today many Americans would do no better if quizzed on the life of the Buddha, and yet today virtually the whole of the Buddhist world has roots in North America, from the Theravada traditions of South Asia to the Vajrayana traditions of Tibet and the Mahayana traditions of China, Japan, and Korea.

On a Sunday in Los Angeles not long ago, I set out with my mother and a detailed city map to explore the Buddhist world in what must be the most complex Buddhist city on earth. At the Wat Thai temple in North Hollywood, hundreds of Thai-American children were learning the Thai language and drawing crayon pictures of the life of the Buddha in the educational wing, while their parents listened to a sermon in the temple or chatted under the trees next to open-air Thai kitchens and snack stalls. At the Kwan Um Sa Korean temple on Olympic Boulevard we saw the large and stately temple room, formerly a Masonic lodge, lined with posh red chairs facing an altar with a huge standing Buddha. At the Sri Lankan temple, a house on Crenshaw Avenue, we spoke with one of the resident saffron-robed monks about his Buddhist chaplaincy at UCLA.

We arrived at the Vietnamese temple on Berendo Street, the oldest of the thirty or forty Vietnamese Buddhist temples in the L.A. area, as a group of volunteers was mailing thousands of invitations for the upcoming celebration of the Buddha's birthday. At the International Buddhist Meditation Center we met an American-born nun who had been initiated into a Vietnamese Buddhist lineage and is an energetic organizer of the city's Buddhist Sangha Council, an ecumenical organization unlike any other in the world, bringing monks and nuns from across the Buddhist spectrum together in a local forum. A few blocks away we visited the Zen Center of Los Angeles, where the houses of half a city block are occupied by the Zen students of Maezumi Roshi. At the Hsi Lai Temple in Hacienda Heights, we met Taiwanese nuns who led the Chinese Buddhist community in the construction of the largest Buddhist temple complex in the Western Hemisphere—a massive and elegant palace-style hilltop temple and convent complex. When my mother went home to Montana with the photographs of her trip to Los Angeles her friends gasped, "This is L.A.?"

The first mosque in the United States was built by Lebanese immigrants in Cedar Rapids, Iowa, in 1934. In the 1950s the same Iowan community of Muslims started the first Muslim publishing house. By 1971, they had dedicated another new mosque in Cedar Rapids. The history of Iowa Muslims is but a part of the history of American Islam, for we now know that long before the rise of the Black Muslim movement in Detroit in the 1930s there were African-American Muslims who had come as slaves from Africa. There are now more than six hundred mosques in the United States—in Houston, Chicago, Toledo, Tempe, Savannah. In Washington, D.C., the Islamic Center is a beautiful building, its minaret rising above the tree-lined streets of the embassy district. The mosque in Quincy, south of Boston, sits in the shadow of the great cranes of the Quincy shipyards, which employed many of the early Muslim immigrants to the Boston area from Jordan, Syria, and Lebanon. It is but a short walk from the birthplace of the sixth president of the United States , John Quincy Adams, and is one of some twenty mosques in the Islamic Council of New England. The nationally organized Islamic Society of North America has its headquarters in Plainfield, Indiana, and has large conventions every Labor Day weekend. There is an Association of Muslim Scientists and Engineers, an Islamic Medical Association, a Muslim Students Association. There are more Muslims in the United States today than Episcopalians. According to some estimates, there will soon be more Muslims than Jews. On June 25, 1991, the U.S. House of Representatives, which opens each day with an act of prayer, for the first time heard a prayer offered by a Muslim religious leader, Siraj Wahaj, an African-American imam from the Masjid al-Taqwa in Brooklyn.

There are also many smaller Asian communities, such as the Jains, the Zoroastrians, and the Sikhs, in the United States. The Sikh community dates back to the early decades of the twentieth century, when the first Sikh immigrant workers arrived in California and the Pacific Northwest. They were disparagingly called "rag-heads" and the newspapers spoke threateningly of a "tide of turbans." Many were among the "Hindus" thrown from their boarding houses in the Bellingham riots. The Pacific Khalsa Diwan Society was founded in Stockton, California, in 1912 and the *gurudwara* (Sikh house of worship) in Stockton is one of the oldest in the United States. There are more than fifteen *gurudwaras* in California and nearly as many on the East Coast, the largest being the Richmond Hill *gurudwara* in Queens, which gathers as many as five thousand Sikh Americans for large festival days. There are some sixty Jain temples and centers in the United States, like the one on Cedar Street in Norwood, Massachusetts.

Both the Jain Association of North America and the Zoroastrian Association of North America have biannual congresses.

Of course there are many parts of the United States where this new world of religious diversity has yet to be visible. But even in those places—perhaps the hills of the Olympic peninsula or the streets of Anaconda, Montana—the cultural awareness of such diversity is generated through the modern media. When my Grandma Anna came from Sweden in 1914, she and her mother, Louisa, brought the family Bible. For them, and for almost everyone in their generations, the Bible was the most important book they owned. For some it was the *only* book they owned. In any case, it was the main book on the subject of religion. Today the bookstores, even in Anaconda and Port Townsend, are stocked with paperback books on the world's religions. There are scriptures such as the Bhagavad Gita and the Holy Qur'an. There are collections of religious poetry telling of the heart's love of Lord Krishna. There are books on Zen Buddhist meditation, Islamic calligraphy, Sufi poetry, and Jewish holidays. There are books describing the legends, rites, and myths of the Plains Indians, the Yoruba, and the Maori. Newspapers, even the Butte *Montana Standard* and the Port Angeles *Peninsula Daily News*, contain stories of the Dalai Lama's Nobel Peace Prize, the Islamic resurgence in the Middle East, the rising Sikh self-consciousness in India, and the opening of a Buddhist peace pagoda in Massachusetts. Everywhere consciousness of the world's religious diversity is greater than ever before.

In North America this plurality is a relatively new phenomenon of the past quarter-century. Even so, it is astonishing that we have paid so little notice. During the 1970s and early 1980s there was a great deal of attention and concern about what were called "cults," some of them being new guru-centered religious movements from India. When young people, Protestant, Catholic, and Jewish, followed enthusiastically after Hindu gurus or new-style Tibetan Buddhist teachers, it was newsworthy and, to some, alarming. An anti-cult movement complete with "deprogrammers" was mobilized. And yet all the while we failed to notice that Hindu Americans were becoming our surgeons, engineers, and newsdealers, Buddhist Americans our bankers and astronauts, Muslim Americans our teachers, lawyers, and cabdrivers. By now we are all virtually next-door neighbors.

The "Old World" is also becoming a new world. Western European countries such as Britain, France, Germany, and Sweden are all struggling with the meaning of their new religious plurality. Britain, long dominantly and officially Christian, is a barometer of the changes that are taking place. When Fielding wrote *Tom Jones* two centuries ago, his Parson Thwackum could say, "When I mention religion, I mean the Christian religion; and not only the Christian religion, but the Protestant religion, and not only the Protestant religion, but the Church of England." Today, however, when religion is mentioned in Parliament or in relation to school assemblies, it can no longer be presumed to be the Protestant religion of the Church of England. In Britain, there are over a million Muslims, 400,000 Hindus, and 400,000 Sikhs. Leicester is said to be the second-largest Hindu city in the world outside India (second only to Durban in South Africa). There are substantial numbers of Muslims in Bradford and Birmingham, of Sikhs in Southall and Handsworth. In the city of Coventry, 10 percent of the population is from the Indian subcontinent. Pluralism is an issue at virtually every level of British life—from the election of city officials and the construction of school curricula to the theological discussions of the Church of England. So persistent have the questions of interfaith relations become that the Church of England issued a 1992 publication entitled *Multi-Faith Worship*, raising questions, exploring dilemmas, and offering advice. How should Hindu and Sikh prayers be included in the annual Boy Scout services? What kind of installation service is appropriate for a newly elected Sikh mayor? How might a memorial service for disaster victims be shaped to include Christian, Muslim, Hindu, and Sikh prayers?[42]

Religious plurality is an older but not necessarily an easier issue in Asia. India's long and legendary pluralism, rooted in a broadly Hindu ethos, was torn by rising communal self-consciousness during the struggle for independence. Religious communalism literally divided the land into India and Pakistan. But the political use of religious identity—Muslim, Sikh, and Hindu—has not waned in supposedly secular India since then; indeed, it seems to be on the rise. Elsewhere in Asia, Indonesia has built its government on what it calls the Panchashila—the "five principles" of a general monothesim and humanitarianism—which it claims unite Islam, the dominant religion, with Hinduism, Buddhism, Christianity, and Indonesian traditional religion. Nearby Malaysia is officially Muslim, but struggling with Hindu and Chinese minorities. The Philippines are predominantly Catholic and struggling with the aspirations of a Muslim minority demanding its political rights. Sri Lanka has seen over a decade of violence between the predominantly Buddhist Sinhalese majority and the Tamil minority population, which is largely Hindu. With the disintegration of the Soviet bloc, the "politics of identity" seems to be the dominant source of energy and of conflict in the struggle of cultures and ethnic groups for independence and for power.

Frontiers of Encounter

The world has always been one of religious diversity and interaction. From ancient times to the present, people have encountered and have had to interpret for themselves the religions of their neighbors. Herodotus, encountering the mysteries of Egypt, identified Egyptian gods as ancestors of the more familiar gods of Greece, assimilating the foreign into the familiar. When early Buddhist monks travelled along the Silk Road from India to China in the third century, they had to speak of the Middle Way of Buddhism in language that would be understood by Taoist and Confucian sages. Buddhism changed and so did China. When the first Muslim generals and their armies came to India in the eleventh century, the scholar Alberuni was with them, taking upon himself the task of trying to understand the religiousness of the Hindus, whom he found "totally differ from us in religion, as we believe in nothing in which they believe and *vice versa*."[43] His *Kitab al-Hind* (Book of India), might be seen as one of the earliest works of comparative religion. It is a book which closes with a prayer to God "to pardon us for every statement of ours which is not true."[44]

The Hebrew prophets interpreted the Canaanite gods as impotent idols, nothing but dust, blocks of wood. The early Christians interpreted their Hebrew background in light of what they saw as a new reality, the Messiah, the crucified and risen Christ. Christianity is an interpretation of Jewish traditions and Jewish hopes, but the church also moved in the Greco-Roman world among people who had never held those traditions and hopes, who did not know the language of the Hebrew prophets, and Christians had to offer an interpretation to them as well. In Athens, Paul stood in the agora and spoke of the god to whom the Athenians had erected a shrine marked "To the Unknown God," and he quoted the Greek poets who spoke of the one "in whom we live and move and have our being" (Acts 17:28). In the second century, the Christian theologian Justin Martyr insisted that the God of the Bible was surely the God of Plato as well, and that the activity of God, the Logos, fully present in Christ, is universal and is seen wherever intelligence and goodness are seen. Interpreting the "other" in light of our own experience and tradition has always been a religious necessity and a religious challenge.

What is new today is not the diversity of our religious traditions nor the task of interpretation. What is new is our sharply heightened awareness of religious diversity in every part of our world and the fact that today everyone—not just the explorers, the missionaries, the diplomats, and the theologians—encounters and needs to understand people and faiths other than their own. In the hundred years since the days of Great-grandma Hilda and the World's Parliament of Religions, all of us have come to a very new place in our religious history. For much of the world's population, our religious ghettos are gone or almost gone, and the question of how we respond to religious difference is unavoidable. Hasidic Jews live in neighborhoods adjacent to those of Korean Buddhists and African-American Muslims. Some may retreat into voluntary isolation again, claiming the loyalties of religion, ethnicity, race, or language ever more insistently, but the exigencies of an interdependent world will not permit such a response for long. The question of difference is not only a cultural, social, and political question. It is also a theological question, as people in each religious tradition think about what it means to embrace a particular faith in full recognition of the power and dignity of other faiths in the lives of their neighbors.

Diversity, of course, is not pluralism. Diversity is simply a fact, but what will we make of that fact, individually and as a culture? Will it arouse new forms of ethnic and religious chauvinism and isolation? Or might it lead to a genuine pluralism, a positive and interactive interpretation of plurality? These are critical questions for the future, as people decide whether they value a sense of identity that isolates and sets them apart from one another or whether they value a broader identity that brings them into real relationship with one another.

Swami Vivekananda ended one of his electrifying speeches at the parliament of 1893 with a flourish of romantic, visionary hope, a tribute to America: "It was reserved for America to call, to proclaim to all quarters of the globe that the Lord is in every religion. . . . Hail Columbia, mother-land of liberty! It has been given to thee, who never dipped her hand in her neighbor's blood, who never found out that shortest way of becoming rich by robbing one's neighbors, it has been given to thee to march on at the vanguard of civilization with the flag of harmony."[45] America has grown up to disappoint this vision in the past century, dipping her hand repeatedly in the blood of her neighbors, discovering in her own way the shortcuts to getting rich. In 1893, the United States used military force in Hawaii, in 1894, in Nicaragua; in 1898, Cuba and then the Philippines. All this before the new century had begun. In fact, American history told from the standpoint of its native peoples would have amply demonstrated the soiling of Vivekananda's vision from the very day that European settlers came to these shores. Even so, there is one part of the vision—the flag of harmony part—that may still be claimed as a distinctively American vision, though not a reality, one hundred years after the Parliament. As rocky and sometimes ugly as the history of immigration has been, with its racism, prejudice, and exclusion, America has kept on growing and changing into an ever-becoming nation of immigrants. This process of growth has created in the United States what is by now the most ethnically diverse nation on earth—and simultaneously one of the most religiously minded. With conscious and energetic attention to the question of difference and diversity, it is just possible that the United States may become a culture not simply of diversity, but of genuine pluralism. This would surely be America's most significant contribution to world civilization.

In 1893 the census declared that the frontier line was no longer traceable on the map of America. But there were other frontiers that were just beginning to be visible. These were the frontiers of encounter, where it was no longer a question of pushing out the known borders of settlement into what was "unsettled land," but of reaching the known borders of one community and encountering others. These were the frontiers that were just beginning to be visible in 1893— in America's encounter with the native peoples of the continent; in European America's encounter with Asian immigrants; and in Christian and Jewish America's encounter with people of other great faiths and civilizations. Today these frontiers of encounter and many others like them are everywhere. They are local and global, east and west, north and south. It is at these frontiers that our common future will be defined.

The Names of God

The Meaning of God's Manyness

THE LAND of the Pacific Northwest, where my great-grandparents homesteaded in the hills one hundred years ago, was for many centuries the ancestral home of the Quillayut, the Klallam, the Suquamish, and the Quinault. They saw the land as sacred, shaped out of god-like ancestors who at the time of the beginning were transformed into the snow-capped mountains, the tumbling rivers, and the clear blue lakes of the Olympic peninsula. As Chief Sealth or Seattle of the Suquamish people is said to have put it on the occasion of the treaty transferring these lands to the government of the United States in 1854, "Every part of this soil is sacred in the estimation of my people. Every hillside, every valley, every plain and grove has been hallowed by some sad or happy event in days long vanished. Even the rocks, which seem to be dumb and dead as they swelter in the sun along the silent shore, thrill with memories of stirring events connected with the lives of my people."[1] The idea that such lands could be privately owned and transferred legally from hand to hand was completely alien to the native peoples of America; the sacred treasure of nature could not be owned by any human being.

To the native peoples of the Pacific Northwest and the Great Plains, the ownership of God was as unimaginable as the ownership of nature. The claims of the missionaries who came in the wake of conquest preaching exclusive access to the true God were as astonishing to the Suquamish and the Blackfeet as the claims of homesteaders and miners to land, forests, minerals, and water. It is important to let their astonishment rise to full relief in our consciousness, for most of us are so deeply rooted in the mythic terrain of property ownership we scarcely think to question it or even to recognize it as one particular way of thinking about humanity's relation to the natural world. The private ownership of land has become a sacred principle of American life. The ownership of God takes but a little more audacity than the ownership of nature.

Whatever we may think of God, the referent of that word, that symbol, is a mystery. God is finally beyond our grasp. God is not ours—even with the grace of God's revealing. There are, however, Christians and people of other faiths who seem to have no trouble speaking of God's ultimacy with one breath and staking out a private territory of God's activity and grace with the next. But what if we presuppose, as do both the inclusivist and the pluralist, that God's activity and grace abound? What if we presuppose, as Hindus do, that the names and forms of the one God are many, limited only by our human capacity to recognize them? What might we learn, then, of the one we call "God," who cannot be owned as we wish to own land and property? In this chapter, I want to explore the meaning of "God," an exploration which I undertake as a Christian whose understanding of God has been both stretched and clarified through dialogue with people of other faiths, especially Hindus.

In India, those who speak of Krishna revere him as the creator, sustainer, and destiny of the whole universe, and yet they simultaneously understand him to be the divine child who was born and grew up in their midst in the area around Mathura called Braj, the Bethlehem and Nazareth of Krishna devotees. Krishna is clearly both ultimate and personal, both universal and particular. For those who focus their eyes on the personal and particular alone, the temptation to cling to a personal God is as strong as it is among Christian exclusivists. However, the predicament, the poignancy, and, finally, the futility of human possessiveness toward God is recognized by Hindus and is the constant theme of the stories of Krishna, who was loved ardently by the villagers of rural northern India.

In one of the most beloved episodes, Hindus recall how Krishna the cowherd used to beckon the milkmaids to the forest in the middle of the night to dance the great circle dance. They came, risking everything, and Krishna miraculously multiplied himself to dance with each and every one of them. There was plenty of Krishna to go around, an abundance of Krishna's presence, but the moment the milkmaids became possessive, each thinking that Krishna was dancing with her alone, Krishna disappeared. Krishna's hide-and-seek in the

Problem right now in society

world enabled the milkmaids to recognize that God is not theirs. The point is one that speaks to us all: The moment we human beings grasp God with jealousy and possessiveness, we lose hold of God. One might add that the religious point here is quite the opposite of God's jealousy, of which we hear so much in the Old Testament; it is God's infinite capacity to love and the problem of *human* jealousy.

In many religious traditions, Hindu and Christian included, people speak of the Divine as both ultimate and personal, beyond and yet within, transcendent and yet near. Hindus speak of Brahman as the impersonal ultimate, the one who is *nirguna*, or "without attributes," and beyond any name we might bestow; yet simultaneously they recognize Brahman as the one who is *saguna*, "with attributes," and in doing so use the names Vishnu, Krishna, Shiva, or Devi, the Goddess. Those who are especially devoted to any one of these gods simultaneously recognize that what they mean by Shiva or Vishnu, Devi or Krishna, is both incomprehensible and comprehensible. So, for example, Shaivas (devotees of Shiva) speak of Sada Shiva, the "eternal Shiva," with an infinite number of heads and arms, truly omniscient and omnipotent. At the same time they speak of Shiva as fully present right here—in this place, in this temple, under this very tree. In something of a similar way, those of us who are Christians use the term *God* to speak of Ultimate Reality. Yet in the same breath what we mean by God is not impersonal and abstract, but intensely personal, with attributes and qualities we can name, such as love, justice, mercy, and forgiveness, and with a face we can recognize not only in the face of Jesus but in the multitude of human faces to which the Christ event constantly refers.

All of us, in almost every religious tradition, live our lives with a theology of sorts, whether we think about God as father or mother, lover or hero, tyrant or thousand-armed protector. Even if we think more abstractly of the "ground of being," "depth dimension," or "ultimate concern," as Tillich would put it, or think of God as absent, meaningless, a foolish idea and an outworn name, we still have a theology in the sense that we have made some evaluative decisions about the meaning of the term *God* for ourselves. Even those who are uncomfortable with the term *God*, who quarrel with God or who reject God, have an idea and an image of God.

Of course, for many the word *theology* sounds a bit lofty, the sort of enterprise necessary and interesting only for priests, rabbis, or perhaps professors. But we are all theologians when we allow ourselves to encounter and ponder real questions about God. Theological thinking is the task of bringing to the surface and examining the ideas of ultimacy and reality that we already employ and in terms of which we live our lives. It is the critical and yet open questioning of these ideas. In this sense, theological thinking is not an idle matter. It undergirds the way in which we think about all questions of value. It is a necessity of life.

What do those of us who are Christians mean when we speak of God in history, in our times, in our world, and in our lives? We cannot simply presuppose the meaning of God as if it were perfectly evident, a given. Our concept of God is not simply given; we learn it, for better or for worse. We develop the operative concept of God with which we live, inheriting God, as it were, from our historical religious tradition as it is taught to us. Learning something of God from our families and teachers, from personal friends and public figures, we develop an impression of what this word *God* means. Perhaps it becomes more than a concept and we experience God for ourselves, but even within a single religious tradition such as Christianity, where the image of God is seen in Christ, people live their lives with vastly different concepts of God. Some live with an angry and vengeful God just over their shoulder. Some live with a God of forgiveness. Some live with a revolutionary God, others with a God who is a pillar of the status quo. We need to acknowledge our own responsibility for the image of God that we are content to believe in.

Not only is our understanding of God not a given, it is also not static. Life continually confronts us with questions and experiences that shove us face to face with what is "real" or "ultimate." When we struggle with serious illness, with death or catastrophe, with violence or racism, when we consider the problems of abortion and genetic engineering, we are continually adjusting, refocusing, deepening or sharpening our use of the term *God*. The encounter with people of other faith traditions, whether directly as personal friends or through the sacred literature that they cherish, also forces us to clarify for ourselves what it is *we* mean by the word.

People of many religious traditions speak of God in the singular or of gods in the plural. Some, like many Buddhists, resolutely refuse to speak of God or gods, either one. While it may be easy enough for Christians to apprehend the Muslim monotheistic understanding of God, the questions become more difficult when we encounter traditions like those of the Hindus, in which God is spoken of in the plural, under many names, or the Buddhist tradition, in which God is not spoken of at all. Whether our friends of other faiths do or don't speak of God or gods, it is important for us as Christians to apprehend as best we can what *they* mean by "God" or "gods" or "no-God." This will sharpen our own operative understandings of God as well.

The "imaginative construction" of the concept of God is a task for which Christian thinkers and laypeople alike have responsibility. It is a task which today must take seriously such issues as the new facts of global interdependence and the new voices of women, the marginalized, and the poor. Theologian Gordon Kaufman writes, "Theology is not merely a rehearsal and translation of tradition; it is (and always has been) a creative activity of the human imagination seeking to provide more adequate orientation for human life."[2] Among the urgent tasks of theology today is to confront seriously the challenge of religious pluralism, including the many ways of speaking of the Divine, about the gods, about God.

Encountering God in Other Traditions

Several years ago I spent an afternoon in Nairobi with the parents of a Muslim colleague at Harvard. They were Sindhis (from the part of the Indian subcontinent known as Sindh) and Ismaili Muslims, followers of the tradition of Islam led today by the Aga Khan. We visited the large mosque and Islamic center in Nairobi and enjoyed a meal at a Gujarati restaurant before they put me on the evening train to Mombasa. Just as they were getting me settled in my compartment, we heard the evening call to prayer. My friend's father glanced at his watch and said to me, "It is time to remember God in prayer. Excuse us." We closed the compartment door and he and his wife sat down to pray. I sat with them. "In the name of God, the Almighty, the Compassionate, the Merciful . . ."—I recognized the first few lines of the Qur'an in Arabic. I bowed my head and entered into the spirit of prayer with them, though I did not know the words they spoke. Is our God the same God? Frankly, the question did not occur to me then. I simply took it for granted.

What we take for granted in our experience is the very stuff of theological reflection. What allowed me to feel so natural in entering into a spirit of prayer with my Muslim friends? When I preached not long ago at a church on the green in Lexington, just across from the famous statue of the minuteman, I reflected on the matter. I spoke of the common monotheistic tradition of Judaism, Christianity, and Islam. Allah is not "the Muslim God," I said, but simply the Arabic word for God. Allah is none other than the one we know as God and is the name Arabic-speaking Christians also use when they pray. After the service, a con-

cerned parishioner cornered me to argue that Allah could not possibly be the
God we Christians worship, for our God includes Christ and the Holy Spirit,
whereas Allah does not. In a sense he was right. Our understanding of God and
the Muslim understanding of God are different in many ways. Given that fact,
how are we to think of Allah and God?

As we discussed the matter together over coffee, the parishioner and I concluded that there were at least three alternatives. We both rejected the idea that
there could be two "Gods," the one we call God and the one Muslims call Allah,
so the first possibility was that there could be one God, ours, with Allah being a
false god. This would be a form of exclusivist thinking: our way of thinking
about God excludes all others. It did not, however, seem to account for the vibrant faith of the fifth of humankind who worship Allah. The second alternative could be that we see God in God's fullness and that Muslims see the same
God less clearly. (Muslims, no doubt, would see it the other way around.) This
would be an inclusivist view—our way of thinking about God includes the
other, somewhat less adequate, conception. The third and perhaps most satisfactory alternative would be to insist that there is one God whom both Christians
and Muslims understand only partially because God transcends our complete
comprehension. As Muslims put it, "*Allahu akbar!*" It means not only "God is
great!" but "God is greater!" Greater than our understanding, greater than any
human idea of God. This would leave room for the self-understanding of both
Christian and Muslim and would be a pluralist view.

The Hindu tradition poses another kind of question: What about the
manyness of God? What about the gods? What about the prolific images of the
gods? When I stand with a Hindu woman, Ranjini, before the great granite image of Vishnu at Sri Lakshmi Temple in Ashland, Massachusetts, my first question is, What does this image mean to her, a Hindu woman? As a scholar of religion, I spend my working days pursuing such questions: How does a Hindu
conceptualize Vishnu and the presence of Vishnu in this image? How does she
think of Vishnu in relation to the other gods of India, even those present in the
two other shrines of the same temple—the goddess Lakshmi and the elephant-
headed Ganesha? But what happens when I push beyond my scholarly work
into my theological thinking as a Christian: How do *I* understand Vishnu? Is
Vishnu God?

My friend Ranjini would say unequivocally that Vishnu is God. She uses the
term *Lord*. She folds her hands in prayer before the image of Vishnu. She
touches her forehead to the threshold of his sanctum. She sings the words of the

"Suprabhatam," a morning hymn to Vishnu, every Saturday morning. She does not, of course, see this granite image as an "idol" if one means an inert stone that is not God. She understands the image as an embodiment and residence of the Divine. We were both at the temple during the week of ceremonies when the eyes of this granite image were ritually opened, when the spirit or breath, *prana*, was established in the image. In Ranjini's understanding, God, out of his gracious mercy, has come to dwell right there in Ashland and in the millions of other places where people have prepared room for God in their temples and in their hearts.

Because the image of God was properly "established" in this temple, it is incumbent upon the community to offer regular worship. The temple is open every day and a priest lives with his family at the temple to perform all the daily rites. People from the community come to these services as they are able, often on weekends, but the services go on, day in and day out, whether they are there or not. This image of Vishnu is a lens through which Ranjini's vision of God is directed and is a means through which her service to God is offered. She has a smaller image of Vishnu in a cupboard-size shrine in her Wellesley kitchen. Rather than having a separate room for worship, she prefers to have the Lord's shrine present where she works and spends much of her time. The presence of Vishnu is a living reality in her life.

The problem of God is raised in yet another way in encountering the Buddhist tradition, for most Buddhists do not speak of God or gods at all. In Buddhist analysis, the very idea of the eternal, unchanging God is one of the many ideas to which we human beings cling in order to avoid seeing deeply into the heart of reality. The Buddha was not a god, but a pathfinder and seer who saw into the nature and causes of human suffering. *Buddha* literally means "one who is awake." The Awakened One saw clearly that change is ubiquitous, moment to moment, year to year, age to age. The source of our perpetual anxiety is our drive to resist change, to somehow try to fence off a piece of the changing river of reality and stake it out for ourselves: this is me, this is mine, and this is my God. Chief Seattle would have a great deal of sympathy with the Buddhist insight that we human beings tend toward a kind of "spiritual materialism," making God into yet another possession.

Most Buddhists would say unequivocally that the Buddha, a historical figure who lived in the sixth century B.C.E., is not God or a god. The golden image of Buddha present in the meditation room at the Cambridge Insight Meditation Center focuses one's attention, but does not claim the devotion of meditators and certainly does not need to be served on a daily basis like the image of Vishnu at the Sri Lakshmi Temple. At the most, three bows of reverence will be made by those who come into the meditation room—to the Buddha, to the Dharma, his teaching, and to the *sangha*, the community of followers. As a pathfinder, the Buddha shows the way to the "far shore" of this river of birth and death. One can glimpse the far shore, one knows that it is there, but one cannot describe it other than to say it is inextricably related to this shore.

What do Muslims, Hindus, or Buddhists mean when they speak of Allah, of Vishnu, of the Buddha? Even those of us who study such matters recognize that these are questions entirely too big to answer, even in a lifetime, but they are questions we must ask if we are to glimpse the worlds of meaning in which other people of faith live. And once one has asked these questions and started down the path of inquiry, there is another equally important question. It is the self-reflexive question that a scholar may or may not choose to pursue: What do these realities, as understood by Buddhists, Hindus, or Muslims, mean to me as a Christian? This is a question we can begin to answer only by delving deeply into the meanings implicit in our own symbols of faith.

Let me reiterate our question rather bluntly. Is Allah the one we call God? Is Vishnu what we Christians mean by this word *God*? Is perhaps the "far shore" God? Of course, the question is not quite right, but we must begin by putting the question in this simple way so that we can see clearly the dimensions of our theological problem. For academic theologians the question can perhaps be made to vanish under the distancing lens of interpretive theory, but for most Christians and Hindus who live their daily lives in terms of these realities it is posed in just this simple way.

In the moments of quiet before the service begins, I enter into my church in Cambridge, sit quietly in a pew, fold my hands in my lap, close my eyes, and pray. Ranjini, my Hindu friend, goes to the temple in Ashland, presses her hands together in prayer in front of the large granite image of Vishnu. Are these two acts of worship structurally or experientially the same, but theologically different? (Of course there are those who would interpret both acts in psychological or sociological terms, but we are asking here about a religious interpretation.) How do those of us who are Christians or Hindus understand the relation between these two acts of prayer theologically? Again, there are at least three possibilities. Perhaps only one of us worships the "true" God, as the exclusivist would say. Perhaps only one of us sees God fully and the other but partially and dimly, which is an inclusivist position. Or, in a pluralist view, perhaps we honor the same God, whom Christians and Hindus know by different names, experience in different ways, and see from different perspectives and angles.

I pose these as stark alternatives, but they are not either simple or simple-minded ways of thinking. Quite frankly, most of us, Christians and others, do not know how to think about the questions these alternatives raise. We do not even know if we should ask such questions or, having asked them, if they are answerable. We need to think about them, however, for this theological thinking, this thinking about God, is not simply an "other-worldly" matter. It is inextricably related to our orientation in this world. It is a matter of considerable importance to us in this global village whether those of us who are Christians believe we understand God fully or think that we might actually learn something new about the one we call God from the faith of our neighbors.

In this chapter I want to focus on my own reflections about what I have learned about God from my encounter with Hindus and the multitude of gods of India, leaving aside for the time being the challenge of non-theistic Buddhism. There is an energetic Christian-Buddhist dialogue these days that has attracted some of the ablest Buddhist and Christian philosophers and theologians, but the Hindu tradition poses quite different questions to us, with its strong emphasis on the oneness of reality and its simultaneous display of the multitude of gods. The Hindu tradition is baffling to most Western theologians—attractive for its articulate philosophical theism and yet somehow repugnant for its astonishing, vivid, multi-armed and multi-headed gods.

The One Across Whom Space and Time Is Woven

Wesley Ariarajah, a Sri Lankan Christian theologian, describes a discussion with one of his students, a Christian girl, about a Hindu festival being held on the campus. "We usually do not go to the festival," she said, "because we don't worship the Hindu God." "The formulation of that statement fascinated me," Ariarajah writes. "'Do you mean that you don't agree with the way that Hindus understand God,' I asked her, 'or are you saying that there is a Hindu God, different from a Christian God?' 'I don't know,' she said with some hesitation. . . . 'But don't the Hindus and Muslims worship their gods, but we worship the true God revealed to us in Jesus Christ?'"[3]

Ariarajah poses the question for us: "In one sense what my student friend said is true. There is in fact a Christian, a Hindu, and a Muslim conception of God. . . . One must say that, even within the same religion, sometimes one's own conception of God is very different from another person's. But how many gods are there in the universe and beyond it? Are there many gods to choose from? Is there room for a Christian god, a Hindu god, and a Muslim god? The whole Bible stands on one firm foundation: there is one God, no other."[4]

One approach to understanding God language is to take seriously and literally the oneness of God, an affirmation which is fundamental to many religious traditions. Oneness is a powerful way of speaking of God's ultimacy. The Sikh daily prayer, the Japji, begins with the word "One." "*Ekhi Omkar,*" "One is God," the Supreme Reality is One. The Shema recited daily by Jews attests, "Hear, O Israel: The Lord Our God, is one Lord; and you shall love the Lord your God with all your heart, and with all your soul, and with all your might." For Muslims, the oneness of God is expressed in the Shahadah, which means literally bearing witness, the affirmation of faith: "There is no God but God, and Muhammad is God's messenger." The utter unity of God, the doctrine of *tawhid*, is central to Islam; God has no associates, no sons and wives, and there is no compromise with polytheism or with the human tendency to identify God with one's own group. In the Hindu tradition there are many attestations of oneness. One of the most popular dates back at least to 1,000 B.C.E., the time of the Rig Veda: "Truth is one; the wise call it by many names."[5]

The language of God's oneness is continuous in the Jewish, Christian, and Muslim traditions. All three faiths faced the problem of how to interpret the oneness of God in the context of polytheistic traditions. In the early years of the Christian community, for example, the task of Paul was to interpret the Gospel in the context of the religious and intellectual life of Greece and Rome. We have already referred to the story of Paul's encounter with the people of Athens and their gods (Acts 17:22–28). He points out the shrine marked "To an Unknown God" and proclaims to the people that the one they worship as unknown is the One God who made heaven and earth, who made the world and everything in it, and who made all the nations from one ancestor so that they would seek God and find him. When Paul wanted to communicate the scope of this unknown God, it was a Greek philosopher that he quoted, speaking of that One "in whom we live and move and have our being." The words are deeply familiar to those of us who are Christians; they are an intimate part of Christian liturgy and prayer. Through Paul, Christians have adopted and thoroughly integrated that language of the Greek philosophers into our very conception of God's ultimacy and God's mystery.

The God language I was first attracted to as a student was that of Paul Tillich, whose words constantly pointed toward the One "in whom we live and move and have our being." He spoke of "ultimate reality," the "ground of being," and "the depth dimension." In an essay called "The Depth of Existence," Tillich wrote, "The name of this infinite and inexhaustible depth and ground of all being is *God*. That depth is what the word *God* means. And if that word has not much meaning for you, translate it, and speak of the depths of your life, of the source of your being, of your ultimate concern, of what you take seriously without any reservation."[6] Depth does not have to be translated into Father, or into Lord and King. God is height, but also depth; transcendence, but also intimacy. God is what Dietrich Bonhoeffer called "the 'beyond' in the midst of our life."

It is not surprising that with Tillich on my mind, the first Hindu literature that attracted my attention was the Upanishads. There too was the language of sheer ultimacy and intimacy, a language that is not the sole preserve of any religious tradition, but is used with consummate power by the Hindu sages of the middle of the first millennium B.C.E. I would agree with the German philosopher Schopenhauer, who called the Upanishads "the most elevating reading the world has to offer." He read Anquetil Duperron's Latin translation of the Upanishads and wrote, "It has been the solace of my life and will be the solace of my death."[7]

For those of us who would speak of God today as well, the language of the Upanishads is compelling theological language. These teachings on the spiritual quest are largely dialogues, queries into the nature of the Divine, or of the Real. They pose some of the most provocative, intriguing, puzzling questions and contain some of the most exciting spiritual discourses in all religious literature. The Svetasvatara Upanishad, for example, begins with the questions "What is the cause? What is Brahman? Whence are we born? Whereby do we live? And on what are we established? Overruled by whom, in pains and pleasures, do we live our various conditions, O ye theologians?"[8] The questions are foundational and refer to that which Tillich would call Ultimate Reality. I have used the word *Divine* here; one might also deliberately use the term *God* to convey the force of this reality to those of us in the Western monotheistic traditions. The terms used in the tradition itself are *Brahman*, the foundational, impersonal divine reality; *Atman*, the foundational, divine reality within, sometimes spoken of as the soul or real self; and *Sat*, or Truth, Reality, Being. These terms all point to the same reality.

For Hindus, knowing Brahman is the most important knowledge of all, the knowledge of "[that] in which we live and move and have our being." As the Taittiriya Upanishad puts it, "That verily whence all beings are born, that by which when born they live, that into which on deceasing they enter—that be desirous of understanding, O pupil. That is Brahman" (3.1). The person who knows Brahman and knows the deepest secret of all—that the Brahman which sustains this entire universe is not different from the deepest reality within the human soul—is truly enlightened. The language of illumination and divine light suffuses the Upanishads. In the Chandogya Upanishad, for example, we are told that for the one who truly knows the secret doctrine of Brahman, the sun neither rises nor sets; it is always day (3.11).

The seekers of the Upanishads turn the religious imagination both outward and inward toward infinity. Looking toward "the Yon," they want to glimpse the One who laid the foundations of the earth. The seekers ask the wisest sages they can find about the nature of "that One" who existed in the beginning and who generated this whole earth. Their questions stretch to the brink of thought: "On what are the elements woven, warp and woof? On what are the sun, the moon, the stars, the gods woven, warp and woof? Across what is space itself woven, warp and woof?" The questions here are those of a persistent woman, the seeker Gargi, who finally asks the sage Yajnavalkya, "That which is above the sky, that which is beneath the earth, that which is between these two, the sky and the earth, that which people call the past and the present and the future—across what is that woven, warp and woof?" (3.8.3).

It could not be a bigger question. Indeed, Yajnavalkya tells Gargi that if she keeps asking such questions her head will fly off. But Yajnavalkya does give an answer—one which describes through a kind of *via negativa* the One across whom past, present, and future are woven, warp and woof:

> That, O Gargi, they call the Imperishable. It is not coarse, not fine, not short, not long . . . odorless, tasteless, without eye, without ear, without voice, without wind, without energy, without breath, without mouth, without name, unaging, undying, without fear, immortal, stainless, not uncovered, not covered, without measure, without inside and without outside. (3.8.8)

Turning inward, the seekers ask after the foundation of human life. Again, the more deeply one delves, the fewer the adjectives that suffice. Finally, "It is *neti, neti,*" "not this, not this . . ." The language of negation is part of both the Hindu and Christian traditions. Christian mystics and theologians alike speak of the *via negativa*, the experiential encounter with the Divine that leaves one speech-less, the intellectual encounter with "that than which no greater can be con-ceived."

But neither Hindus nor Christians let our understanding of the Divine rest with enormous words like Being, Truth, and Ultimate Reality—ineffable and indescribable. The divine reality, God, is made known in ways that are accessible to human beings. If Hindus systematically use the negation of every image to evoke the wideness of the Divine, they also systematically use the accumulation of every image to evoke the particularity of the Divine. If they speak of Brah-man as *nirguna*, "without qualities," they also speak of Brahman as *saguna*, "with qualities." From one standpoint, they say, there is no adjective, name, or form we can use to speak of Brahman; on the other hand, we do and must use adjectives, names, and forms. They speak of the Divine as *svabhava*, God's "es-sence"—God in God's self, stripping away every limiting conception, if we can imagine what that would mean. But they also speak of God as *svarupa*, God's "own form," meaning God in relation to us, and we can use words like *love* and *service* to describe this relationship.

In both the Hindu and Christian traditions, only the real spiritual pioneers strike out on the trackless path toward God's essence. Most of us use our speech, our emotion, our conception as best we can, in poetry and prayer and action, to apprehend the One "in whom we live and move and have our being" in the con-text of our day-to-day lives. In both traditions, Hindus and Christians affirm that God is revealed in ways that we humans *can* apprehend. We encounter not just "the unknown god" of the philosophers of Athens, but the many ways in which the Divine is known, face to face.

Quite frankly, the idea of "many ways" of divine revealing is a problem for many Christians, and for our Muslim and Jewish neighbors as well. It is just at this point that the Hindu tradition presents all of us in the monotheistic West with the world's most energetic challenge to take the multitude of God's names and forms seriously. Yes, we do have many gods, says the Hindu to the accusing Western monotheist, 330 million, to be precise.

The Habit of Oneness and the Challenge of the Many

Most of us from the West have an easier time thinking about oneness than about manyness. Oneness is the basis of our monotheistic traditions and we are gener-ally happy with the notion that value comes in ones. I had never thought about

God being more than One until I went to India. In Banaras, the sages read the Upanishads, with their language of the oneness of Brahman, surrounded by a bewildering array of deities manifesting God's manyness. I have tripped repeatedly upon the problem of manyness and the depth of our Western convictions about oneness, not only as I encountered the gods in the streets of Banaras, but also as I discovered the presuppositions of my own mind.

I first chose to do academic work on the meaning of the city of Banaras because it was widely held to be the most important of the religious centers of India. Hindus call it Kashi, the luminous City of Light. The lavish Sanskrit praises of the city intrigued me and I was fascinated by the accounts of nineteenth-century British visitors like Norman Macleod, who wrote, "Benares is to the Hindoos what Mecca is to the Mohammedans, and what Jerusalem was to the Jews of old. It is the 'holy' city of Hindostan. I have never seen anything approaching to it as a visible embodiment of religion; nor does anything like it exist on earth."[9] Indeed, living in Banaras as a college student, and later as a doctoral student, I too had never seen anything like it on earth.

In the course of my research on the sacred geography of Banaras, I began to glimpse in my peripheral vision some indications that Banaras was not *the* sacred city of the Hindus, at least in the way I had imagined. This luminous Kashi was said to be the earthly embodiment of Shiva's *linga* of light, the *jyotirlinga*, but so were eleven other places in India; there are twelve *jyotirlingas*. Kashi was said to be a place where death brings liberation, but such a claim was also made for Mathura, for Dwaraka, and probably for countless other sacred places in India. Banaras was circled by a famous pilgrimage route of circumambulation called the Panchkroshi Road, but so also, I found, were there Panchkroshi circuits around many pilgrimage places.

For a time I resisted fully acknowledging these glimpses from my peripheral vision, convinced that the praises of this place, Banaras, ought to be unique; such is the stake that academics often invest in the importance of their own subject. Yet I became increasingly aware, and with some irritation I must admit, that almost nothing of the praises of this sacred place really was unique. Kashi itself was duplicated all over India in cities, temples, and temple complexes that touted themselves as "Kashi of the South," or "Kashi of the North," or "Secret Kashi." The River Ganges, on which my sacred city sat so proudly, was also duplicated. There were said to be seven rivers as sacred as the Ganges, and actually called by the name Ganga, and to each was ascribed the heavenly origin and the gracious power of the Ganges I knew at Banaras.

By the time I extended my pilgrimage work in India to the wider scope of Indian sacred geography, I was not surprised to find that Mount Meru, the mythic cosmic mountain said to anchor the universe at its very center, was duplicated throughout India and lands influenced by Indian culture, such as Indonesia. I was astonished, however, to find that this cosmic mountain joining heaven and earth, described so carefully in the mythological texts, was said to have a greater circumference at the top than at the bottom. Who had ever imagined such a mountain? Its proportions were an inversion of our usual image of a mountain peak. Rather than culminating in a single point, it spread out at the top, making enough room for the cities of a whole host of gods.

For those of us schooled in the religious imagination of the West, a mountain peak is not a spacious place. If there is a God on the mountaintop, there is room enough for one only. And anything truly important should be unique, singular, not part of a set of seven or twelve. What I discovered and confronted in the course of my work was my own distinctively Western habit of thought, grounded primarily in the Western tradition of monotheism: the expectation of singularity and uniqueness, and the valuing of such singularity and uniqueness. It is a way of thinking equally pervasive in the three great monotheistic traditions of the West—Judaism, Christianity, and Islam. In monotheistic consciousness, the singular is the proper number for questions of Truth: There is one God, one Only-Begotten Son of the Father, one Seal of the Prophets, one Holy Book, one Holy Catholic and Apostolic Church. It might be called "the myth of monotheism": that there is one and only one holy story to be told, to be reflected upon by theologians, and to be participated in by the faithful.

The monotheism of the West is not simply the intellectual concern of theologians or the doctrinal concern of the faithful who begin their creed with the words "I believe in one God ... " It is presupposed throughout our culture as only our deepest and most basic myths are presupposed. It is a myth in the sense that it is the powerful story we tell about reality, so powerful we do not recognize it as our story. It is not the world-shaping myth of religious people alone, but is a particular way of seeing and evaluating that has shaped equally the worldviews of Marxists, secularists, and atheists in the West. James Hillman, the Jungian psychoanalytic thinker, speaks of what he calls a "monotheism of consciousness," which has to do not only with our way of thinking about God, but with our way of thinking about persons as "individuals," our way of thinking about authority in the structures of family, church, and state, and our way of thinking

about questions of truth.[10] Nietzsche spoke of monotheism as the "rigid consequence of the doctrine of one normal human being—consequently the belief in
a normal God, beside whom there are only false, spurious Gods."[11] He speaks
of this underlying monotheism as a great danger to humanity, for it leads to the
rigidity and stagnation of the human imagination. And, in its most extreme
forms, rigid monotheism is a way of thinking that has few resources for coping
with the world of religious difference in which we live, and few resources for
moving beyond the dangerous polarization of opposing fundamentalist monotheisms, each convinced of the supremacy and exclusive truth of its own point
of view.

The Hindu tradition is both monotheistic and polytheistic. Oneness and
manyness are not seen as true opposites. In the Hindu tradition, matters of importance are thought of quite naturally in the singular *and* in the plural. Singularity or uniqueness is not the sole mark of significance. Indeed, many of the
most important aspects of the Hindu tradition are *not* unique, decisive, and final. If something is important, it is important enough to be repeated, duplicated,
and seen from many angles. There are many gods (*devas*), many divine descents
of the gods (*avataras*), many ways of salvation (*margas*), and many philosophical
systems (*darshanas*). There are also many scriptures: the ancient "wisdom," or
Vedas, including collections of hymns, like the Rig Veda, and philosophical dialogues, like the Upanishads; the two Hindu epics, the Mahabharata and the Ra-
mayana; the Bhagavad Gita, "Song of the Lord," which forms a part of the Mahabharata; and the "old stories," the Puranas, which include mythologies of the
gods as well as the lore of kings, heroes, and heroines. The profusion of gods and
scriptures is matched by a polycentric religious life, social structure, and family
structure. There is no one clear, unmistakable center. Manyness is valued; indeed, it is seen as essential.

Hindu polytheism is simultaneously one of the most significant and one of
the most difficult matters for Westerners to grasp in attempting to understand
Hindu religious life. Students of Hinduism and visitors to India confront it in
the astonishing fact of the presence of so many gods, each with so many facets,
so many heads, arms, and eyes. Hinduism is, in one sense, a radically polytheistic
tradition. But what is meant by this polytheism is not, as one might crudely put
it, that Hindus "believe in many gods." One might, in fact, question whether
Hindus "believe in" gods at all. Rather, Hindus perceive the manyness of the Divine in a way that is both complex and helpful in our inquiry into the meaning of

God. India's thinkers have explored the complexities of manyness more thoroughly and persistently than any on earth. Whether one is charmed, perplexed, or repulsed by India's unabashed polytheism, Hindu theological strategies for thinking about the manyness of God might enable us to get out of our conceptual ruts and think about God in new ways.

Darshana: Point of View

The first "strategy" for thinking about manyness in relation to the One focuses on the question of point of view. Where do we stand? Where do we look? How large is the frame of our vision? Hindus speak of one God, though they sometimes say there are 33, or 3,306, or 330 million gods. As is often the case, the Hindu tradition exaggerates to the point of profundity. Suddenly the meaning of manyness becomes more complex.

The word *darshan* means beholding or seeing, as one beholds the deity in a temple. It also means point of view, and in a very specific sense it refers to the points of view represented by the various Hindu philosophical systems called *darshanas*. I use the word here in its more general sense, however, simply as "view" or "point of view." If the Christian woman prays to God shaped by the image of Christ and the Hindu woman to God shaped by the images of Vishnu, Lakshmi, and Ganesha, we can understand this best by reference to their different contexts and viewpoints. From one point of view their understandings of God are very different, for they are standing in different places. The attributes they ascribe to God are different; the images they hold in their minds are different. And yet from another standpoint their understandings are clearly similar. They both stand as human beings before one they speak of as God, recognizing their human limitations, recognizing a God who transcends the images, expressing attitudes and intentions of love or of service, of supplication or of thankfulness toward the Divine.

In addressing the fact of manyness, the polytheistic Hindu tradition has recognized the relevance of the point of view from which one sees. One might say that there is one God, or three, or thirty-three, or millions, but to make such claims is not really to speak of numbers of gods—it is to recognize perspective. Is one speaking of the perspective of this earth, the perspective of the heavens, or the perspective of the Ultimate? Is one standing in village India or village America? Indeed, Hindu polytheistic consciousness has little to do with the number of gods a person recognizes; it has, rather, to do with that person's ability to take multiple perspectives.

In the Brihadaranyaka Upanishad, a student named Vidagdha Sakalya poses the question of manyness to Yajnavalkya, one of the visionary sages:

> "How many gods are there, Yajnavalkya?"
>
> "As many as are mentioned in the Hymn to All the Gods, namely 3,306."
>
> "Yes," said he, "but just how many gods are there, Yajnavalkya?"
> "Thirty-three."
>
> "Yes," said he, "but just how many gods are there, Yajnavalkya?"
> "Six."

The dialogue continues. There are three gods, two gods.

> "Yes," said he, "but just how many gods are there, Yajnavalkya?"
> "One and a half."
>
> "Yes," said he, "but just how many gods are there, Yajnavalkya?"
> "One."

That one is the One called Brahman, "the Yon." Yajnavalkya goes on to explain what it means to say there are 3,306, or 33, or 6. What is the perspective from which one might say that there are three? two? one? The question of how many is not really a question of numbers, but of viewpoint.

Being aware of the point of view from which one sees the manyness of God is not a consciousness which is exclusive to the wisdom of the sages. This awareness of *darshana*, or *drishti* as it is sometimes called, is part of the common structure of thinking. Most major Hindu temples host shrines to a number of deities, arrayed in the circumambulatories or in the side shrines. While there is always a primary deity in the inner sanctum, everyone who worships there will know that the temple across the street or next door will have a different deity in the inner sanctum. Some years ago, in visiting a Hindu temple in the old part of Delhi, I fell into company with an old woman who took me from shrine to shrine—to Hanuman, Lakshmi, Krishna, Ganga, Ganesha, and finally to the central sanctum which housed the simple stone *linga* of Shiva. "There are many gods," she said, naming a dozen. "How many?" I asked, thinking of Vidagdha Sakalya's question to Yajnavalkya. "So many . . ." she said, her words drifting as if to remember them one by one. "But all these gods are *namarupa*, name and form. From our viewpoint we see many, but truly there is One."

What she expressed is simply the ability to symbolize consciously, to take two viewpoints at once. She used the Hindi term for "point of view," *drishtikona*. From one point of view these gods are many; from another they are One. This capacity to think symbolically means that, like this Hindu woman, one does not relinquish one viewpoint for another. Plurality is not given up in favor of oneness, nor oneness in favor of plurality. Both viewpoints are held—and are understood to be held—simultaneously.

The Naming of God

A second way of dealing with manyness is to understand it in relation to the nature of language. One of the most commonly quoted lines of the Rig Veda is *"Ekam sat vipraha bahudha vadanti,"* "Truth is One; the wise call it by many names" (RV I.64.46). The word is not *Brahman* here, but *Sat*—Reality, Truth, Being—"ultimate reality" in Tillich's sense. Here manyness is a question not only of point of view, but also of the fact of language and naming. How are human beings to speak of the Ultimate? The verse indicates that not only ordinary folk, but even the sages who see deeply into the truth speak of Sat using various names. Even though words like *Sat* and *Brahman* indicate the foundational depth dimension of Reality, we human beings must recognize, finally, that our language is simply that—our language.

The full context of this verse of the Rig Veda makes clear the role of language and naming:

> Speech hath been measured out in four divisions,
> the [priests] who have understanding know them.
> Three kept in close concealment cause no motion;
> of speech, men speak only the fourth division.
>
> They call him Indra, Mitra, Varuna, Agni, and he is
> the noble-winged Garutman.
> To what is One, sages give many a title:
> they call it Agni, Yama, Matarisvan.[12]

Human speech is limited. It may be profound, rich, and imaginative, but finally it is limited. All the speech human beings have, according to the Rig Veda, is only a quarter of all the speech there is. And with this human speech we human beings give many names to what is One. From this perspective, the difference between the Hindu and Christian women at prayer might best be understood by recognizing the limitation of all God language and prayer language. It is not just that they use different names, different language, but also that the very act of naming and speaking is a limitation. All the limited language of human speech and conception is fractional and unable to comprehend the unfractured whole.

The sense of the limits of speech is part of a wider sense of the limits of sense perception and, indeed, of the bounded nature of this world in relation to the wider world of "the Yon." The limit of imaginative vision is recognized profoundly by the seer-poets of the Rig Veda. In the famous creation hymn, the *Purusha Sukta*, for instance, the entire universe is conceptualized as *Purusha*, a cosmic being or person.

> A thousand heads had Purusha,
> a thousand eyes, a thousand feet:
> Encompassing the earth on every side—
> He exceeded it by ten fingers' breadth.

The act of creation is an act of self-limitation. The hymn goes on to say that three quarters of Purusha "went up," and remains beyond our ken; one quarter of Purusha became, by means of sacrifice, the substance of this whole world we know. Divided up, Purusha became this world:

> From his mind the moon was born,
> And from his eye the sun,
> From his mouth Indra and the fire,
> From his breath the wind was born.[13]

Thus the tradition is embued with a sense of the limitations of the world of language and the world of the theological imagination. Put in Vedic terms, the scope of our language and imagination is but one quarter of reality as it is. With the quarter of speech that we know we stretch the mind to comprehend the quarter of reality that we know. But the fullness (*purnatva*) of divine reality exceeds what we can speak or imagine by three to one, by "ten fingers' breadth." The Upanishads, which are concerned with knowledge of the Ultimate, also make clear that our language has a limit in its capacity to symbolize the Divine. As the Taittiriya Upanishad puts it, Brahman is that limit "whence mind and speech, having no hold, fall back" (2.4). The Kena Upanishad speculates, "There the eye goes not; speech goes not, nor the mind" (1.3).

Despite and because of this sense of the limit of language, the poets and seers of the Vedas use a great number of names to speak of this Reality. One of the hymns of the Maitri Upanishad is a classic instance of this multiplication of names:

> Thou art Brahma, and verily thou art Vishnu
> Thou art Rudra. Thou art Prajapati.
> Thou art Agni, Varuna, and Vayu.
> Thou art Indra. Thou art the Moon.
> Thou art food. Thou art Yama. Thou art the Earth.
> Thou art All. Yea, thou art the unshaken one![14]

Here again it is clear that the manyness of God does not have to do with the number of gods there are, but with the language human beings have for naming and speaking of the Divine. The manyness of God testifies not only to the shifting of viewpoint, but also to the human sense of limit: that the Real—God—exceeds the various ways of naming and imagining. Human language for God is just that—human language. It is, so to speak, only a quarter of the language there is.

Not only are there many "names and forms" of God, but each single name and form of God has many names or epithets. Hindus can sing a thousand names of Vishnu alone. More important, however, than the mere multiplication of names is the persistent reflection on what it is that we *do* when we give God names. When it comes to naming Reality, theological language must be multiple. According to the Rig Veda, even the language of the wise must be multiple, not because of the nature of Reality, but because of the nature of language. Without in the least diminishing the soaring power of language, both poetry and prose, Hindus have insisted that the full extent of speech sails far beyond the language we know.

We cannot know, cannot even speak in an adequate way of God's essence (*svabhava*) or about the Reality to which adjectives will not stick (*nirguna*). And yet we can and must speak of the forms of God we know (*svarupa*) and artfully employ those adjectives and names that evoke our experience of God (*saguna*). According to the Hindu, there are beautiful names and forms of God, terrifying appearances and manifestations of God, faces of God, glimpses of God. But these are not exclusive; they are multiple. They are like streams that carry us in the direction of the ocean of God's fullness. As a south Indian folk song puts it:

Into the bosom of the great sea
Flow streams that come from hills on every side,
Their names are various as their springs,
And thus in every land do men bow down
To one great God, though known by many names.[15]

Modern Western theologians have recognized that the concept of God is a symbol. The "available God," as Gordon Kaufman puts it, is a symbolic construct, historical and cumulative, ever reshaped in our understanding. The "available God" is what the Hindu theologian would call *svarupa*—God as we know God. As the Hindu philosopher Radhakrishnan put it in his Oxford lectures of 1926, "We cannot think of God without using our imagination. . . . These different representations do not show God in himself, but only what he is to us."[16] We must not claim, however, that God as we know God exhausts the reality of God. To do so, and to claim ultimacy for human symbols and language, is truly idolatry.

The Hindu tradition, from the Rig Veda to Radhakrishan, has clearly recognized the nature of God language. It is human language which constructs, approaches, and apprehends, but never exhausts or fully comprehends the Divine. That is not to diminish it, for our God language is still the most precious and important language we have. So when Hindus use multiple God language, as they do with abandon, we must understand that this polytheism is not simply a question of the plurality of gods. It rests on an understanding of the very nature of the language used to speak of God.

Mahatmya: The Greatness of Each God

When Hindus speak of the manyness of God, they also understand that our language for God is often the language of praise and love. The abundance of human love multiplies our language toward God, just as in love we multiply the names and epithets of the one we love. It is also the abundance of love that overflows into the language of uniqueness: You are the only one in the world for me! In the Hindu tradition, this way of speaking is called *mahatmya*, a word which means "praise." It is divine exaggeration. When people address God in a particular image or with a particular name, they do not say "O thou partial and fragmentary manifestion of God." They do not worship God as but one of the 330 million. They do not, in a real sense, speak of the immediate name and form of the Divine before their eyes, but of the One that particular name and form enables them to see. The names and forms of the Divine are not partial, and do not therefore "add up" cumulatively to the One. And though Ranjini and her friends may sing the Vishnusahasranama, "The Thousand Names of Vishnu," the thousand names do not necessarily come closer to the truth than each single name. Each single name and form can fill the whole horizon of invocation. Each name is great. Each, indeed, is the greatest.

Hindu religious literature is filled with *mahatmyas*. Hymns of praise express the greatness of something—a god, a place, or a ritual act. When a particular god, or image of god, is glorified in a *mahatmya*, that one is praised not as a partial manifestation of the Supreme, but as the Supreme One. In and through the particularity of this one god or image, the fullness of Reality is seen. Thus, to speak of many does not diminish the fact that the fullness of Reality can still be seen through a single lens. Both Ranjini and I speak of God with the language of fullness, completeness, and omnipresence. Both of us speak the language of praise, a genre that emerges from love and does not submit to the judgments of truth and error.

The language of praise has an ancient history in India. In the hymns of the Rig Veda, composed as long as 2,500 years ago, there are many gods named and praised. There is Surya, the Sun; Agni, the Fire and the messenger who moves between heaven and earth; Indra, the Thunderer who released the waters of life from the heavens; Varuna, the keeper of contracts, the watchful guardian of order and of conscience. Such gods have often been called nature gods, and their relation to natural phenomena is clear enough. It is a relation, however, not an identification. Indeed, the attributes of Surya, the Sun; Agni, the Fire; and Indra, the Thunderer, overlap one another considerably, especially where the poets amplify their songs to each god as if to stretch toward the limit of the imaginative horizon.

When Max Müller, the great German scholar of Indian civilization, tried to describe the nature of the Vedic pantheon, he said, "I could not even answer the question, if you were to ask it, whether the religion of the Veda was polytheistic, or monotheistic."[17] It is decidedly not monotheistic in the usual sense of that word, for there are many gods named to whom prayers are lifted. And yet, as Müller recognized, this is not a "system of polytheism." It is not really a system—certainly not in the sense of the ancient Greek or Roman pantheons, in which the gods had clear functions and relations, and were subordinate to a monarch among the gods, Zeus or Jupiter. Furthermore, the Vedic "polytheism," he argued, is not really polytheism because each of the many gods is exalted as if that one were the one God. Max Müller used special terms for this type of religious consciousness—*henotheism*, not the worship of "one" god, but the worship of "single" gods; or *kathenotheism*, the worship of one god after another, one god at a time.[18] He cites the praises of Surya, for example. Surya, the sun god, is seen not merely as the light of the chariot-driven sun, which wakes the earth from slumber, but also as the giver of daily life, the one who brings both light and life, the defender and protector of all living things, the one who sees both good and evil. In the superlative, Surya is called "the god among gods," "the divine leader of all the gods."[19]

Müller puts the matter this way: "When these individual gods are invoked, they are not conceived as limited by the powers of others, as superior or inferior in rank. Each god is to the mind of the suppliant as good as all the gods. He is felt at the time as a real divinity, as supreme and absolute, in spite of the necessary limitations which, to our mind, a plurality of gods must entail on every single god. All the rest disappear from the vision of the poet, and he only who is to fulfill their desires stands in full light before the eyes of the worshippers." Underlying the poetry of the Vedas is the sentiment "Among you, O gods, there is none that is small, and none that is young: you are all great indeed."[20]

In the context of *mahatmya*, therefore, each god is seen and worshipped as the one God—at least as much of the one God as human beings can know, given the nature of language and imagination. Each god, no matter how specific or apparently limited his or her characteristics and tasks, fills the whole theological horizon at the time of worship—be it for an hour, a day, or a festival time. In India today each temple, no matter how obscure, has its great festival day, each deity its moment in the sun.

I watch women in the morning at Asi Ghat in Banaras, worshipping in the various ways they worship. One woman comes from her chilly morning bath in the Ganges. With clean clothes and a plastic basket of offerings she enters the temple of Asisangameshvara. There she pours Ganges water on the Shiva *linga*, daubs some red *kumkum*, sprinkles some rice, lights a small light and circles it round, places a marigold and some bilva leaves on the *linga*. She sings her prayers. She does not honor a god whose province is limited to the domain of Asi Ghat in Banaras but through this particular form sings praises to God.

Christianity is also a tradition of praise. Bishop Krister Stendahl introduced me to the genre of Christian language that is called doxological, after the ascriptions of glory that are part of the psalms and hymnody of the church.[21] When

Christians sing *"Gloria in excelsis Deo"* or "Praise God from whom all blessings
flow," it is a kind of *mahatmya*, giving praise out of the fullness of one's heart. In
the Methodist tradition in particular, doxologies or *mahatmyas* have long been
the dominant vehicle of devotion and of theology. Both John and Charles Wesley were hymnists, and their songs of praise were a vibrant and distinctive part
of the early Methodist movement. In one of his most famous hymns, Charles
Wesley opens his heart with the words

> O for a thousand tongues to sing
> My great Redeemer's praise,
> The glories of my God and King,
> The triumphs of his grace!

This is the spirit of *mahatmya*, the yearning for a thousand tongues to sing the
praises and glories of God. And any Hindu would sing along fervently.

Trimurti: The Many Forms of Each God

The Hindu notion of the Trimurti, the "three forms" of the Divine, also provides a vehicle for helping us think about the question of God's manyness. Simply put, there are three forms of God—as creator, sustainer, and destroyer—
and each form is all three. At the most elementary level, Brahma is seen as the
creator, Vishnu as the sustainer, and Shiva as the destroyer. One might say that
the three gods add up to a single Godhead, and taken together they accomplish
the full range of divine duties; however, Hindus do not tend to think of it this
way. It is not a uniting of three gods into one, for each of the three is whole, not
partial. The creation, the undergirding, and the dissolving of all that exists constitute three aspects of Godhead. The three modes of divine activity are not
separable.

It is striking to those of us who are Christian that the Trinity, like the Trimurti, is more complex than it seems at first. The Trinity also has nothing to do
with three gods. Like the Trimurti, it has to do with God's mystery and multiplicity. When Christians use the word *God* they mean *all* of that mystery and
multiplicity, not just the "Creator" part, or the "Savior" part, or the "Spirit" part.
God is not parceled into three distinct bundles, one of which created, one of
which lived on earth as Jesus, and one of which moves about invisibly as the Holy
Spirit. Each of these facets of the Divine is involved in all three modes of activity.
Of course, the famous Russian Orthodox icon of the Holy Trinity by the artist

Rublev has the three seated like individual persons around a table, three angels looking vaguely at one another. And the hymn "Holy, Holy, Holy" speaks of "God in three persons, blessed Trinity." But three "persons" does not mean three Gods, even though both Jews and Muslims have sometimes harbored suspicions that this Trinitarian language was slightly polytheistic. Christians do not believe that the three are separate, or even separable. God is triune—three and one. They all belong together and through any one of these divine facets the whole of the mystery of God can be seen.

The Trimurti is often dismissed by Christians as so different from the Christian notion of the Trinity as to be irrelevant. I am not so sure. In a simplistic way, the Trimurti has never been relevant even to Hindus. No one worships the Trimurti of Brahma, Shiva, and Vishnu as such. In fact, Brahma is scarcely worshiped at all. And Shiva and Vishnu are worshiped as if each were creator, sustainer, and final resting place of the universe. Seeing them as separate is, in fact, explicitly rejected. As the Harivamsha puts it, "He who is Vishnu is Shiva; he who is Shiva is Brahma: the substance is one, the gods are three, Shiva, Vishnu, and Brahma."[22] Perhaps the spirit of the trinities is not so different. Both Trinity and Trimurti point to a complex notion of God. Complex and yet inextricably related. The parts of the Trimurti, like the parts of the Trinity, are not really partial. Each is whole. The great gods of the tradition around whom elaborate theologies and mythologies developed were Shiva, Vishnu or Krishna, and the Goddess. The hymns and praises of each ascribe to that divinity full divine power and omnipotence, as creator, as sustainer of all that is, as the source of the cosmos in the beginning, and as its final resting place in the end.

Similarly, in Trinitarian thought one cannot separate the creation aspect of the Divine and assign it to the Father, for it is clear that the Son, the Logos, was also there "in the beginning" and the Spirit (*Ruach*) was there as the wind that moved upon the water. Creation is an aspect of each of the "members" of the Trinity. The threefold nature is not a numerical plurality, but a matter of facets or distinguishable but not separate aspects of the Divine. Wrestling with the language of the Trinity occupied the early church fathers for at least three centuries. Justin Martyr saw the Logos as "other than" the Father but inextricably related to the Father, as one torch is lit from another. Ireneus saw the matter historically, as successive missions of the Son and the Spirit in God's plan of redemption. Countering what they thought was a tendency in Justin toward a two-God theory, the Modalists (or Monarchians) saw the Father, Son, and Spirit as modes of being that in no way reflect any distinction or division in the Godhead. Tertullian spoke of one being with three *personas*, a term which suggests the aspects, faces, or vital energies of God.

But the Trimurti brings us a further complexity. In the understanding of the Trimurti in the Hindu tradition, each one is not only "the greatest," in the language of *mahatmya*, each one is also many. Each name, each god, is understood as multiple and complex. Each "individual" god is *trimurti*. It is not that Brahma, Vishnu, and Shiva are woven together into a kind of over-god who transcends them all. In the minds of Hindus who worship them, each is threefold, or perhaps even fourfold or fivefold. When Ranjini stands before Vishnu, she knows Vishnu alone to be the One who creates, sustains, and destroys, and who manifests himself in numerous divine descents or *avataras*. Shiva too is *trimurti* for those who worship him—creator, sustainer, and destroyer.

It is not simply that the many gods together give expression to the multiplicity of the Divine, or that each of the many gods may be praised as God Supreme, gaining the full consciousness and attention of the worshiper during the time of worship. It is important to realize that as theism and theological thought developed in India, each "individual" god was seen as complex. Each was seen as the thousand-headed One, Purusha, who includes the others. Each expresses the full range of God's multiplicity. Further, each is not seen as penultimate, limited to the one quarter of Reality that we know; each is seen to stretch the theological imagination beyond the world-unworld limit of name and form. Each is Brahman.

For instance, the hymnist of the *Narada Purana* sees Vishnu alone as the primal Purusha, the One of a thousand heads, eyes, and feet, saying of him, "I salute Lord Vishnu who is immanent in all living beings, is quiescent, omniscient, who has thousands of heads, and who is very real. I worship that unaging Supreme Ruler, who stands the breadth of ten fingers above the universe of both past and future."[23] It is the vision of such a world-spanning Vishnu / Krishna that is presented in the theophany of Krishna in the tenth and eleventh chapters of the Bhagavad Gita, when Krishna appears to Arjuna with a thousand heads and a thousand arms. From the point of view of the theology of Shiva, however, the configuration is different. For instance, the Ishvara Gita, which comprises part of the *Kurma Purana*, provides a Shaiva version of the Bhagavad Gita in which Shiva is the luminous One of a thousand arms, a thousand feet.[24]

In one of the most important and often told myths of Shiva, the two gods Brahma and Vishnu encounter one another in the time before the beginning of creation and the luminous Shiva appears to them.[25] Vishnu is described as the One of a thousand eyes, feet and arms, and he announces plainly to Brahma that he is *trimurti*. "I am the creator, the sustainer, and the destroyer of the universe." Brahma is annoyed by this claim, and responds, "I am the creator, eternal and unborn, the origin and the soul of the universe." In most versions of this myth, the two begin to battle fiercely over the issue of primacy until Shiva appears to them in a blaze of light.

In one particularly interesting version of the myth, however, Brahma and Vishnu enter into competition in a most extraordinary manner. Brahma enters Vishnu's body, and travels around inside for many thousands of years, seeing the entire universe there within Vishnu, ready to be made manifest. He is impressed, and honors Vishnu when he makes his exit. In turn, Vishnu enters into the body of Brahma, and he too travels around for many thousands of years, seeing the entire universe. He too is amazed and he honors Brahma. Rather than continuing their contest, the two mutually perceive the extent and grandeur of one another.[26]

In all versions of this myth of divine competition, however, as the two gods stand confronting one another, a great shaft of fire splits through the ground between them, coming up from the deepest waters beneath and extending as far up as the heavens reach and beyond. The two attempt to find the extent of this dazzling light, but after searching for its top and bottom for many thousands of years they are unable to fathom it. It is Shiva who appears to them from the light. And it is Shiva, here, who is said to be the supreme *trimurti*. "He who is Shiva, Brahma, and Vishnu is called Shiva in the Puranas by virtue of his eternally and intrinsically enlightened and pure nature."[27]

The internal dynamic of the language of *trimurti*, its members shifting depending upon the perspective from which it is viewed, is scarcely a modern theological discovery. For many centuries Hindus have been well aware of how this way of theological thinking works. In the fifth century, the poet Kalidasa put it beautifully when he wrote, in the context of a passage praising Shiva as supreme,

> In these three persons the one God was shown,
> Each first in place, each last—not one alone;
> O Shiva, Vishnu, and Brahma , each may be
> First, second, third among the Blessed three.[28]

It is not only Vishnu and Shiva that are each seen individually to be the One who is expressed in three forms. The Goddess, called Mahadevi, the Great God-

dess, is also seen in this way. In one of the rich scriptural sources of Goddess mythology and theology, the Devibhagavata Purana, the story is told of how all the
other gods, having ascended through the many levels of the heavens, reach
the highest heaven and enter into her royal hall for *darshan*. The gods behold the
Goddess with a thousand heads, a thousand eyes, a thousand arms. They bow
down to touch her feet, and suddenly they see reflected in her toenails the whole
of the universe. They sing,

> Thou createst, preservest, and destroyest this Universe. . . .
> O Mother! I now realise fully well that this whole Universe rests
> on Thee; it rises from Thee and again melts away in Thee. . . .
> O Devi! The rumour goes that Brahma is the Creator, Vishnu is the
> Preserver, Shiva is the Destroyer! Is this true?
> O Eternal One! It is through Thy Will power, through Thy force,
> that we create, preserve, and destroy.[29]

. . . .

> Those who say that Vishnu, Shiva, and Brahma are
> respectively the Preserver, the Destroyer and the Creator of this
> whole Universe do not know anything. All the three, above
> mentioned, are created by Thee; then they perform always their
> respective functions; their sole refuge being Thyself.[30]

Ishtadevata: The Chosen God

There is one more Hindu strategy for thinking about God's oneness and
manyness: each of us chooses one from the many. From among the many names,
we human beings are responsible for choosing one. From the many facets, we
choose one to focus our Godward gaze. It is well known that Hindus have a notion of "chosen deity"—*ishtadevata*. The "chosen god" is that one a particular
person has taken for special honor and devotion. Choosing may differ from family to family, even within a family, depending on tradition, circumstance, and
temperament. The Hindu tradition has long recognized that in imagining and
speaking of God, we human beings choose the idea of God that will ground our
being. Through our language we choose the center.

For those in the Jewish and Christian traditions of the West, this language is
especially striking, since the Bible speaks of God as having chosen us, and not we

God. And yet perhaps the idea of the "chosen god" is not all that alien to us. As Christian theologians continally remind us, our particular language for God, Christ, and Spirit is not bestowed from on high. It is shaped by particular cultures and by particular times. In a very real sense we do choose it. The church has struggled for twenty centuries with its language and its understanding. For example, the language of God as King comes from cultures where the notion of king is meaningful. Recently many Christians, particularly women, have found the language of "King" too hierarchical and have ceased using it. Many have ceased to speak of God as the one whose banner Christian soldiers bear into battle, for this is not what they mean by God. Many have also found that to speak of God as Father is inadequate or distorting, both of God's reality and of their own. Do we speak of God as monarch or shepherd, as breath or word, as YHWH or Elohim, father or mother, as creator or redeemer? All of this is a language of images which we use more or less frequently depending upon how well they express our sense of God. When we think about it, it is clear that we Christians do our own share of choosing.

What is striking in the Hindu understanding of the "chosen god," however, is that the multiplicity of divine names and embodiments is not suppressed once one has made the choice. A man or a woman does not choose a single God and exclude the others. Indeed, all other forms and images are related to the chosen image of God. When one god is imaged, when one is praised, when one's story is told, it is not to the exclusion of the others, but in relation to them. As in a kaleidoscope of complex colors, the pieces of the divine multiplicity are arranged and rearranged, with one and then another clearly at the center—but no pieces are eliminated.

In a particular painting, for example, Krishna may be portrayed dancing in a circle with the milkmaids (the *gopis*), having multiplied himself so that each milkmaid has Krishna as her partner, but the other gods are not simply absent from the scene. They are depicted in heaven above, watching the cosmic dance and sprinkling flower petals of blessing upon it. Or in a granite image one might see Shiva standing forth in eight-armed form from the fiery *linga*; Vishnu and Brahma are not absent, but present on bended knee, doing homage. In another image Devi might stand triumphant on the head of the bull-demon Mahisha, whom she has slain when all the gods were powerless; in her many hands are the distinctive emblems and weapons of all of the other gods. So each god can be seen as positioned at the center. A center does not exclude what surrounds it, but rather anchors and integrates the entire field of the circle.

The Hindu tradition, as it is handed on in popular literature, comments explicitly upon the human tendency to make one's "chosen god" the rival and suppressor of others. Such conscious comments surely arise from the fact that there was, at times, sectarian deprecation and antagonism. In response, Hindu texts often preach a strong message of tolerance. In the very same hymns that exalt and praise one god, the devout are often warned not to deprecate other gods. Indeed, one of the signs of what Hindus call the Kali Age, the age of darkness in which the world is now plunged, is the tendency to despise the chosen god of a rival community. In many mythic contexts, the gods themselves take up this question by praising one another and thus challenging the narrow religious imagination. For example, in the Ishvaragita, Shiva speaks in praise of Vishnu: "Vishnu, which dwells in the very souls of all beings . . . is known as Imperishable. Those who, due to their false notion of distinction in the world, think otherwise, cannot visualize me and are reborn again and again. Those who find this Vishnu, the unmanifest, and Me, the Supreme Lord, as completely identified and one, are never reborn."[31] If Shiva praises Vishnu, Vishnu also bows down to Shiva. The story of how Vishnu daily offered a thousand lotus flowers to Shiva is well known. When one day he discovered he had but 999, Vishnu plucked one of his own lotus eyes to complete the offering.[32]

God's manyness and oneness in the Hindu tradition has been conceptualized in a variety of ways which are not parallels to Christian thinking, but which provide a variety of theological strategies for thinking about God in a world in which the "names and forms" of the Divine are many. All of them may not be helpful to us, but they shake us from a bewildered or condemning dismissal of "polytheism" and enable us to learn something new about this mystery we call God.

How do we think of the manyness? First, it is a matter of *darshana*, of the perspective from which one views the Divine. There are many facets of the crystal, each of which gives a complex vision of the whole. Second, it is a matter of language; manyness is an essential part of the project of naming the Divine. Third, it is integral to the genre of praise, *mahatmya*, that each of the many names or aspects of the Divine is praised as supreme, the All. To the eyes of the beholding worshipper, each is the One. Fourth, not only is each the One, each is many; each of the multiple ways of perceiving the Divine is not only unitary but also complex. Finally, each name and form is chosen, and once chosen is related to others, not exclusive of them. The exaltation of one's chosen deity lies not in the condemnation of other images of the Divine, but in the multiplication of meaning through the appreciative recognition of others, a kind of mutual inclusivism. This is the point we are invited to consider in the great prayer attributed to the philosopher Shankara in the Haristuti, a hymn offered in praise of Hari, one of the thousand names of Vishnu:

> May Vishnu the ruler of the three worlds,
> worshipped by the Shaivites as Shiva,
> by the Vedantins as Brahman,
> by the Buddhists as Buddha,
> by the Naiyayikas as the chief agent,
> by the Jainas as the liberated,
> by the ritualists as the principle of law,
> may he grant our prayers.[33]

Recognition: Reflections on God at Padmanabhaswamy

If we insist that God is One, with all the complexity, plurality, and multiplicity that oneness entails, it is not surprising that we—whether Christians or Hindus—might have many moments in which we "recognize" God in the forms and modes of worship of religious traditions not our own. Many have had the experience of what I would call recognition—glimpsing the God we know through windows framed by people of other faiths, and extending our understanding of God thereby.

Close to the southern tip of India in the city of Trivandrum is the vast temple of Padmanabhaswamy, with its many circumambulatory corridors lined with majestic carved stone pillars. It is one of the most extensive and splendid temples in southern India. At the center, in the inner sanctum, lies a great granite image of Vishnu, eighteen feet long, resting upon the coils of the serpent called Endless. It is said that Vishnu supports the whole universe with but a fraction of his being. All of what we know of the universe is manifest from the body of the Lord at the dawn of creation. A lotus grows from the Lord's navel. It opens into flower. And so our world begins.

One spring evening in 1988, I was near the end of another research trip in India. I had spent two months on the road, visiting temples large and small, trying to gain some sense "on the ground" of the pilgrimage patterns of Hindu India. Standing at the outermost entry to the temple of Padmanabhaswamy, I gazed through doorway after doorway, each opening into one circumambulatory corridor after another, each doorway receding toward the inner sanctum in the distance, each lit with oil lamps casting a glow upon the darkened corridors. In the inner sanctum, a splendid twelve-tiered tree of oil lamps lit the court immediately in front of the image. The play of light and darkness, lamp and shadow, so typical of the temples of the state of Kerala was here profound.

As I walked around and around the concentric corridors of Padmanabhaswamy, getting closer with each round to the sanctum of the temple, the words of Psalm 27 came to mind and stayed with me. "One thing I have asked of the Lord, that I well seek after; that I may dwell in the house of the Lord all the days of my life, to behold the beauty of the Lord, and to inquire in God's temple." Though I am not part of the community of Hindu worshipers, it is true that I inquire in Hindu temples. And from time to time I have been able to behold there the beauty of the Lord. That evening at Padmanabhaswamy was one of those times.

I lined up with the other women at the north door of the central shrine as the time approached for the *arati*, the evening offering of oil lamps. The drums began to beat and the bells clang; the reedy *nadaswaram* so typical of South Indian temples began to whine. The attendant drew back the bar and we all seemed to move en masse, propelled by the surge of a wave of bodies, into the inner sanctum. As the bells rang with an increasing sense of crescendo, suddenly the central pair of doors to Vishnu's chamber were flung open to reveal part of the huge reclining image. Then the pair of doors to the left were flung open, revealing the upper portion of Vishnu; then the doors to the right, revealing his feet.

I could not see the image very well at all, but as the many different multi-wicked lamps of *arati* were waved to honor Vishnu, I could see the suggestion of his presence there. It was a sense of enormous presence, dimly seen, illumined for a moment by oil lamps and by the intermediary grace of the priest who moved the soft light before the long body of the Lord. The lamps were lifted high toward his face. In the center doorway they were raised on high as an offering to Brahma, coming forth from the navel of the sleeping Lord. Finally, in the last doorway, the lamps were offered to Vishnu's feet. When with the quickening of bells the *arati* reached its climax, the last lamp presented to Vishnu was brought out to be given to the people as a blessing. Four hundred pairs of hands stretched out to touch the flame and then touch its blessing to the forehead. Mine were among them.

A restraining cord that kept the worshipers a few feet away was removed and we were allowed up on the platform itself, where we could look through each set of doors for a closer view of each section of the image. At one end, a priest moved me into just the right position to look up and see the face, a countenance of peaceful repose. But the image is really too large to take in with the eyes. I felt a sense of huge presence, like the sage Markandeya, who is said to have roamed the whole world as it is contained within the body of Vishnu until one day he fell out of the mouth of the sleeping Lord and beheld the Lord from the outside, a sight simply too vast to comprehend. Vishnu mercifully swallowed him again and Markandeya once again found himself in the comfortable and recognizable world categorized by name and form.

I had spent most of the day trying to gain permission to enter this temple. Padmanabhaswamy, which was a thriving temple long before the first European ever set foot in India, is closed to non-Hindus today. Sometime during the years of colonization, the temple closed its doors to those who so profanely misinterpreted its holy things. A great many Christians, and not only the missionaries who traveled in the company of the Raj, would have used the term *idolatry* had they stood there in the inner sanctum. There it was, after all, a huge "graven image." It is no wonder Hindus would prefer not to expose their heart's worship to such misunderstanding.

Deep within the consciousness of Christians are the vestiges of language learned in Sunday school about pagans who bow down to graven images. Moses returned from the mountaintop with tablets of scripture to sweep away the idols to which the Children of Israel had falsely addressed their prayers. The word gained primacy over the image. And yet words were also shaped into images. The king, the lord, the shepherd, the father, the God with a mighty arm outstretched through history—these, as we have seen, are images, too. Even so, many of us who are Christians and Jews have preferred to think that those who address God through material images are idolators, while those whose images are shaped by words are not. There is idolatry on both sides, but it has to do with the shortsightedness of those whose vision stops at the image. The image is a window, not an object. The eighteen-foot image of Vishnu is no more an idol than the cross, the "Our Father," or the bread at Holy Communion. And no less. Idolatry is in the eye of the beholder.

Seeing that tryptich in the temple in Trivandrum, with its three glimpses of a God larger than one could fully comprehend, was a moment of recognition for me, and the experience of God's presence there was describable only as worship. My experience as a Christian was surely different from that of the Hindus

pressed against me on either side. But we shared the sense of delight and revelation as the doors were opened, and perhaps some sense of both the majesty
and mystery of the Divine. I thought of nothing at the time. It was a moment
of total presence, not of reflection. But as I left the temple, looking frequently
back through door upon door, light and shadow, in the direction of Vishnu resting upon the serpent called Endless, I began thinking about what we Christians
call the Trinity, the threefold vision of God as creator, redeemer, and spirit. I
could not get it out of my mind—this triple yet singular revelation of the one
God, the glimpses we had through the doors that were opened upon his presence, the overwhelming sense that no vantage point could enable us to see the
whole.

The image of Vishnu at Padmanabhaswamy both challenged and enlarged
my own concept of God. I remember a title on the shelf of the library in the
Methodist church in Bozeman: *Your God Is Too Small*. And he was. As one theological liberation movement after another has discovered, "he" was also too
male, too white, and too much at home in Western culture. India's theological
gift to me has been the discovery that God can be addressed as Mother, can wear
the ashes of the cremation pyre, or can beckon us to dance. It should not surprise
us to recognize the God of Abraham and Sarah in Trivandrum or Banaras if
God is indeed the One we say God is—the creator of heaven and earth and all
that is therein. As Swami Chidananda, one of today's sages of Rishikesh, in
northern India, puts it, "The Christian churches are only two thousand years
old. Before that God was not in hibernation!"[34]

Each of us brings religious or ethical criteria to our understanding of the new
worlds we encounter. When I "recognize" God's presence in a Hindu temple or
in the life of a Hindu, it is because, through this complex of God, Christ, and
Spirit, I have a sense of what God's presence is like. Recognition means that we
have seen it somewhere before. I would even say that it is Christ who enables
Christians—in fact, challenges us—to recognize God especially where we don't
expect to do so and where it is not easy to do so.

Reciprocally, we must realize that Hindus also recognize the God *they* know
in Christian churches and ways of worship. A few years ago, a Hindu Shaiva
friend, Dr. Shanmugam Gangadaran, studied with us for a year at Harvard
University. He had come from southern India and had never lived in a predominantly Christian culture before. Separated from his religious community, he
came regularly to worship with me at the Harvard-Epworth United Methodist Church. It was moving and humbling to have a devout worshiper of Shiva

ɟ us that year, and many in the church who had no inkling of the sophistication of Shaiva Siddhanta theology nonetheless commented on how they appreciated his presence. It was surely because of his knowledge of Shiva and the sense of divine presence nurtured by that knowledge that he was able to recognize God's presence in the worship of our church.

Like Chief Seattle, people of ancient traditions all over the world have seen European colonialism, bearing a particular image of a universal and sometimes colonial God. Despite the difficulty of seeing beyond the white tribalism of the settlers and the distorting lens of colonialism through which Christianity was presented, many of these people came to see that the God of whom the alien Europeans spoke was one they could recognize. They would say, "Our God is the same God." Similarly, David Broome, an Aboriginal Australian and a Christian minister, speaks of the ancient vision of the Dreaming, which has held Aboriginal culture for over forty thousand years. The Dreaming is the spiritual foundation of Aboriginal religion. It is religious life and vision grounded in the hills, the rocks, and the springs of the Australian landscape. The Dreaming is the time, the source, the place, and the spirit of revelation all in one. As Broome put it, speaking of Australia's 1988 bicentennial, "God did not come to Australia two hundred years ago. God has always been here. God was here in our Dreaming."[35] The Aboriginal theologian Djiniyini Gondarra writes, "Is the God of the Bible active in the Aboriginal history and the Aboriginal dreamtime? This is the question that is asked by the Christian churches today. The Aboriginal Christians are convinced and believe that the God of the Bible was with us and our people in the dreamtime. He was very active in our history. He has come to us in many different ways and many different forms to reveal His presence. He is the God of the Aboriginal race in Australia."[36]

Recognizing God is not an easy task. It is not the simple affirmation that all these visions of God are the same—they are not. And there are places and communities where I as a Christian do not have the experience of recognition. For me to recognize God as I know God in Vishnu or Shiva and for Mr. Gangadaran to recognize Shiva in Christian worship and language, or for the Aboriginal to recognize something of the Dreaming in the God of Abraham and Sarah and the Christian to recognize God as we understand God in the Dreaming can only be the fruit of a real encounter. There are no easy, uncritical theological equations here. Yet as we are open to real encounter in the give-and-take of learning and un-learning our recognition of the one we call "God" can only become larger and clearer.

The Faces of God

Discovering the Incarnation in India

O NE DAY in Banaras Pandit-ji's cousin came to visit. He was introduced to me as "Uncle." Like Pandit-ji, he was in his eighties, but
unlike Pandit-ji he had rarely met a Westerner. Uncle was fascinated
to discover I was a Christian; I may have been the first he had ever met. He asked
me to tell him about my *ishtadevata*, my "chosen god," Jesus Christ. I must admit I was not quite sure what to say. I had not practiced this Hindi vocabulary,
and for a fleeting second I found myself wishing I had done a Hindi study
course at Landour, the old mission station in the hills north of Dehra Dun
where the lessons were geared to the explication of terms like "Son of God" and
"the Word made flesh." I told him that Christ was fully God and fully man. I
used the words *Parameshvara*, "supreme God," and *manushya*, "man," as they
would be used in the Hindi translation of the Bible. The word *incarnation* does
not appear in the New Testament, but I decided to try to convey that sense of divine embodiment. Jesus Christ was the incarnate presence of the supreme God,
right here on earth. I used the term *avatara*, which is only approximately accurate, and means, literally, a "divine descent" of God into the world of name and
form.

The *avatara* notion is a powerful one in the Hindu tradition. According to
the Bhagavad Gita, when righteousness has declined and injustice prospers,
God comes into being, in age after age, to reestablish order. The stories of the
"divine descents," *avataras*, of the supreme Lord Vishnu are stories of rescuing

the righteous and protecting the faithful. In the sequence of *avataras*, God
weaves his saving power through all the realms of creation. As a fish he guides
Manu, India's Noah, through the great flood. As a boar he dives deep to rescue
the sunken earth from the bottom of the sea. As a man-lion he kills an arrogant
demon and rescues the young boy Prahlada, his most ardent devotee. As a dwarf
he humbly asks for three paces of land from a world-conquering demon and
then expands to stride through all the earth, the heavens, and the beyond with
his three steps. As the fully human Rama, he nobly embodies righteousness, re-
nouncing his kingdom on a matter of principle and protecting humanity by
slaying the demons of the forest during his fourteen years of exile. As Krishna
he ecstatically lifts the heart to love.

I do not for a moment doubt the transforming and sustaining power of these
stories for Uncle. Indeed, they are moving stories for me. There is much that I
find captivating, but, to be honest, much that I don't find captivating: the endless
battles; the *avatara* Parashurama, who killed his mother and then slew all the
world's warriors seven times over. There is much that I find appealing theologically: the fact that the forms of God's embodiment move through the strata of
life with a kind of theological Darwinism—a sea-going fish, a land- and sea-
going tortoise, a mammal, a half-man / half-lion, a dwarf, a human, a superhu-
man. Among them all, it is especially Krishna who moves my heart religiously
and expands my mind theologically.

"Is it true," Uncle asked as if verifying an outlandish rumor, "that Christians
believe Jesus was the *only* avatara?" I recalled in my mind all the language about
the decisiveness, uniqueness, and finality of Christ—language I was uncomfortable with, but which I knew was still the common Christian understanding.
"Yes, most Christians do," I responded. "Christians say he was unique, the only
one." "But how is it possible," he asked, "to believe that God showed himself
only once, to one people, in one part of the world, and so long ago?" The implications were clear in the expression on Uncle's face: What kind of stingy God
would that be? What kind of small-minded, self-centered people would believe
in such a God? To him it was clear that the full, embodied disclosure of God to
men and women was not only multiple in time and place, but potentially infinite. Uncle went on to ask about the story and attributes of Jesus. Did he have a
goddess or consort? Did he have a vehicle or animal mount? Did he have special
powers? I did my best, but between my inadequate Hindi and my inadequate
theology, I am afraid Uncle was disappointed in Jesus.

Immanuel, "God with us," is scarcely an unfamiliar notion to Hindu thought. I know of no neighborhood in Bozeman or in Boston that is as filled with a sense of the presence of God, always and everywhere, at every corner and every turn, as Banaras or Brindavan or Ujjain. God is abundantly present in countless names and forms, and the acknowledgment of that presence is the dominant theme of the religious life of Hindus. When Uncle expressed a certain dismay at the notion of the singular incarnation of the Divine, he was not only thinking of the many mythic events of the *avataras* of Vishnu, but of the events of divine embodiment that are part of the religious life of every temple, every wayside shrine, and every household.

The idea that the image properly sanctified is a form of divine embodiment is commonplace in India. It is elaborated most fully in the Shri Vaishnava notion of *archa avatara*, or "image incarnation." Through rites of installation, the Divine is invited to be present and "established" in an image. The key rite is called *prana pratishtha*, the establishing of the breath in the image. Once the breath is established, God's presence is perpetual and one must honor God in and through that image on a daily basis. Other images are not "established," and so when they are honored the Divine is invited to come and be present through an "invitation," or *avahana*; at the end of the period of worship, the worshipper gives leave for the Divine to go again. Some image incarnations are utterly transient—a clay image, shaped in the palm of one's hand, into which Shiva is invited at the beginning of worship and given leave at the end. The clay, being no more than clay again, is disposed of in a river or temple tank. I am often puzzled with the stereotypical view of India as "other-worldly," for in the Hindu tradition there is nothing in the substance of this world that cannot display the presence and glory of God—an enlightened person, a cow, a tree, a basil bush, even a lump of clay. There are those in Hindu India even today who are seen as human embodiments of the Divine. Gurus like the woman Anandamayi Ma or the popular Sathya Sai Baba, for example, are often revered as more than mere saints; they are *avataras*.

Many in the West today struggle with and reject the very idea of incarnation. They take the myth and the mystery out of the Christ event to make it simply the story of a visionary human teacher. Incarnation is the stumbling block. Not so for Uncle or for most Hindus. Incarnation is assumed. Of course God takes form in this world. Of course God comes into being in flesh. Of course God is embodied. Uncle's problem is not with incarnation, but with the seemingly impossible notion that incarnation is an event in the singular—only once and so very long ago and far away. I felt that Uncle was right, in a sense. God could not be made captive to the "Jesus story" of first-century Palestine. To insist that there is no other possible way of apprehending the fullness of God than through Jesus did not do justice to the faith of a man like Uncle. And it did not do justice to the wideness and mercy of the one I call God or the one I speak of as Christ.

And yet to line up Jesus Christ with all the other *avataras* did not do justice to my faith as a Christian, either. For those of us who are Christians, Jesus Christ is not simply one among many, but the fullness of God-with-us, the mirror in which God is revealed to humanity and in humanity as love. We can appreciate the meaning that Jesus has had even for those who call themselves Hindus. Gandhi, for example, saw Jesus as a great teacher and moral exemplar, "so patient, so kind, so loving, so full of forgiveness that he taught his followers not to retaliate when abused or struck, but to turn the other cheek."[1] I am glad to share this Jesus with Gandhi and I am glad that Gandhi could share this Jesus with us through the example of his own life. Even so, for me as a Christian, Jesus is not simply a great teacher, nor is Jesus simply and flatly God.

It is sometimes hard not to be possessive about Jesus, especially when we feel the point of the incarnation is being missed. This was made quite clear to me a few years later when I received the following invitation from the International Society of Krishna Consciousness to a Christmas celebration at the rural center called New Vrindavan in West Virginia:

> It is with great pleasure that we announce the inauguration of the veneration and worship of Lord Jesus Christ and His teachings under the direction of our teacher Srila Kirtanananda Swami Bhaktipada. We are preparing to perform an installation ceremony for the murti (holy form) of Lord Jesus Christ at our Radha Krishna Temple in New Vrindaban. One of our devotees who is an expert sculptor has created a beautiful murti of Lord Jesus sitting in the lotus posture.... This occasion will mark a significant interfaith event in North America for Christian-Hindu understanding. You are cordially invited to attend this exciting and historic installation ceremony as our special guest.

The service was to include a Vedic fire sacrifice and a Bach organ recital. My curiosity as a student of the history of religions was aroused. That an image of "Lord Jesus Christ," seated cross-legged in wine-red robes on a lotus cushion, his beard neatly trimmed, should be installed next to the image of Krishna and the other gods in a Hindu temple in West Virginia and his worship inaugurated there was a fascinating event in the history of religions. As a scholar I was tempted, but as a Christian something in me recoiled from the invitation. I was surprised at my response. I suddenly sympathized with the few picketers who carried placards outside the movie theatre on Boylston Street when *The Last Temptation of Christ* was playing. "Not My Jesus!" one placard read. No, this cross-legged image was not my Jesus. Why not?

In the first place, Jesus the carpenter's son did not sit peacefully on a lotus, but walked the roads of Galilee and challenged the powers of Jerusalem with such boldness that he ended up crucified with two thieves. And that intersection of life with death is at the heart of the Christian message. He did not transcend the body. He did not grow to gigantic proportions and crush his enemies beneath his feet. He did not have the magical weapons of Lord Rama, nor did he have Rama's helper, the valiant Hanuman, who came flying in with a mountain of medicinal herbs from the Himalayas to bring the decimated armies of his master back to life. When Jesus hung dying on the cross, bruised and bleeding, there was no miraculous intervention. He really died—no miracles and no magical herbs —a fully human death, as we all will die.

There was another problem with this transcendent Jesus on the lotus cushion. This image was to be in a temple. Hindus worship the image in the temple with daily offerings of flowers and water, incense and sweets. I think I understand this kind of worship. I have studied it and written about it. I admire it with what Krister Stendahl often calls "holy envy"—the appreciative love one has toward the mysteries of another faith. When I stand in a Hindu sanctuary during the *arati*, when the oil lamps are raised toward the deity, I feel drawn into an attitude of worship. It is not the worship of idols, but the honoring of God through focused attention to the consecrated image in which God is graciously present. This form of worship, called *puja*, has an integrity and beauty all its own, and it must surely be one of the many ways in which God truly enjoys a relationship with men and women. But as Christians, even in those churches where incense and images abound, we don't do *puja* to Jesus. We don't offer incense so that Jesus may enjoy the fragrance and then waft that fragrance into our own nostrils. We don't offer water to wash his feet and then sip that water as sanctified by his touch. We don't offer him food and then receive the remains of that food offering ourselves as God's grace. We do not worship Jesus in quite that way and we do not because of the mystery of his humanity. It is because in Jesus God has become truly human that it would have felt odd to me to worship him sitting in wine-red robes on a silken cushion, to offer him flowers and water. Even Mary of Bethany, who anointed Jesus' feet with a pound of perfume, would not have brought the perfume to an image of Jesus. Jesus of Nazareth, who revealed divinity in humanity, so clearly directs us to God on the one hand and to our neighbors on the other: "If you have done it unto the least of these, you have done it unto me."

Divinity and Humanity: The Uniqueness of Christ

When Christians speak of the "incarnation" of God in Christ there are two important implications. One is that "God" becomes much clearer through this self-revelation and self-limitation in human form. The *svabhava* of God becomes *svarupa*, God-in-essence becomes God-in-relation, God-invisible becomes God-visible. The *nirguna* becomes *saguna*; unspeakable and indescribable Reality becomes speakable and has a form. The mystery is made plain, at least for a moment, and we see God face to face. Those who knew Jesus of Nazareth, as attested in the synoptic Gospels, spoke of him as Immanuel, "God with us" (Matt. 1:23), as the expected and anointed one, the messiah, or, in Greek, the Christ. And Thomas, seeing with his eyes the risen Christ, exclaimed, "My Lord and my God!" (John 20:28).

There is a second implication: In taking human form God sanctifies the human as well. As the three wise men say in chorus in W. H. Auden's "For the Time Being: A Christmas Oratorio," "To discover how to be human now is the reason we follow this star."[2] Incarnation means that God finds us, and we find God, in the human faces of one another and in the human fabric of our lives. Christians cannot help but be inclusivists in Christology. As Christians see it, the "Christ event" of incarnation altered the meaning of the human condition not only for the tribe of Christians but for everyone. It disclosed a new image of the human as well as a new image of God. As the British Methodist lay-leader Pauline Webb put it, "To name Jesus Christ as the focal point of the meeting of divine and human nature means to me that through him all human life has been dignified. Whether he is named as such by others does not for me in any way diminish my recognition that they share in the benefits of his having dignified our humanity in this way."[3]

Perhaps it is in the mystery of this double revelation of divinity and humanity that Christians might speak about the "uniqueness" of Jesus. Like Uncle, I am sometimes uncertain about the language of uniqueness, for it often seems to be a declaration of exclusivity rather than an invitation to faith, discovery, and dialogue. When the "uniqueness" of Jesus Christ is used to exclude the stranger of another faith, it ceases to be Christian language.

Christians give many arguments for the uniqueness of Jesus Christ. Some I find quite unpersuasive. Lesslie Newbigin, who served for years as Bishop of Madras, insists on the historicity of Jesus as unique. "The Hindu can speak of many avatars, because none of them is part of public history; they are all ideas in the mind. There is no event in public history that can or could replace those events that we confess to have taken place under Pontius Pilate."[4] Karl Barth called upon Jesus Christ as the decisive criteria for truth. When asked about the meaning of the Pure Land Buddhist concept of the grace of Amida Buddha, he responded, "Only one thing is really decisive for the distinction of truth and error. . . . That one thing is the name of Jesus Christ . . . which alone constitutes the truth of our religion."[5] Roger Nicole asks, "Why was it necessary for Christ to come at all if salvation can be obtained apart from him? When we reflect on the immensity of his suffering and the paramount significance of the incarnation, it appears incongruous, to say the least, that these great deeds should represent only one of several ways of being reconciled to God."[6] Dr. W. A. Visser't Hooft, the first general secretary of the World Council of Churches, said, "If Jesus is not unique, there is no gospel."[7] But I wonder. Does the "Good News" of the Gospel really depend upon its being the only Good News there is, the only real history, the only criterion for truth? Can't the Gospel stand simply and humbly on its own merits, without the fortress of "only-ness" about it?

Other Christian theologians are beginning to question an exclusivist understanding of Christ. As the Indian theologian Stanley Samartha puts it, "Through the incarnation in Jesus Christ, God had relativized God's self in history. Christian theologians should therefore ask themselves whether they are justified in absolutizing in doctrine him whom God has relativized in history."[8] Or, to put it in the language of Tillich, who makes a similar point, "What is particular in him is that he crucified the particular in himself for the sake of the universal."[9] Wesley Ariarajah points to the variety of statements about the Jesus of history and the Christ of faith found in the New Testament itself and asks us to take seriously the contexts in which they occur.

> The claims that Christ is the only way, the only Saviour, the one Mediator, etc., are made in the language of faith, and should be understood within the context of the church's faith commitment. The excessive emphasis on

only is part of the early Christian polemics against the Jewish people from
whom the Christians were growing out as a separate community. That
community was a small one. Its faith was strong and secure, on the one
hand; it was constantly under attack, on the other. The community was
under immense pressure to justify its faith in Jesus, the crucified master
whom they now experienced as the risen Lord. As much by the logic of the
circumstances as by the strength of their convictions they were led to make
claims for Jesus which he would not perhaps have made for himself.[10]

From the very beginning there have been many Christologies, many interpretations of what it meant to speak of Jesus of Nazareth as Christ. The Jesus of history and the Christ of faith are both central to the testimony of the early church
as found in the New Testament. It is not one Jesus who is depicted in the Gospels,
and it is a credit to the insight and honesty of the early church that several interpretations of Jesus were preserved in the New Testament. In the synoptic Gospels, for instance, Jesus himself does not claim to be one with the Father as he
does in the Gospel of John, but points continually to God as his Father and challenges his followers to a God-centered life in which ethical action clearly counts
more than belief. Yet the Gospel of John opens by describing the Word, the
Logos, who was present and with God even at the dawn of creation, and it is
filled with theological discourses on the meaning of Jesus as the Christ to the
faith community. Saint Paul, in the context of the new and growing community
of faith, does not focus on the teachings of the historical Jesus but on the meaning
of the Christ event for the early church. All of this is the treasured heritage of the
Christian community, but it does not point to a single and seamless view of Jesus Christ.

   What does it mean, then, to speak of the uniqueness of Jesus? Does uniqueness mean that this story of Jesus is the *only story* of God's saving presence here
on earth? I could say so in faith, but it flies in the face of the evidence of the history of religions. As a scholar of religion, I couldn't speak of uniqueness in the
sense of the "only story" without ignoring what I know of other religious traditions. There are clearly many stories of God's presence in what we might gener-
ally call "incarnations" and "divine embodiments" which shape the life-worlds
of both tribal cultures and whole civilizations. Does uniqueness, then, perhaps mean that it is the *only true story* or the *only saving story*, while the others
are incomplete or mistaken? Again, I could hold this view as long as I never en-

countered someone like Uncle, who would speak of the loving and revealing presence of Krishna, the Lord who lures those who love him away from conventional pride and possessiveness, who overturns the human hierarchies of power and social order. I could say so as long as I never met Mr. Gangadaran, who speaks of Shiva's boundless grace and mercy. In encountering such a faith, I find myself asking, as the principal of Madras Christian College did at the International Missionary Council in 1938, "Is there any such thing as a religious faith which in quality and texture is definitely not Christian, but in the approach to which one ought to put the shoes off the feet, recognizing that one is on the holy ground of a two-sided commerce between God and man?"

Uniqueness, to me, does not mean that the "Jesus story" is the only story of God's dealings with humanity, nor the only true and complete story. The language of *only* is the language of faith, not of statistics. Faith in Christ rests on two remarkable affirmations: Jesus Christ reveals to us the face of God, which is love. And Jesus Christ reveals to us the meaning of the human, which is love. This double revelation is enough. I do not need to know that it is the only true story on earth to affirm that it is worth giving my heart to. I do not need to convince myself or anyone else that Uncle's stories are wrong. Indeed, the God whom Jesus reveals is not a tribal god or a stingy one, but has surely sought and loved the sheep of every fold. And the humanity which Jesus reveals is not narrow, arrogant, or dogmatic, but boldly open to claiming the stranger as neighbor. Both sides of this double revelation—the Godward and the human—must push Christians beyond the narrow obsession with uniqueness as singularity.

On the human side of this double revelation, Bishop Newbigin is right. We *can* say just when Jesus lived and when he died. The "historical Jesus" lived and died during the time of Pontius Pilate. As a human being, Jesus, the man of Nazareth, was unique as all human beings are—born of particular parents, at a particular time, in a particular place, and with a wholly distinctive physique and personality. There are many documents and one can cite them with footnotes. His life is, in that sense, part of public history. For those of us who are Christians, the revelation of the Christ event is far more radical than this, however. On the divine side of the double revelation, we say that this particular human being also reveals the fullness of God as love. How that could be so is a mystery. By definition there are no documents or footnotes to verify a mystery. That is the radical faith of the church, and those of us who are Christians live our lives in terms of that faith.

It is not the case, however, that, as Lesslie Newbigin has suggested, Hindu stories are only "ideas in the mind" and that because they are not what we call "history" they are therefore inferior. Uncle's experience of God's presence is not an "idea in the mind," but a reality that has grounded the lives and deaths of millions of Hindus like him for many centuries. It is a reality in which he and his family have nourished children in love, faced grief and pain, and rejoiced in what they too call the "grace" of God's revealing. We all live by powerful, resounding stories, stories so true that they reveal to us God's purpose for the whole creation and the whole human family. Not every story is a story up to that revelatory task. There are inadequate and even destructive stories that may be compelling for a generation, but cannot sustain the ongoing life of a culture. Some stories have proven to be up to the task of anchoring an entire life-world, of sustaining generations of faith and nourishing whole cultures and civilizations. Some of them are even what we in the modern West call history, with names, dates, and footnotes: the story of the Siddhartha Gautama, whom Buddhists call the Buddha, the one who is truly awake; the story of Muhammad, who recited God's living word as the Messenger; and the story of Jesus of Nazareth, whom Christians speak of as the Christ, the Son of the Living God. Some do not have documented names, dates, and footnotes—like the incarnation of Lord Krishna, for instance—but their reality in the lives of people of faith is no less powerful for that reason.

As a Christian, I confess that Jesus enables me to see something of God that I do not know in any other way: God truly grounded in the soil of human life and death. Krishna, enchanting and revealing, is much larger than life even as a baby; his foster mother Yashoda, opening his mouth with her fingers to remove a bit of dirt he had playfully eaten, glimpsed in his mouth the whole of the universe with its worlds and stars. In the whole sequence of *avataras*, only Rama is said to be fully human, and yet his was a super-humanity, suffused with supernatural strength and divine weapons that always hit their mark. The humbling of God to "earthen vessels" is unheard of in the mythic heritage of the Hindu tradition. The *avatara* is a divine descent, God coming "down" into this world, but yet as God. It is not really *incarnation* with the full meaning of taking on the body of flesh and blood.

Jesus did not point the way out of suffering, as did the Buddha. Jesus did not rescue humanity from suffering, as did the *avataras*. Jesus took on suffering himself, experiencing suffering and death as all of us do. Only in going through the valley of the shadow of suffering and death did Jesus overcome the grip of suffering and death. Not only Hindus, but Muslims as well find this humbling humanity of Jesus disturbing. As my Muslim friend from Nigeria, Is-Haq Oloyede, a law professor, once put it in conversation, "God cannot be helpless! It is not befitting of God." Indeed, in the Muslim tradition, which very much reveres Jesus as a prophet, there are those who insist that he did not die on the cross, but came down from the cross and lived to old age.

It is understandable that the early church struggled with the doctrine of incarnation, eliminating extreme views in order to find a middle way between those who minimized Jesus' humanity and those who minimized his divinity. Some of the second-century Gnostics held to a matter-spirit dualism and a negative evaluation of matter, including the body, which made it impossible to imagine that the Divine had become flesh. Jesus as embodied was a mere semblance (*dokesis*), hence the term *Docetism*. Though he sat in the shade of a tree, he only seemed to experience the heat; though he hung on the cross in the sun, he really did not feel the thirst; though his hands were pierced with nails, he did not really know the pain. This view of Jesus was rejected by the early church. So too was the third-century doctrine called Arianism after its spokesman, Arius of Alexandria. In this view, Jesus was not equal to God, but a creation or emanation of God the Father. This idea is also called subordinationism, for both Jesus Christ and the Holy Spirit were seen as subordinate to God the Father. As Arius put it, "The Son who is tempted, suffers, and dies, however exalted he may be, is not to be equal to the immutable Father beyond pain and death: if he is other than the Father, he is inferior."[11] Docetism and Arianism are but two instructive examples of views of Christ that were rejected by the early church. In 325, the Council of Nicaea carefully formulated a creed that insists on the full divinity of Christ, who is called "God from God, Light from Light" and "True God from True God . . . of one Being with the Father," *and* the full humanity of Christ, who "became truly human . . . suffered death and was buried." That creed is still the most universal creed of the church.

From the first century to the twentieth, Christians have continued to wrestle with the meaning of Jesus Christ, the double revelation of the divine and the human. Some interpretations, called "high Christologies," emphasize his divinity; it is through the disclosure of God's presence in Jesus that Christians "see" God. In Jesus, Christians glimpse the face of that "ground of being" to which Tillich points. Speaking as a Christian, I can say that I think about God or "see" God through the centering focus of Christ. But I do not think it is the *only* way to think about God or the only transforming *darshan* of God available to humankind. I do not think that a life centered on Christ needs to eliminate, ought to eliminate, or even *can* eliminate the experience of the *avatara*, the divine descent, that has been attested to by Hindus in the many ways that Uncle has seen. I fully believe that God is also revealed in the ways that Uncle has glimpsed—and that I also have glimpsed—in the villages and temples of India. Uncle is right in thinking that God is not miserly but merciful. God's revelatory presence is not singular but plural, indeed infinite. In every tradition of faith, people point to the overflowing plentitude of God, who extends "ten fingers' breadth beyond," as the Rig Veda puts it. But Christians also attest to the fact that this plentitude includes our humanity—life and death, his life and death, our life and death.

Other interpretations, sometimes called "low Christologies" or "Christologies from below," emphasize the humanity of Jesus who is, above all, God-with-us. In W. H. Auden's "For the Time Being," it is Simeon who says it perfectly when the newborn child is presented in the temple: "And because of His visitation, we may no longer desire God as if He were lacking: our redemption is no longer a question of pursuit but of surrender to Him who is always and everywhere present. Therefore at every moment we pray that, following Him, we may depart from our anxiety into His peace."[12] God is not lacking in this world, but present, always and everywhere. This is the meaning of the incarnation. Karl Barth puts it well when he speaks of the incarnation as God's "friendliness to humanity." He seems to include the whole of humanity in the consequence of incarnation, not just Christians. "One thing is sure," he writes, "that there is no theological justification for setting any limits on our side to the friendliness of God towards humanity which appeared in Jesus Christ."[13]

Christians should not be fearful or suspicious, therefore, of discovering the presence of God, which we know in Christ, in the religious lives of people of other faiths. If we follow the Indian theologian Stanley Samartha toward what is called a "Christology from below," one that begins with the man Jesus of Nazareth, we follow a route to the discovery of incarnation that leads us to the poor, the ordinary, the unremarkable and yet remarkable humanity that Jesus loved and shared. The route to affirming Jesus' divinity passes through his humanity. As Samartha puts it, "At a time when there is so much degrading dehumanization in the world and such a great need to bring out what it is to be human in such a world, to minimize the humanity of Jesus is to diminish seriously the resources for supporting the struggles for human freedom, dignity, and self-respect."[14]

Insofar as India has been drawn to Jesus, it is not so much because of the miraculous divinity of Jesus as the Christ, for divinity abounds in the life-worlds of Hindus, but because of his compelling humanity. It was this that found resonance in Gandhi when he said, "Christ died on the cross with a crown of thorns on his head defying the might of a whole empire. And if I raise resistance of a non-violent character, I simply and humbly follow in the footsteps of the great teacher."[15] Tagore's "religion of man" breathed the same spirit, and his verses from *Gitanjali* are often quoted by Indian Christian theologians.

> Leave this chanting and singing and telling of beads! Whom
> dost thou worship in this lonely dark corner of a temple
> with the doors all shut? Open thine eyes and see thy
> God is not before thee!
>
> He is there where the tiller is tilling the hard ground and
> where the pathmaker is breaking stones. He is with
> them in sun and in shower, and His garment is covered
> with dust. Put off thy holy mantle and even like Him
> come down on the dusty soil![16]

"I am the Way": Inclusive Love

Some Christians speak not only of the "uniqueness" of Christ but of the "exclusiveness" of Christ. It cannot be said too plainly, however, that exclusivity is utterly contrary to the Jesus we meet in the synoptic Gospels. If Jesus is a lens through which we glimpse the nature of God, we certainly cannot say that he reveals a God whose mercy and compassion are focused exclusively on one people. Or that he reveals the kind of God that Uncle was wary of—stingy with appearances. Not at all. Jesus kept company with everyone in the world of his day. He freely and boldly crossed the barriers that might separate one ethnic group from another—Samaritans, Jews, Romans. In fact, many who are exemplars of faith and recipients of loving mercy in the Gospel narratives are those we might call "people of other faiths": the Roman centurion, the Syrophoenician woman, the Greek Cornelius, the good Samaritan. Jesus did not see "Christianity" and "Judaism," or the other "isms" we use to categorize people of faith today. He saw faith. There is no question but that he would have kept company with Patwardhan and Krishnamurti, with Gandhi and Tagore.

Inevitably, when I speak of these matters to church people, someone asks about the well-known passage from the Gospel of John: "I am the Way, the Truth, and the Life. No one comes to the Father but through me." For many this seems to close the case: No other religion can be a true way to God. I am often tempted to take the approach of simply quoting another verse: "I have many sheep that are not of this fold" (John 10:16). Or "I truly understand that God show no partiality, but in every nation anyone who fears him and does what is right is acceptable to him" (Acts 10:34). The problem with this approach, however, is that the Bible should not be used as an ammunition belt full of verse-size bullets to be fired off as they are needed. To do so does violence to the text and to the context of the early church out of which it came—a tiny church, struggling for a sense of its own identity in the Jewish community and in the Hellenistic world. The meaning of the Bible is not to be found in its individual verses alone, but in its undergirding message as appropriated through the questions and struggles of each community of faith.

So I try another approach. If "I am the Way" is the answer, what exactly was the question? I once asked a class of 150 religion students to state it. Nobody remembered the question, but most everyone knew the answer. However, "I am the Way" is not the answer to any question one might wish to ask. It is the pastoral response to an anxious question. It was poor uncertain Thomas who asked the question that night, as John tells it. It was the last night Jesus spent with his disciples. After having washed their feet, he spoke to them in words of farewell: "I am going where you cannot follow, not just now. I am going to God's house of many rooms to prepare a place for you, and you know the way where I am going." And what did Thomas ask him? Did he ask, Lord, are Hindus to have a room in God's heavenly household? Did he ask, Lord, will Buddhists make it across the sea of sorrow on the raft of the Dharma? Lord, when the Prophet Muhammad comes six hundred years from now, will he hear God's word? No, on that night of uncomprehending uncertainty he asked, "Lord, we do not know where you are going; how can we know the way?" And Christ answered, "I *am* the Way, . . ." It was a pastoral answer, not a polemical one. It was an expression of comfort, not condemnation.

For the tiny minority of Christians like the Johannine community, who committed themselves to the Way of Christ, who experienced the resurrection of new life in Christ, this was essential language of faith. It was, and it remains, the expression of our commitment to what we have seen and known. And it is in our commitment to the Way of Christ and Christ's love that we will find our way ahead, as Christians, in the earth-household. Our tradition, like our family, is precious in its particularity for us. No other family will do. But that does not mean that no other family of faith belongs to God. Whole-hearted commitment to Christ's way is worthy of the faith to which Christians are called; the denigration or demonization of our neighbors is not.

And who is this "I" in the Gospel of John? "I" is not simply I, Jesus of Nazareth, born of Mary, suffered under Pontius Pilate. John's nativity story is cosmic and makes no mention of Bethlehem. It is a very "high" Christology. "In the beginning was the Word, the Logos, and the Word was with God, and the Word was God—through whom everything was made; without whom nothing was made." It is a world-spanning Christ who speaks this "I." To see the Logos, the Word, *is* to see God. The disciples did not yet understand. Phillip asked, "Show us God and we shall be satisfied." Christ answered, "Have I been with you so long and yet you do not know me, Phillip?" Christ is the Logos, the Word, the divine intention to speak, to disclose, to reveal. There is no "way" to God: God *is* the Way, the Truth, the Life.

Christians cannot speak of Christ as exclusive, but perhaps we can speak of commitment as exclusive. While we can recognize both the truth of other glimpses of the Divine and the power of other communities of faith, we cannot be seriously committed to multiple centers, as much as we may appreciate them. The language of faith is the language of affection, of affirmation and commitment. It is, as we have seen, the language of *mahatmya*, of untrammeled praise. It is, as Bishop Krister Stendahl puts it, "love language," analogous to the language we use when we say to someone we love, "You're the only one in the world for me." It does not mean, "I have systematically surveyed everyone in the world and have chosen you." It means, simply and powerfully, "I love you." Faith requires the cherishing and deepening of commitment that is fundamental to any relationship. And the language of faith is the language of love, not of judgment.

Credo is the word with which the great creeds of early Christendom begin. "I believe . . ." we say. The Latin *credo* means literally "I give my heart." The word *believe* is a problematic one today, in part because it has gradually changed its meaning from being the language of certainty so deep that I could give my heart to it, to the language of uncertainty so shallow that only the "credulous" would rely on it.[17] Faith, as we have seen, is not about propositions, but about commitment. It does not mean that I intellectually subscribe to the following list of statements, but that I give my heart to this reality. *Believe*, indeed, comes to us from the Old English *belove*, making clear that this too is meant to be heart language.

To say "I believe in Jesus Christ" is not to subscribe to an uncertain proposition. It is a confession of commitment, of love.

How is it that the vibrance of love language and heart language became starched and stiffened over time into the language of dogma? How is it that *credo* seemed to become a set of propositions rather than an expression of commitments? How is it that positive commitment to what is true for us has been twisted through the centuries into the negative insistence that nothing else in the world could possible be true? We must ask these questions, especially when the great love language of the New Testament is taken out of context and used to throw up walls against our neighbors.

The Gospel of John contains another of the best-known verses of the entire New Testament, John 3:16: "For God so loved the world that He gave his only Son, that whoever believeth in Him should not perish, but have eternal life." The point of this verse is surely the plenitude of God's love. For God *so loved* the world that this greatest of gifts was given. *Love* is the great word of the Gospels and the one plumb line of Christian life. There are many Christians, however, who take this affirmation, turn it inside out, and make it a condemnation of everyone who does not believe in Christ. In doing so, they turn the second part of the verse into a non sequitur: For God so loved the world that He gave his only Son, that whoever does not believe in him will perish and suffer eternal damnation. This is *not* what the Bible says, and I want every Christian who has been tortured by this kind of theological abuse to know that, and I want Uncle to know it too.

I do not believe that our faith in Christ can lead us any longer along the road of intolerance and exclusivism. That road runs contrary to the spirit of Jesus of Nazareth. Faith in Christ means that I live my life, and will surely die my death, in terms of my commitment to Christ. It does *not* mean that no other experience of God's presence and mercy could possibly be true and serve to anchor someone else's life and transfigure someone else's death. It does *not* mean that I am somehow unfaithful if I also delight in the vision of playful, ecstatic, and tender love that Krishna reveals of God, for a visit to the community of Krishna in Brindavan brings all the pleasure of a visit to someone else's warm extended family. It does *not* mean that those Buddhists who do not use the word *God* at all but steadfastly cultivate stillness of mind toward the twin goals of wisdom and compassion are lost on the path. Indeed, they are on a path more profound, more spiritually serious, than that of many Christians.

Far from insisting on the importance of his continued personal presence, Christ said to his disciples, "It is good for you that I go." And Christ has gone. He is far up the road, out ahead of us.

The Faces of Christ

Christ is not separable from the Trinity—from the might and majesty of the Creator, from the mystery and restless movement of the Spirit. In the Christian tradition, these three aspects of the Divine belong together to perpetually remind us that God will not fit in our pockets or even in our churches. As we have already seen, all the great monotheisms, however unitary they may seem from a distance, become more complex the closer we get. As different as they are, the formulations of the Trinity and the understandings of the Trimurti express the many-sidedness of our symbolic expressions of Ultimate Reality. The one we call God is both beyond the reach of the human imagination and at the same time present in very tangible, seemingly mundane, and human ways.

Even this presence of God is not experienced in one single way, but is complex. Hindus speak of God's multidimensional presence in terms of "the many faces of Shiva" or the many "tastes" of Krishna. Though Christians do not use this language, we nonetheless shape our experience of Jesus as the Christ through a number of distinctive images—the child, the teacher, the healer; the one who suffered, who died, who rose from the dead. These images evoke in us different religious sensibilities and emotions—all parts of the experience of what we call the presence of God in Christ.

The complexity of God's presence is one of the great themes of the Hindu tradition, played in a dozen ragas. Worshippers of Shiva often speak of the faces of Shiva, the utterly transcendent one, whom human beings cannot fully describe, but who nonetheless shows his face, indeed his five faces. His first face is as creator: Shiva is revealed in creation itself. His second is as sustainer: Shiva upholds the world and its natural and moral order. Third, he is also destroyer: Shiva sometimes turns the human sense of order on its head, lifting up as holy the very things human beings might despise as polluted or frightening. Shiva's fourth face is that of concealment or mystery: Shiva appears even where men and women are unable to recognize him. Fifth is Shiva's face of revealing grace: Shiva bestows upon his devotees what seems like the completely unmerited gift of his presence. Shiva's five faces are moments of human vision—in creation, in sustenance, in destruction, in concealment, in grace. It is difficult indeed to say they are "his" faces, for Shiva is often depicted as half-male, half-female.

The faces of Shiva are often made explicit ritually. For example, at the great Shiva temple of Mahakaleshvara in Ujjain in central India, the smooth stone shaft of the *linga* of Shiva is decorated at different times of the day with Picasso-esque faces drawn by the priests in red *kumkum* powder and beige sandal paste to show the various faces of Shiva. During certain hours of worship they can be seen. These faces are called *jhankis*, or "glimpses." And at other hours the faces are all washed off and only the bare stone remains. The rhythm of glimpsing the face of Shiva and seeing the faceless Shiva is a regular part of temple worship. It expresses liturgically the inextricability of the *nirguna* and *saguna*, God transcendent and God revealed.

Vaishnavas who worship Krishna also speak of five such moments in the human vision of the Divine. They are called *rasas*, literally "tastes." Because Krishna is said to have been born on earth and to have grown up among village folk, people know and love him in many different ways. First, Krishna is a baby, a child, even a mischievous child, and our human relation to him is as a mother. This form of relationship to God is called *vatsalya*, literally the love of a mother cow for her calf. We human beings love God, they say, with the spontaneous self-giving love that mothers bear their children. It should interest those of us from the patriarchal traditions of the West that the human love toward God is not compared here to the love of child toward parent, specifically the father, but rather the love of parent, specifically the mother, toward child. It is a love that emphasizes not obedience, but joyful, irrepressible, tender love, ever astonished and delighted by the divine child. Second, Krishna is a friend to his village cowherd pals, who love him with the honest, companionable, admiring love between friends. He is a hero-friend, who protects and defends them. This "friendship *rasa*" of the love of God is not unfamiliar to Christians.

Third, Krishna is a lover, at least to those young women, the *gopis*, or milkmaids, who used to steal away from their homes to dance with him in the grove at night and who loved him with the pure, focused, risking love of lovers for the beloved. In Christianity, only our mystical traditions speak of Christ as lover, and even so they might be challenged by those who insist that our relationship to God has as its best analogue the "illegitimate" love of a lover to whom one is not married. After all, loving God has some risks—one will not get any compliments for this kind of love. It makes one vulnerable. It is not socially sanctioned.

It generates no family of heirs to carry on one's good name. This love is totally between oneself and God alone—and that is enough. For those uneasy about this, I should say that even Vaishnavas do not agree on the illicit nature of this love. Some insist that Krishna and his favorite milkmaid, Radha, were married. Others insist they were not.

Krishna's fourth aspect is somewhat more formal. Krishna is called Lord, even King, by those who love him with obedient, respectful love, those whose way of loving is service. Serving God is a noble calling and is a "taste" of the love of God that is also present in the Christian tradition. Finally, Krishna is utterly transcendent, the supreme God in whose presence one tastes the taste of peace, abides with God. In sum, Krishna is the child, the friend, the lover, the lord, and the supreme one. These are different faces of the same Krishna, who enables human beings to love him with whatever love comes most naturally to us. The way in which one worships Krishna is not as important as the realization that there are many such ways, just as human beings are good at loving in many different ways.

The five faces of Shiva or the many tastes of Krishna indicate to Hindus, and to us, the complexity of God and of human relatedness to God. God, though supreme, is not faceless, but out of abundant grace shows forth, shines forth. There is no one single way to see and experience God's grace. When one moves in close to any expression of the Divine, it becomes multifaceted. This is what the Trinity is about. This is what the five faces of Shiva or the many *rasas* of Krishna are about. The closer one gets, the more one sees. The singular becomes many-sided.

Seeing these faces and tasting these *rasas* requires practice. My own capacity to see and understand the meaning of *incarnation* in Christ has been extended greatly by the faith of Hindus. I have learned to see something of what Hindus see by following along with them in what are by now tens of thousands of miles of backroads pilgrimage travel in India to the places and temples where they go for the *darshan* of the Divine, the "seeing" or "beholding" of the image of God. It might be a famous and powerful, or really a very ordinary, divine image. The physical image is understood as a divine embodiment. As we have seen, it is sometimes called an *archa avatara*, an "image-incarnation." Sometimes it is "established" ritually, but often it is said to be *svayambhu*, spontaneous, self-manifest. Of a *svayambhu* image, Hindus say essentially, "We did not put this image here. We did not invite God to be present here. God was already here. God came here of God's own accord and we discovered it." No matter how it came to be, the image is not something *at* which one looks and therefore at which one's vision stops; it is a lens *through* which one sees, which focuses and directs one's vision to God.

The image makes the presence of God available to human beings, and in serving the image—offering food and water, clothing and ornaments, a fan or a fly whisk—Hindus practice every single day the language of hospitality that the divine presence in the world requires of us. The arts of both Martha and Mary, of loving daily service and of lavish adornment and praise, are practiced in the worship of a Hindu temple. After all, it is not as if the Divine *needs* the food, water, and clothing that human beings offer. The emphasis is the other way around. Human beings need to refine the arts of service and caring, and, according to the Hindu tradition, the Divine graciously condescends to be present in every temple, on every home altar, precisely that they may do so.

Christians don't speak of faces as a way of evoking the many perceptions and images of Jesus Christ, but we could. We could also speak of the many tastes of the Divine that are awakened in us each year through the repetition of the story of Christ in the Christian liturgical calendar. First, Christ is not-yet, and the taste is of hope, one of the most radical words in the Christian theological vocabulary. Second, Christ is the divine child, and the taste is of delight and tender, unconditioned love. Third, Christ is healer, and the taste is of liberation and wholeness. Fourth, Christ is the one who struggles with temptation and with death, and the taste is that of suffering. Fifth, Christ is risen, and the taste is the taste of joy and faith. One could go on and on, of course. There is the open and accepting face of love, there is the bold face of the teacher who stood with the poor and powerless, there is the angry face of the prophet who could not abide hypocrisy. But let us begin with just five. As we will see, some are like faces we might glimpse were we to get close enough to one of the Hindu visions of the Divine. There would be a moment of real recognition, of having seen this face before. Others, however, like the face of suffering, are quite different from any face we will glimpse in the temples of India, at least they are different from any divine face.

Every year, beginning in Advent, Christians practice seeing the faces of God in Christ and moving through the phases of that revelation. We repeat yearly the story of hope, birth, teaching and healing, testing and death, resurrection and life. Over and over, we refine our capacity to live life in terms of these multiple glimpses of God. Christ is present to us not in one simple way, but in many ways in the complexity of life and struggle. Not only in birth, but also in death. Not only in hope, but also in trial. Not only in glory, but also in mystery and hiddenness.

Waiting in Hope

In the season of Advent, Christians focus on the not-yet, the face of expectation. The angel announced to Mary, "You will conceive in your womb and bear a son, and you will name him Jesus." Mary was troubled, no doubt frightened, but she agreed: "Here am I, the servant of the Lord; let it be with me according to your word" (Luke 1:31, 38). And she waited. We do not know what those months of waiting were like, but in our common life, yearly we recognize the fact that there are many seasons when God's presence is not-yet. All we can do is prepare and hope. In a world where tragedies, catastrophes, and violence greet us with each morning's headlines, to sing "Let every heart prepare him room" is to stand in radical hope. We have to practice and refine our human capacity for such expectant and wakeful hope.

It is hope that is sustaining in times of despair and discouragement. The anguish of Job is not only that of a man who suffers, but also that of one who complains that his hope has been destroyed, "uprooted like a tree" (Job 19:10). The greatest loss is hope. "My days are swifter than a weaver's shuttle, and come to their end without hope" (Job 7:6). Hope in God, which is the bedrock of the faith of the Psalms and of the apostle Paul, is not naive optimism. It is the wakeful and confident expectation of God's presence. To lose that hope is to lose everything.

Some years ago, when I was living in India, I received a letter from my friend Ken back in Cambridge at just this season. "Somehow this year's Advent really comes at the right time," he wrote. "I found myself in church this morning very troubled and pessimistic about the world. At first I felt this entry into a season of hope was a bit of 'going through the motions.' But I find myself convinced that 'the motions' are most needed at just such a moment. Otherwise I would simply give up. The season is no panacea, but it reminds me to be still and wait a while. So, these eternal motions of Advent's hope did begin to work on me." God is revealed in hope, in the affirmation of waiting. The simple rites of Advent refine our capacity to wait in expectation with the mystery of anticipation. A candle is lit, then two candles, three, four.

In a sense, we already know the outcome of our hope. But there are seasons

when the not-yet really is a mystery, as it was to Mary, when we do not know
what our waiting will bring. And yet it is hope in confidence, it is not hope in the
vague sense of wishing for what one wants to happen. It is hope shaped by the
story, the holy history, of Christ's birth, life, death, and resurrection. Hope is a
resonant word within the Christian tradition; it does not seem to be nearly so resonant for Hindus. Lesslie Newbigin writes of his years in South India,

> When I was learning to read and speak the Tamil language I slowly came
> to realize that it had no word for "hope." When I questioned my Hindu
> teacher about this, he asked me in turn what I meant by hope. Does hope
> mean anything? Things will be what they will be. . . . This conversation
> helped me to realize that in English also the word "hope" often stands for
> nothing more than a desire for what may or may not be. In contrast to this,
> the New Testament speaks of hope among the great enduring realities—
> an anchor of the soul entering in beyond the curtain which hides the fu-
> ture from us, something utterly reliable.[18]

It is true that the conventional use of "hope" is often empty, unconvinc-
ing. But the hope of the New Testament is a radical, wakeful waiting-in-
expectation. It is standing on tiptoe and "waiting in eager longing," as Paul put
it in Romans 8. Paul uses the term *hope* as if it were the heart leaning forward
toward the horizon of dawn, ready for the sunrise. In Ephesians, he prays that
the people of Ephesus may have the knowledge of God "so that, with the eyes
of your heart enlightened you may know what is the hope to which he has called
you" (1:18). Newbigin had trouble finding a word in Tamil for this meaning,
and we would have as much trouble in Hindi or Sanskrit, where the word *asha*
means "hope, wish, desire," but with only the resonance of benediction and
blessing, not that of eager expectation. Perhaps the one place where this sense
of eager expectation is cultivated as a religious sensibility in the Hindu tradition
is in the longing love of the milkmaids for Krishna when he has gone away. It
is the strong taste of love-in-separation, yearning love, love that awaits fulfillment.

The sense of waiting in eager expectation for the one who has not yet come is
the dominant theme of Advent. It is not only the coming of Jesus, but the "Second Coming" that is anticipated, casting an eye far ahead toward the horizon of
God's fulfillment. Historically, for much of the Christian tradition, the waiting
in expectation includes the expectation of God's judgment. A colleague at Har-

vard, George H. Williams, tells the story of a research stint in a small town in Poland where the Advent season was taken as a season of penitence in preparation for the return of Christ in judgment. There was no pre-holiday bustle of feasting and excess, not even the singing of carols, but only the most serious austerity. And then, on Christmas Eve after the midnight mass, when the family had returned home for a simple meal and a special wafer was broken and shared around the table, the rejoicing and caroling began. "Hallelujah!" they exclaimed. "He has come not as a judge, but as a child. We have one more year to get ready!"

The Child

Christ is a little baby, a child. Part of the cycle of the Christian year is to marvel at the mystery of birth. The Christmas story sounds so familiar, so purposive, too purposive, really, as it is told year after year: How they went to pay taxes and ended up in a stable. There are no surprises. We see the scene so clearly in our mind's eye—as orderly as the crèche scene set up on the side table in the living room. Joseph, Mary, the manger, the shepherds, the friendly beasts, the angels, are each in place as if they all knew what was going on. But of course they did not know what was going on, there in Bethlehem, any more than we know what is going on when God moves in our lives in small yet utterly decisive ways.

What W. B. Yeats called "the uncontrollable mystery on the bestial floor" was the mystery of birth itself.[19] Birth is experienced as a mystery and that particular birth was a great mystery. Even the "glorias" of the angels and the testimonies of the shepherds could not make it clear to the company in the stable what kind of birth this was. "Mary treasured all these words and pondered them in her heart" (Luke 2:19). Today there is perhaps too much certainty, too little pondering, among both the religious and the irreligious.

In only two of the four Gospels does Jesus appear as a baby, and even then he is something of an emblematic baby. We don't hear him cry or see him crawl. We don't know if he was ever up to mischief. The story takes us straight from birth to young adulthood. But the divine child somehow stole into the Christian imagination anyway, in Gnostic Gospels that told of his childhood; in medieval devotion to the mother and child and to the child himself, as in the elaborate cult of the Infant of Prague; and in the development of Christmas, with all the yearly trappings of the crèche. God did not first show his human face as the young and fearless prophet, but as a child. A world in which children are the most vulnerable victims of poverty, malnutrition, and violence is surely in need of the refinement and enlargement of our capacity to see Christ as a child.

Hindu Vaishnavas insist that the most spontaneous and unconditioned love is that of parents for a child, and the adoration of the child Krishna in the Hindu tradition is very popular. In every Vaishnava household one would very likely find one particular figure among the *murtis*, the "images," on the home altar: the child Krishna on his hands and knees, crawling with a ball of butter in one hand. He is affectionately called *makan chor*, the "butter thief" who manages to get his little hand into the pot of freshly churned butter no matter how assiduously his mother tries to keep it out of his reach. She scolds him, but even in her scolding it is clear that the naughty little Krishna has stolen more than butter. He has stolen hearts. The loving affection and seemingly endless tolerance that is directed toward all children and their pranks is a measure of the holiness of this taste of love.

In Vishvanath Gali, the most crowded of Banaras commercial lanes, there is one store that sells nothing but clothing and adornments for the child Krishna. It opens into the lane like a cupboard stocked with dazzling piles of color: blue, pink, and gold satin outfits, trimmed with silvery ribbon; tiny ornaments and necklaces; crowns and headdresses, tiny peacock feathers to top off the crowns; little silver flutes; little enameled eyes to add to an image at the time it is installed on the home altar. Visiting that shop with a friend and trying the little outfits on the brass image of the crawling Krishna, I had to admit that there is something in all of us that loves this sort of thing. There is a lightness and playfulness to it that is consonant with the spirit of Krishna devotion. No one imagines for a moment that Krishna needs the little blue satin outfit we have just slipped on around his arms or the tiny strand of beads we have put around his neck. Indeed, no one imagines that the world-spanning Krishna is confined to this little brass image at all. This acting out, this "playing house," has to do with us and the ability to bring our affections and sensibilities to the service of God. I wondered somewhat irreverently what it would mean to harness the tremendous energy of the Barbie doll and G.I. Joe industry to the refinement of the religious imagination.

One August morning in Kankroli in rural Rajasthan, my Christological thinking was stretched a bit more by this Hindu vision of the child Krishna. I was visiting a temple that is not called a temple at all by the Pushtimargis, the "people of the path of grace," who worship there. It is called a *haveli*, which means a big household, a household large enough for and inclusive of the whole joint family. It is telling that the Pushtimargis call their places of worship households, for Krishna is honored and served and loved as part of these households, as the divine guest. Among the Pushtimargis, Krishna is especially honored as a child. From inside the *haveli* in Kankroli, the bells rang for the midmorning worship and the faithful gathered around the door of Krishna's chamber. I too craned my neck for the first glimpse of the child god. As the bells clanged, the priests opened the big temple doors and flung back the curtain from the inner sanctum.

Usually when the sanctum is opened in this way, oil lamps are lifted up to God, and simple offerings of food and water are made, which are then returned to the people as God's *prasad*, or grace. That morning, however, something else was offered as well—toys. Two elderly priests stood before Krishna and proceeded to take out Krishna's toys, his silver tops and miniature cows, and play with them in front of Krishna. I was startled—dumbfounded really—at the notion that one might worship the Lord by offering the gift of play. The Christmas festivities surrounding the child Jesus seemed very solemn by comparison. I wondered how much it really matters to most Christians that Jesus must once have been a child and was not always simply a miniature messiah. The stories of the childhood of Jesus are few and most of those that are preserved are narratives that did not quite make it into the canon of the New Testament.

I discovered there in Kankroli a new dimension of incarnation. What does the language of God-with-us, the incarnational language of my own tradition, really mean? The offering up of play is not really any different in nature from many daily Hindu temple rites—offering the Lord food, water to wash his feet, a soft bed for rest. How else would one worship the child god? How else show love and hospitality? Doesn't all of this familial, ritual language of love and hospitality toward God enable people to "practice the presence" of the incarnate Lord in all of life? I thought of my many visits to Brindavan as a guest of the temple community at Radha Raman. The attention lavished on the child Krishna blends seamlessly with the love of children in these families and in this community, where it is impossible even to imagine the abuse of children. And the arts of hospitality that are cultivated in the worship of Krishna as the divine guest are extended openly and generously to all guests, as I have many times experienced.

The Healer

One of the camp songs that I crooned as a teenager repeated the refrain "I have touched the hem of his garment, and his love has made me whole," drawing the language of healing from the story of the woman of faith who thought that if she could but get close enough to touch Jesus she would be healed. The Gospels are filled with such healing miracles, stories of those who were cured of illness, blindness, and madness by the power of their contact with Jesus.

Summer camp aside, I was never much attracted to Jesus as healer in anything but a symbolic or spiritual sense, and there were no healings that I was aware of in our First Methodist Church in Bozeman. The healing services I saw on television in the fifties, with the hands-on prayers of the shirt-sleeved televangelists, were to me an utterly alien version of Christianity. It was in India that I discovered a culture that assumed a deep relationship between spirit, mind, and body, and that enabled me to understand in a new way the very clear Gospel message of healing and to appreciate the face of the healer in Christ.

Interestingly, the healing miracles of the Gospels do not astound my Hindu friends. India is filled with healers and tales of miraculous healing. Everyone knows someone who was healed somewhere. There are countless pilgrimage shrines where silver amulets of legs, arms, breasts, and hearts are sold to faithful pilgrims who offer them in the temples as pledges of faith along with their prayers for healing. They are like the silver arms and legs presented to the saints or to Our Lady of Guadalupe in Mexico—tokens of faith and intention toward God. And for those not given to healing pilgrimages, India's long tradition of yoga is built upon the assumption that body, spirit, and mind go together. The stretching of the body, the disciplines of balance and of stillness, are not simply physical, but involve those aspects of ourselves that we speak of as mind and heart. The traditions of yoga are not ascetic in the sense that the body is denied or punished in order to somehow free the spirit. Not at all. The body is seen as a vehicle of spiritual growth. Perhaps that sounds too instrumental; more accurately, the body-spirit-heart-mind is seen as one interrelated whole.

One Thursday morning in October a few years ago, I went into the hospital for the first time in my life as customer. I had a lump in my breast and was to have a biopsy that morning. I was anxious, but somehow I managed to channel my anxiety into the curiosity of a researcher. I billed it as a field trip into a world all its own—with its own space, rituals, hierarchies, and rules. I put on the required clothes and walked into the operating theater and sat on the table. My surgeon came in, turned on a Mozart tape, and held out her arms straight in front of her while a nurse put on her operating gown. She quipped, "This is ninety percent ritual and ten percent science." I was relieved. "Most of what happens is determined by this space," she said, since she knew I was teaching a seminar on sacred space that very term. "Both of us have to dress this way and I have to observe certain rules because I have the use of this operating room this morning."

I was flat on my back on the table, lights glaring, Mozart reassuring. She cut, snipped, gave me a little more novocaine, and cut and snipped some more. I told her about India, about the little silver body parts, the arms and legs, the breasts. She recognized it all from Mexico. She had grown up in Mexico. She was a Catholic. I told her I had met the pope. If I winced a bit she said, "I'm sorry," and then laughed at how we, as women, are socialized to say "I'm sorry." The operation was longer, went deeper, and—when I looked around afterwards—was a little bloodier than I had imagined. It was my blood, too—a stark reminder that this was me, bleeding but not hurting. It interested me that the predominant feeling I had was not of being hurt, but of being cared for—a surgeon and two nurses "attending" in the fullest, most Buddhist sense, really paying attention.

When the doctor phoned the next afternoon, she said it was cancer. "I have cancer," I said when I put down the phone, but almost immediately I wondered what it meant to say those words. Breast cancer grows slowly. I had perhaps had this lump for several years—years when I felt ebulliently well, years when in fact I had had cancer. This was really the first day in a long time I had been without that lump, and yet I was saying, "I have cancer." I wondered about the power of words and locutions to position us in relation to disease. Whether I decided to use the possessive "I have" about cancer or not, I would have to make friends with the word. It could no longer be an alien term with a frightening penumbra around it, for suddenly it was an intimate acquaintance. On one level I knew perfectly well that sickness, old age, and death are not intruders into life, but are part of life. Leaning into that truth and really seeing it would be another matter.

The idea that faith, the restoration of right mind and heart, is an inextricable part of what it means to be healthy is a good biblical idea. I do not believe that anyone who has lived into the middle years of adult life would contest this. The healings of Jesus were not the display of sheer other-power, for again and again he said, "Your faith has made you well." Faith is the Godward leaning of the heart and mind. It is the ability to open the heart and let it move toward a center that will truly hold. The close relation of mind and heart and body is beginning to be reclaimed in the modern West, even among those who have been estranged from their religious roots. Oddly enough, it is science that is the catalyst.

After the long radiation treatments and during the course of chemotherapy, I picked up a brochure entitled "Discover the Mind / Body Connection that Reduces Stress and Illness." It was from the Mind / Body Clinic set up in the Deaconess Hospital by Dr. Herbert Benson, whose research on the "relaxation response" I had been following from a distance for several years. As a student of Indian traditions, it had fascinated and slightly amused me to see Western scientists and doctors hook up TM meditators, yogis, and Tibetan lamas to technical monitors to demonstrate the physiological changes that take place when the mind is concentrated in meditation. The concentration of the mind brought down their blood pressure and enabled them to raise their body temperature sufficiently, even in frigid environments, to dry out wet sheets wrapped around them. I found it somewhat amusing that at last the experimental wisdom of perhaps three thousand years of Indian practice could be "proven" by modern medical science in the West. I imagine it amused the lamas and the yogis, too.

The mind / body groups were not open to just anyone. You had to have cancer to get in. This was my chance, so I signed up. There were about fifteen of us seated in chairs around the circle that first day. We received simple instruction in the "relaxation response." Sit in a comfortable position, back straight and feet flat on the floor. Close your eyes. Focus the mind on the breath or on a word or phrase. When thoughts arise—worrying thoughts, or "awfulizing" thoughts, as they called them—simply notice them. Witness or observe them, as it were. And then bring the mind back to the focus. The chatter of the mind, the ceaseless inner dialogue has quite a dominant voice when the sense and feeling of cancer is part of one's life. The doctor told us that first day, "We all know that the thought of frightening or stressful things can actually produce physiological changes associated with terror or stress. If our thoughts can make us frightened or anxious, they can also heal us and give us peace."

We were asked to choose a "focus word" and were given a list of possibilities:

GENERAL: "One," "Peace," "Love," or "Ocean"
CHRISTIAN: "Come Lord," "Lord have mercy," "Hail Mary, full of grace," or "Maranatha"

JEWISH: "Shema Yisroel," "Shalom," or "Hashem"
EASTERN: "Hamsah," "Om," or "Shanti"

In my cancer group, Sylvia and Rachel certainly chose something from the Jewish list. I speculated that Sam and Michelle each went with an Eastern focus word. I wondered if Louise, being Catholic, chose the Hail Mary. Several probably took the more generic words. I knew about these focus words. In the Hindu tradition, they are called mantras. I had studied about them and could give a bit of an impromptu lecture about them, if called upon. But that was not at all what I was being asked to do here. Like everyone else, I was being asked to try it out. I hesitated just a moment and picked from the Christian list.

There we all were, week after week for eight weeks, with Hodgkin's disease, lung cancer, brain tumors, lymphoma, and breast cancer. We sat together at the beginning of each session, settling into our Shema Yisroels, our Oms, our Lord have Mercys, our Loves. Settling past the words into inner stillness, doing as a matter of course there in the hospital what the popes and nervous bishops of the world dared not to do—praying together—in a very profound sense. And it was clear to me that the divine healing of faith, which Jesus elicited and pointed to wherever he found it, was not a gift directed only to those who had the name of Jesus as their focus word.

Dr. Benson is an evangelist of sorts. He began his research with TM meditators who knew from experience what they were certain Benson would discover if he measured their pulse and breath during meditation. Gradually he has extended his interest from East to West and has begun asking Christian ministers to participate in colloquia on the mind / body in the context of prayer. His message is straightforward: Pray, pray every day. It's good for your health! Open the "knots of the heart" and let go of the anger, the resentment, the hurt. Open the heart, and let it move Godward. This is an old gospel that we learn anew. Our medical "missionaries" have found it in the East and are bringing it home.

One more point is important, however: Jesus as a healer, a worker of what people called miracles and wonders, did not focus that power upon himself. According to the biblical story, Jesus spent forty days and nights in the wilderness, clearly meant to recall and affirm the forty years the people of Israel spent in the wilderness with Moses. He is said to have been tempted by divine power and princely prestige, tempted by the easier fork in the road, tempted by what Hindu yogis call *siddhis*, miraculous powers that come from having an utterly concentrated (we might say God-centered) mind. Should he turn stones to bread? Should he throw himself from the temple wall and land uninjured?

These "miraculous" powers are real, according to my Hindu friends. Real yogis have the power of levitation, supernatural knowledge, the ability to walk on fire or lie on a bed of nails. I saw such a yogi one summer afternoon in Banaras. I had gone to the river for a walk and made my way down the lane that joins the river at Chet Singh Palace, a somewhat delapidated property of the Maharaja of Banaras. There on the palace grounds a crowd gathered around a formidable yogi who lay stoically on his bed of nails. Someone put an iron slab on his chest and then a strong young man stepped up with a sledgehammer to swing at the slab. I was bug-eyed with horror. After receiving a few mighty blows, the yogi stood to show his chest—ribs apparently intact and no sign that the nails had penetrated his skin at all.

For the most part, however, the Hindu and Buddhist traditions reject the *siddhis*. Only an ostentatious yogi such as the one I encountered at Chet Singh would make a show of these powers, and real spiritual adepts warn of being fascinated by them. The Buddha was told of a man who had practiced his yoga for years and could now walk across the river, and he is said to have responded, "Yes, but the ferry costs only three cents!" So it was with Jesus. He would not perform miracles simply to satisfy the curiosity of his accusers.

No doubt Jesus was really tempted. God could surely have removed the cup of suffering. When they scoffed at the foot of the cross, "He saved others; let him save himself if he is the Messiah of God, his chosen one!" there could have been a miraculous show of strength worthy of Rama or any of the *avataras*. But that is not the Christian story.

The Face of Suffering and Death

The fourth face of Christ is the suffering face of the one who is tempted and tested, and who finally suffers death. The season of Lent dwells on this testing and suffering. This too is God's face, and I think this is the one my Hindu friends comprehend the least. That God becomes one of us in birth, in life, and in love is one thing. That God becomes one of us in death is quite another.

The Gospels tell us of Jesus's feeling of loneliness and abandonment as all of his friends were asleep in Gethsemane, unable to watch with him one hour. They tell us of anguish, of tears, of real fear. He faced death. It was not simply the death of old age and sickness, to which the Buddha finally succumbed. It was the untimely, violent death of the young and the good. Studying this face of Jesus is very important. It will not do to miss the death and show up for the resurrection on Easter morning. We need the practice of the yearly drama of Holy Week, especially Good Friday, for the time will surely come when in the darkness and grinding grief of death we will need to be able to glimpse God's face.

By the time I was forty-five, death was no stranger. There were the relatively peaceful and timely deaths of all of my grandparents and of my two octogenarian teachers in Banaras. There were the untimely deaths of Aunt Irene, who died of cancer, and Aunt Elizabeth, who had a seizure and fell on the floor in her apartment. My best friend from graduate school, Ken, who had written so hopefully about Advent, was killed in a motorcycle accident in Ahmedabad. My friend Dean died of AIDS. My teacher from India, J. L. Mehta, born within a stone's throw of the Ganges in Banaras, died entangled in tubes in Mt. Auburn hospital in Cambridge while I kept watch in the hall. My father, suffering from three years of acute depression, parked his car by the banks of the Gallatin River and shot himself. It seemed as if suffering and death were everywhere. And it came to matter deeply that God wears the face of death, not as Yama, the Hindu functionary god with a noose who leads souls off to death, but as one who faced suffering and death himself. That is what the incarnation is about. And when people die in all the terrible and untimely ways they die, young and old, God is the first to weep. God does not justify our suffering, God participates in it.

Banaras is a city famous for its cremation grounds. Manikarnika Ghat, the principal cremation ground, was once outside the city to the south, as is appropriate in a culture that is concerned with purity; everything associated with death is considered impure and should not normally be mixed in with the rest of life. As Banaras grew, however, it stretched out along the Ganges to the south and gradually surrounded Manikarnika. More important, the sacred city embraced and sanctified death, not just geographically, but spiritually. In Banaras, the cremation ground is holy. Banaras is a place where people come to die in the hope of crossing over to the "far shore" of this worldly life. "Death in Kashi is liberation," they say. So the elderly and infirm come to Banaras to die. I never spent an afternoon in the heart of the city without hearing the chanting of a funeral party on its way to the cremation grounds.

One morning as I sat with Pandit-ji, translating Sanskrit on his front porch on Asi Road, a funeral procession came by carrying a corpse bound with cloth on a bamboo litter. They were headed for Manikarnika. It was nothing special. In Banaras, death is just part of the traffic. Pandit-ji smiled broadly and raised his eyebrows as he often did when he was about to impart a truth. He quoted to me from the Mahabharata: "What is a great wonder?" It was the passage where the righteous king Yudhisthira was being tested by a forest spirit. "What is a great wonder?" the spirit asked. "This is a great wonder," replied the wise Yudhisthira. "Every day we see people go to the city of death, and every day we go on thinking we will live forever." And so it is—a great wonder. We confront and yet do not confront death. We know that we will die. There is evidence every day in the lanes leading to Manikarnika. And yet we go on leading our lives as if it were not true. It is both a blessing and an astonishing feat of delusion.

In the United States, however, we do not see people go to the "city of death" on a daily basis. There is an acceleration of deaths that begins as one's parents and their generation begin to die. We begin to read the obituary pages with regularity. Even so, our cultural "denial of death," as Ernst Becker has called it, is widespread. We do not confront death daily, at least when we are young, at least if we are lucky. When I first went to India, I was both young and lucky. Or was I? I had scarcely seen death. In India, however, I lived for the first time in a culture which did not attempt to cover up the pain and anguish of life and which did not deny the reality of death. Birth and growth, joy and celebration, disease, old age, and death—all of it is so visible, in fact overwhelming, in Banaras. Every aspect of life—beginning, fullness, ending—is present at an intense pitch.

In Banaras, death and suffering are visible in daily life as nowhere else in the world. Banaras is also Lord Shiva's holy city, which Hindus speak of as the divine incarnation of Shiva's radiant light. As I came to know Banaras, I asked over and over, How could this city, which displays the wares of death, be seen as so holy by Hindus? And its Lord, Shiva, seemed to elude description. He was called Vishvanatha, Lord of the Universe. Sometimes he was depicted as regal—adorned as the Lord of the Universe might be, with jewels, the scent of sandalwood, and the crescent moon as an ornament in his hair. And yet the moment one expected him to be regal, said my Hindu friends, he would appear as a beggar, living on the cremation grounds, adorned with snakes as his ornaments, smeared with ashes.

Gradually, in the face of this Shiva, and in this terrifying and bewildering city so closely associated with Shiva, I cam to ask again the question of the incarnation: How did I, in my mind's eye, *expect* the Divine to appear? Should God be pure, bright, clean, and probably Protestant—the resident glorious, invisible Holy of the beautiful white churches of New England? Somehow I felt certain that Jesus the Christ would be more at home here, in Shiva's city. I began to see that it is precisely in this place, in the very presence of suffering and death, that Hindus affirm the abiding presence of Shiva and the certainty of passage to the far shore. If I could not see the point of the faith of Hindus in Banaras I had missed the point of my own faith in the incarnate Christ, who is present not only in light and life, but also in suffering and death.

Resurrection

Death is not the last word. The fifth face is that of the resurrected Christ. It does not look just like the face of Jesus of Nazareth. It is easy to mistake him for the gardener or the fellow traveler on the dusty road to Emmaus. Early in the morning, Mary went to the tomb where Jesus had been laid and the stone had been rolled away from the opening. She ran to get Simon Peter and the disciple whom Jesus loved. Simon Peter and the other disciple looked inside and saw the linen cloths that had been on Jesus' body, and the napkin that had covered Jesus' head rolled up in a place by itself. After the astonished disciples had left, Mary lingered, weeping, and stooped to look into the tomb. She turned around and there was a man standing. "Woman, why are you weeping?" he said to her. "They have taken him away," she said, not recognizing him. "Tell me where you have laid him." He called her by name—Mary. She recognized him as Jesus. It was Mary who broke the news to the disciples: "I have seen the Lord." The tomb was and is empty.

In Kashmir a few years ago, I was visiting the Srinagar valley and saw in my guidebook that there was a place said to be the tomb of the prophet Jesus, Yuz Asaf, who did not die on the cross but lived and spent his last forty years in northwest India. I was astonished to find that there was quite a literature on this subject. According to one writer, there are at least twenty-one historical documents bearing witness to Jesus' stay in Kashmir.[20] I read this with great interest, following what seemed to be some extremely elliptical reasoning about the Kashmiris being the lost tribe of Israel. When my taxi driver stopped at the tomb of Yuz Asaf in the Khanjar quarter of Srinagar, I was filled with curiosity. He accompanied me into the tomb. As a Muslim, he knew the story. "There is a Muslim saint buried here as well," said the driver, "but his grave was placed on the north-south axis as is customary, while the grave of Yuz Asaf was on an east-west axis according to Jewish custom." The gravestones had been covered with cloths. Next to the stone of Yuz Asaf was a slab carved with footprints, not unlike the many footprints of the Buddha or Rama that one might find elsewhere in India. The taxi driver was careful to point out how these footprints bore the crescent-shaped marks of crucifixion.

I was tempted for a moment. What if it were true? What if the gardener had been a gardener after all and had shown Mary the place where Jesus was laid? She would have rushed to that place to do whatever was necessary. All the tenderness and caring that the aftershock of a death calls forth could spring into action. For just a split second, standing on the cool stone slabs of that sanctuary in Srinagar, I felt the kind of kindred love that one might instinctively feel in discovering the long lost grave of a brother missing in action. For just a split second, I felt inadequate to the moment. Here I was, barefoot and empty-handed at a grave in Kashmir rumored to be that of Jesus. I had not even so much as a garland of flowers.

There is something in us that would like to have the grave of Jesus. As at the tombs of Muslim saints, there would be a kind of blessing, or *baraka*, to be had from being so close to the powerful and blessed dead. Such a faith, however, would not hold us for very long. The moment passed. In the end, I stood reverently with my taxi driver there at the gravesite in Srinagar and breathed a sigh of relief that this was not the final word of the Christian faith. The Easter affirmation "Christ is risen!" is the final word. As inveterate a researcher as I am, eager to stop at any shrine, temple, or mosque, I must admit I was uncomfortable at that tomb of Yuz Asaf. I was glad to leave.

The Ferry to the Far Shore

That death could not hold Jesus comes as no surprise to my Hindu friends. Death cannot hold anybody. As a Hindu friend once said to me, standing on the ghats in Banaras, looking down at the cremation ground, "You people think that death is the opposite of life, but we think of death as the opposite of birth." In the Hindu view, the soul's pilgrimage is a long one, and we are born time and time again. Krishna tells Arjuna in the Bhagavad Gita, "Death is certain for anyone born, and birth is certain for the dead; since the cycle is inevitable, you have no cause to grieve" (II.27).[21] The incarnation and reincarnation of the *atman*, the spirit or breath, is presupposed in the Hindu view. Birth and death are milestones, not the starting gate and the finishing line of a single race.

Reincarnation and resurrection have some things in common as ways of thinking. Both are affirmations that death is not decisive. Both presuppose a life, a Godward life-energy which, as the Bhagavad Gita puts it, "does not die when the body dies." Both address the mystery of that ongoing, irrepressible life that cannot be done in by death. But there are critical differences as well. Reincarnation is not what I as a Christian mean by resurrection. Reincarnation has to do with a wide understanding of life, one that includes both birth and death. Resurrection has to do with the meaning of life itself, no matter how long its trajectory might be.

Reincarnation makes us take a longer, more deliberate view of birth and death. Along the Ganges at night one can see the glow of the cremation grounds at Manikarnika Ghat and Harischandra Ghat. Gradually, I found their presence not a horror but a relief, a reminder not of finality, but of passage. This affirmation of the soul's long pilgrimage is an appealing view and it is little wonder that so many, even in the Christian tradition, find it attractive. This Hindu view takes seriously our sense of the "immortality of the soul," our sense that we come to this life "trailing streams of glory," and our sense that what we call "life" is usually too short a time in which to grow up. It gives us a sense that we do indeed reap what we sow, though it may not be evident in this life. The soul bears the imprint of the deeds, attachments, and emotions that drive this complex being we call "me." Genius like that of Mozart is accounted for. The death of a child, the mental illness of a loved one, is somehow more explicable in the larger context of this long drama we cannot fully see or understand. It is a plausible and attractive worldview for those of us who would like a little justice done, whether we ourselves can see it or not.

This is not the resurrection view. As contradictory as it seems, the resurrection of Christ has to do with life now, not later. It has more to do with whether there is real life before death than with whether there is life after death. Total transformation is possible now. Indeed, it has already happened if we were but wakeful enough to see. In the ebb and flow of birth and death, the interplay and rivalry of good and evil, justice and injustice, war and peace, obedience and apostasy that characterizes the human community, there is a decisive event that flies in the face of orderly cause and effect. It is new life, rising right out of the midst of death. It is a real crossing over. Death finally is overcome.

It interests me that almost as soon as the ancient Indian sages had formulated the idea of rebirth, either in heaven or on earth, they became restless with it. What disturbed those thinkers was not so much rebirth, but re-death. Being

born again and again was not so unappealing, but the prospect of dying over and
over was deeply disturbing. The cycle of birth and death was not in itself spiritually satisfying and final liberation became the ultimate goal. Even for Hindus
who presuppose that "death is certain for anyone born, and birth is certain for
the dead," there is a yearning to cross over to the distant shore of freedom, to cross
over "from death to deathlessness." The closer counterpart of the message of
resurrection is *moksha*, liberation from the long trajectory of birth and death.
Birth and death will end. We will cross the river of birth and death, and there
will be ultimate transformation. There is some convergence of the reincarnation view and the resurrection view after all, and especially in Banaras.

I learned something about both death and the conquering of death in Banaras. For all its cremation grounds, Banaras is not a morbid city where everyone is
focused on death. What is distinctive about the city is the daily juxtaposition of
death and life. The festivals, the brilliant crowds at the bathing ghats, the lanes
bursting with commerce—all are interspersed with the pulse of processions to
the cremation grounds. Even the tourists who come to see the city at dawn are approached by zealous, enterprising boatmen whose sales pitch is "Boat 'round?
Dead bodies burning, madam?" To live life, affirm life, and celebrate it, death
does not have to be denied. Having looked death in the face, perhaps more
closely than any of us in the modern West ordinarily look, the Hindus of Banaras also claim for their faith a victory over both re-death and rebirth.

In the Hindu world, Banaras is seen as a place of illumination and liberation.
The Hindu tradition insists, on the whole, that liberation can come only from
the illumination of wisdom. One does not get it for free. The sages and philosophers sought that wisdom. Wisdom—the deep knowledge of the soul's inextricable relatedness to the Supreme Reality—takes a long time. But the moment
Hindus have finished setting the highest and most elite standards for liberation,
they set about finding the means of grace to circumvent them and making the far
shore accessible to all. It is their belief that Banaras is one of those means of grace.
The task of imparting illumining wisdom to the dying and dead is undertaken,
so they say, by Lord Shiva himself. He is seen, in the mythic mind's eye, bending
over the dead at the cremation ground, whispering the *taraka mantra* into the ear
of each one. *Taraka* means "the boat," and this is the word of illumination that
ferries one across the river of birth and death to the far shore. Hindus are not at
all exclusive about who receives this liberating wisdom from Shiva in Banaras: it
is a gift to everyone who dies there. The Lord says, here on the banks of the Gan-

ges so far from Galilee, "Come to me, all ye who labor and are heavy laden, and I will give you rest."

Pandit-ji always said with a twinkle in his eye that he would never leave Banaras. He would not even go to the hospital at Banaras Hindu University, on the leafy campus grounds just outside of the traditional boundaries of the sacred city of Kashi. He had given instructions to the whole family. He had lived his entire life in Banaras, but for a brief period of travel as a young man. He loved the city and he wanted to die there. He loved to think about dying there and to talk about it. I asked him once what would happen to me if I died in Banaras. I am not a Hindu, so would I also receive Shiva's ferryboat *mantra* and be delivered to the far shore? His eyes lit up. He loved the question and loved to expound on how everyone would be liberated by Shiva—even Christians, even Muslims, even atheists. He was the widest of inclusivists and his faith was in a God of spacious grace.

I was to be included in the crossing-over to the freedom of the far shore that was Pandit-ji's most cherished vision. And I am certain that there is plenty of room in God's household of many mansions for Pandit-ji as well. The prayer of the Upanishads is, finally, one we both share:

> *Asato ma sat gamaya*
> *Tamaso ma jyotir gamaya*
> *Mrityor ma amritam gamaya*
> *Om shanti, shanti, shanti*

> From untruth, lead me to truth.
> From darkness, lead me to light.
> From death, lead me to immortality.
> Om, peace, peace, peace.

The Breath of God

The Fire and Freedom of the Spirit

IN AUGUST of 1983, at the sixth general assembly of the World Council of Churches, in Vancouver, I was amazed to find picketers and pamphleteers stalking the sidewalks outside the University of British Columbia gymnasium, which served as a plenary hall, pressing their views on the doctrine of the Holy Spirit. As a veteran of the sixties, I had seen quite a few demonstrations on a wide range of issues, but this one took me quite by surprise. The Holy Spirit? Their placards and handbills were either supporting or denouncing something called the *filioque*. While most of us were perplexed, the ecclesiastical brass—the bishops in their purple vestments, the metropolitans and patriarchs in their flowing black robes—would certainly have known at a glance what the slogans and the leaflets were all about. There has long been a controversy about the Holy Spirit. We could have been at the Council of Toledo in the sixth century or the Council of Florence in the fifteenth century, two places where the issue was hotly contested in the past.

In brief, the question is how does the Holy Spirit move in the world? Does the Spirit "proceed," or go forth, from God the Father, or does the Spirit proceed from the Father and the Son? *"Filioque"* is the "and the Son" clause in Latin. In the Middle Ages the Church of Rome added this word to the creed. The controversy over this addition became one of the major sources of tension between Eastern and Western Christendom. The Orthodox Church insisted that the Spirit goes forth from the Father, while the Roman Catholic Church insisted that the Spirit goes forth from the Father and the Son. For the East, the *filioque* amounted to a subordination of the Holy Spirit to the Son; for the West, it was a protection against the dangers of natural theology, the discerning of God from reason and nature alone. The Orthodox insisted on the freedom of the Spirit to "blow where it wills," as the Gospel of John puts it, while the Roman Catholic church decided, in effect, that the wind of the Spirit could blow only through Christ.

For most of the hundreds of lay delegates and the thousands of assembly visitors who found a leaflet on the Holy Spirit and the *filioque* handed out to them that summer day, the controversy was elusive at best. Most of us do not think much about the Holy Spirit, even those of us who speak of the experience of the Spirit. Does it really matter whether the Holy Spirit "proceeds" only from the Father or from both the Father and the Son? For many the doctrine of the "double procession" of the Spirit no doubt seemed arcane and far removed from the urgent issues of the church in the twentieth century. As I started to think about it, however, I found in this theological furor a fascinating challenge to my own thinking about God.

The controversy over the freedom, the movement, and the presence of the Holy Spirit is really, after all, a controversy about the freedom, the movement, and the presence of God. When Christians speak of God as Spirit, we do not speak of "one third" of God, but of the full presence of God. To speak of God as Spirit conveys the power and mystery of God's universal, active, relational presence. Spirit language is not abstract language about a vague God, elusive and far removed. On the contrary, it is intimate language, conveying to us the sense of God's presence—within us, surrounding us, right here. How we think about the Holy Spirit is an important part of the theological thinking of Christians in relation to a world of many faiths and peoples. Is the Holy Spirit channeled only through Christ, as the "double procession" folk would have it? Or is the Holy Spirit truly an expression of God's constantly revealing mystery and freedom? Can we speak of the Holy Spirit as that sense of God's presence in nature? In solitude? In the experience of transforming power? In the sanctuaries of many faiths? What *do* we mean by the Holy Spirit?

I thought of dawn in Banaras and the palpable sense of what I would call the presence, the breath, the Spirit of God that attends the prayers that have been offered there daily for perhaps three thousand years. I thought of the words of the prophet Malachi, "From the rising of the sun to its setting my name is great among the nations, and in every place incense is offered to my name, and a pure offering; for my name is great among the nations, says the Lord of hosts" (Mal. 1:11). And I thought of the many other Christians through the ages who have stood there on the Ganges ghats in the morning and sensed God's presence, like the German traveller Herman Keyserling in first decade of the twentieth century, who wrote, "The breath of divine presence hangs over the Ganges more mightily than I have ever felt it anywhere else. Especially in the morning when the faithful cover the ghats in thousands, when their prayers flow in golden waves towards the rising sun ... the whole atmosphere seems to be divinely transfused."[1]

Christian theologians have both struggled with and avoided the Holy Spirit. Paul Tillich called the Holy Spirit the "almost forbidden word," and it is true that theologians have often given a wide berth to the Spirit. When they do begin to construct a systematic doctrine of the Spirit they describe their formulations with the formidable term *pneumatology*, from *pneuma*, the Greek term for spirit. The word itself sounds more appropriate to tire sales than to spirituality, but perhaps the use of the term is meant to lend an intellectual aura to an enterprise that is inherently difficult, for the investigation of the Spirit does not lend itself to philosophy as much as to poetry. It is elusive of our mind's grasp—vital, powerful, and yet insubstantial. The biblical passages describe its activity in powerful verbs: the Spirit falls upon, descends, fills, inspires, sanctifies, teaches, reminds, and comforts. The presence of the Spirit is spoken of as a power and a joy, an outpouring and a gift. Many Christians claim the gifts of the Spirit in ecstatic worship and prayer, speaking in tongues. Others might indeed claim that the Spirit's presence is most profoundly experienced when the mind has ceased its grasping formulations and speech has settled into stillness.

There are at least three strong and resonant images associated with the Spirit: breath, fire, and the dove. They are all vibrant images, life images, visible and invisible icons. Breath evokes the sense of the intimacy and presence of the Spirit, with us always, even when we are unaware of it. Much of the Spirit language in the Bible is breath language. In Hebrew the word for spirit is *ruach*, literally "breath" or "wind." It is a feminine noun, and it is employed in the very first verses of Genesis to speak of the mothering, life-giving Spirit of God that hovered, brooded, over the deep at the dawn of creation. Fire evokes the sense of power and empowerment that was the experience of Pentecost and that energized the mission of the early church. Fifty days after the resurrection of Christ, the disciples experienced the outpouring of the Holy Spirit, with the rushing sound of a mighty wind and the descent of what seemed to be flames of fire settling upon their tongues and giving them the ability to speak of the mighty works of God in all the languages of earth.

Breath and fire may be distinct images, but they belong together as intertwining images of the Spirit. The Spirit both nurtures contemplation and empowers action; the Spirit guides us into a life in which these moments of stillness and action, silence and energy are balanced. Finally, there is the bird, the dove, which has become the preeminent icon of the Spirit in the church. The dove's flight is the image of the Spirit's freedom; she is not tethered to the church. As Metropolitan George Khodr of the Orthodox church in Lebanon put it, "Other religions too come under the wings of the Spirit."[2]

There are moments in all human lives of what Martin Buber called the "I-Thou experience"—where eyes meet, where truth meets truth, where one being meets another. Love and suffering, beauty and horror provide us with the experience of such moments. The I-Thou experience of full presence is what Krishnamurti calls "choiceless awareness"—awareness without the grasping, naming, categorizing, and polarizing that distances us from experience. Full presence living. Ordinary human experience can name such moments. They are times of insight, recognition, and awareness. Christians give a name to this powerful sense of full presence: the Holy Spirit. It is what Bishop John V. Taylor has called the "Go-Between God," the invisible "current of communication" that streams between us when we truly recognize the presence of the other.[3] Breath, fire, and the dove all, in different ways, are annunciations of the presence of this "Go-Between God."

Breath: The Invisible Icon of the Spirit

The most pervasive and intimate presence of the Divine has often been expressed with "breath language." The Jesuit theologian Donald Gelpi speaks of *ruach* as "Holy Breath," which he feels is more accurate and less misleading than "Spirit," with its flavor of matter-spirit dualism.[4] Indeed, he says, "breathing" is perhaps even better than "breath" because it conveys the energy and activity of movement. It inspires, it fills, it "clothes" the prophets with power, it enters into their hearts. The Bible is filled with the descent and the infusion of this divine breath. It was the Spirit that came upon David when he was annointed by Samuel (1 Sam. 16:13). It was the Spirit that inspired Bezalel, the chief architect of the tabernacle, with his creativity and artistry: "And I have filled Bezalel with the Spirit of God, with ability and intelligence, with knowledge and all craftsmanship, to devise artistic designs" (Exod. 35:30 ff.) And it is the same Spirit that came upon Mary, descended upon Jesus, and poured out upon the church at Pentecost.

In the Gospel of John, the risen Christ is said to breathe upon his disciples and thus transmit to them the Holy Spirit as they were gathered together (John 20:22). The Divine within us is not exactly our own breath, our own process of respiration as such, but breath is surely the closest possible analogue to what we mean when we speak of the human "soul" or "spirit." Breath is enlivening, it sustains us even when we forget it, even when we are asleep. Breath is vital to our individual existence, and yet it is not "ours," for we share the fact of that vital presence with all that lives. Biblical theologians, such as those on a recent doctrine commission of the Church of England, argue that "the use of the word 'spirit' with reference to God is borrowed from its use with reference to human beings, who are all animated by breath. In this case, 'spirit' is first applied to people and is then applied by extension to God, who has a divine, a holy spirit, not the feeble kind of spirit which we have and which deserts us at death."[5]

Breath is the invisible icon of the Divine. In breath-centered meditation, one rests the mind in the breath, returning again and again to the breath as the mind wanders. It is the breath that draws one back to awareness, to awakeness, to presence. In Christian meditation, it is the breath that draws one again and again to the awareness of God. To speak of our human breath as an icon means that it is both a reminder of God's presence and a window through which we may be drawn toward God's presence at any time and place, for the breath is the most portable of icons. It is indeed the go-between, rising and falling, tracing an invisible thread of connection between the respiration of the body and the Spirit of God.

Spirit or breath language is naturally a way of speaking about our own true nature. When we look within, whether we are Christians or Hindus, sooner or later we have to ask, seriously and not just intellectually, the inescapable question, Who am I, really? It is everybody's question. As the sage of the ancient Svetasvatara Upanishad put it, "Whence are we born? By virtue of what do we live? On what are we established? Guided by whom, in pleasure and in pain, do we live in our various ways?" (1.1). The breath is a vehicle for investigating such questions. People of many traditions speak of the breath of life as God given or even as God-within. There is something sacred about that which enlivens us, breathes in us. Those of us who look to Genesis say that God "breathed the breath of life" into Adam and that first human being became "a living soul"

(Gen. 2:7). The *ruach* of a person is the God-given breath of life. The Quakers call it "that of God in us." As Job puts it, "The spirit of God has made me, and the breath of the Almighty gives me life. . . . If he should take back his spirit to himself, and gather to himself his breath, all flesh would perish together and all mortals return to dust" (Job 33:4, 34:14). In many religious traditions, breath is a primary image for the divine presence within.

The ancient seekers and sages of the Upanishads were relentless questioners, exploring the limits of both outer and inner space. Who are we human beings, really? What is the essence of human life? What seems to depart at death? Is it heat? Is is sight? They tried out various answers to the probing questions about that inner reality, including the charming idea that there is a person the size of a thumb who sits within our bodies as the subject of experience. But they knew finally that we are more subtle than a thumb-sized midget and more vibrant than what we might find by analyzing our physical and mental components. Really we are *atman*, the soul. The word *atman* also means "breath," but not literally the breath of respiration. That is called *prana*, a coarser breath, but nonetheless one that points us in the direction of the Real. The awareness of *prana*, however, is but a vehicle for the realization of *atman*.

One of my favorite passages in Hindu speculative literature is from the Brihadaranyaka Upanishad (6.7 ff), where the teacher demonstrates the "firm basis" (*pratistha*) of all life. He tells the story of a dispute between the various vital senses of the body. Speech and eye, ear, mind, and breath—all argue with one another about their relative superiority. They decide on a contest to determine which is most vital to human life. First, speech leaves the body for a whole year, and when speech returns it asks, "How have you been able to live without me?" The other senses affirm that the body lived in the interim, as the mute live, not speaking, but breathing with the breath, seeing with the eye, and so forth. Then the eye went off for a year, and when it came back it asked, "How have you been able to live without me?" The other senses affirmed that the body lived, as the blind live, not seeing with the eye, but breathing with the breath, speaking with speech, hearing with the ear. The other senses each went off for a year, one by one, each convinced that it would be impossible for the body to exist without its presence. Even the semen went off, and the body lived with no difficulty. Finally, the breath was about to leave. As the breath began to depart from the body, all the other senses began to be pulled up along with it. The text describes it powerfully: "Then Breath was about to go off. As a large fine horse of the Indus-land might pull up the pegs of his foot-tethers together, thus indeed did it pull up those vital breaths together. They said: 'Sir, go not off! Verily, we shall not be able to live without you!'"

Breath, *prana*, is a powerful image of the spark of life within, for truly when breath departs we die. Living beings are called *prani*, literally "those who breathe." *Prana* is so important that it is explicitly and provocatively set side by side with *atman* in the Kaushitaki Upanishad: "I am the breathing spirit [*prana*], the intelligential self [*prajnatman*]. As such, revere me as life, as immortality. Life is the breathing spirit. The breathing spirit, verily, is life. The breathing spirit, indeed, is immortality. For, as long as the breathing spirit remains in this body, so long there is life" (3.2).

The seekers and the teachers of the Upanishads know that the breath of respiration is only the signal and symbol of a more mysterious foundation. Real breath, real sight, real hearing is that which does not leave when respiration ceases, when sight is gone, when hearing is no more.[6] "This life [*prana*] is born from the Spirit [*atman*]" (Chandogya 7.26). If we try to attune our ears to the resonance of the word *atman* for the seekers of ancient India, we find that it is finally said to be none other than the Ultimate Reality which undergirds the whole universe—Brahman. When the sage Yajnavalkya finally moves from the 3,306 gods to the one God, he is asked, "Which is the one God?" He replies, "Life Breath; he is Brahman." *Atman* is Brahman, that "in which we live and move and have our being," to borrow, as Saint Paul did, the words of the Greek philosophers. The foundation within and the foundation of the vast universe are not different.

The early speculations of the thinkers of the Upanishads are much like those of the pre-Socratics in ancient Greece, probing the origins of the universe and stretching the mind, as cosmologists in the sciences do even today, to the first seeds of life. Was it fire, or heat, or light, or water? What was that primordial substrate from which all originated, on which all is woven? Finally, as we have already seen, that ground of all being is named with the word *Brahman*, the Ultimate Reality, "across which space and time are woven, warp and woof" (Brihadaranyaka 3.8). It is a term which names that which ultimately cannot be named, and which is perhaps better implied by the consistent stripping away of all imaginative constructs with the evocative words *"neti, neti, neti"*—"not this, not this, not this, ..."

The sages and seekers of the Upanishads also probed the foundations of life within, asking what really is at the heart of life, engendering vitality. One teacher, Uddalaka, taught his son about this reality with a series of analogies.

"Bring me a fig."

"Here it is, father."

"Break it open. What do you see inside?"

"Some rather tiny seeds, father."

"Break one of them open. What do you see inside?"

"Nothing at all, father."

"From the inside of this tiny seed, which seem to be nothing at all, this whole fig tree grows. That is the Real. That is *atman*. That art thou, my son."

Again, Uddalaka said, "Put some salt in this water and bring it to me in the morning." So the son stirred salt into the water and the next morning he brought it to Uddalaka.

"Fetch me the salt that you put there yesterday."

"I cannot, father."

"Then, taste the water from this end. How does it taste?"

"Salty."

"Taste the water from that end. How does it taste?"

"Salty."

"That which you cannot grasp, but can taste in every drop, That is the Real. That is *atman*. That art thou, my son."   (Chandogya 6.12–13)

The *atman*, the spirit within, is not to be seen or grasped, and yet it is the source of all life. It cannot be seen, but the whole of the varied world grows and flowers from it. It cannot be grasped, but it can be tasted in every drop.

The Real is One, whether we probe within ourselves toward the interior or beyond ourselves toward the infinite. The within and the beyond have two distinct names—*atman* and Brahman—but yet are so related to one another that they cannot really be said to be two. Just how they are related is the source of as much philosophical discussion in the Hindu tradition as the relation of the various "persons" of the Trinity has generated within the Christian tradition or as the relation of the human spirit and the Holy Spirit might generate. Biblically, it is clear that the creative impulse and initiative is God's; the Spirit is breathed into creation by God and the Spirit is breathed into the disciples and the church. But having received this breath, is that which enlivens the soul other than, identical with, or similar to God? These questions of the relation of the human and the Divine in the Spirit are very much those of the Christian tradition as well.

As for the Hindus, the monists among them insisted *atman* and Brahman are identical. The dualists said they are two and that their relatedness in love requires that they be two. The non-dualists refined the language, abandoning the claims of "one" for the more nuanced formulation "not two." The "qualified non-dualists" further refined the understanding. The "difference-and-non-difference" school saw it both ways, and the "unimaginable difference-and-non-difference" school saw the unspeakable mystery in that position. All saw, however, the inextricable relatedness of that *atman* which lies within and the unfathomable Brahman which takes the mind to the outer limit of its imagination.

Whatever the exact relationship of *atman* and Brahman, of soul and Divine, our human problem is that we are unable to see that inextricable relatedness clearly. Because we do not see clearly, we human beings continually live with a notion of self, world, and God which is illusory, *maya*. It is not at all that the world is an illusion, as some would characterize *maya*. Rather, *maya* refers to the fact that we live with a generalized case of mistaken identity, like the traveler who sees something coiled on the path and thinks it is a snake, only to find when he sees more clearly that it is a rope. Or the beach walker who sees the bright glitter on the beach and thinks it silver, only to discover as he reaches down to grasp it that it is a shell. This is *maya*. Something is there, but we have made a mistake about what it is, and the process has elicited in us very real responses such as terror or greed.

To sharpen our consciousness of the truth, both Hindus and Buddhists have always begun with the breath, as we shall see when we explore the paths of spiritual discipline. Breath is the go-between, the thread of connection that leads both inward and outward. In Hindu yoga traditions, for example, *pranayama*, "breath control," is one of the first steps of the discipline of yoga. It is the breath that can begin to lead us to clarity of mind. The ancient sage Patanjali's one-line description of yoga is this: "*Yoga citta vritti nirodha*," "Yoga is stopping the whirlpools of the mind." To gain spiritual freedom we must break the tendency of the mind to attach itself to one object and then another, to claim and classify everything with reference to the self, as "me" and "mine." This does not mean mindless living, but rather the enabling of the clear vision of the mind, unclouded by the currents that swirl us perpetually into whirlpools of possessive attachment. Breath is a way to begin, they say. Ordinary breath is not conscious or voluntary. We breathe without thinking about it. But if we bring it into the realm of conscious and intentional action it becomes, then, the first image or icon, so to speak, of God, the Real. The breath is the link between the body and the mind. It is the breath that harnesses the body and enables it to be still. And it is attention to the breath that calms the whirlpools of the mind and creates the still pool of consciousness necessary for clear seeing, for breaking the grip of *maya*, for releasing us into the presence of Brahman.

The importance of breath in the Hindu tradition enhances our understanding of the Spirit. It is that spirit within, the inside of the inside of the fig seed, which cannot be seen or grasped, but can be known by the fig tree that grows from it. It is called the unseen seer, the unknown knower, the un-understood understander. For Christians, the Holy Spirit is that of God which moves within us and enables us to apprehend God, enables us even to know what we know of Christ. It is the Spirit, as Jesus puts it, that will continually remind us of all that Jesus has taught (John 14:26). Spirit language is not the language of the incarnation. And yet Spirit language is also not the distant, mind-stretching language of Ultimate Reality. It is intimate language. It is deeply personal but not personified. To speak of God as Spirit is to speak in the most immanent and immediate way of God's presence. It is the mystery of God, as close to us as our very breath.

Christian Orthodox traditions of prayer also use the breath with prayer as a vehicle of linking our consciousness to God. As Theophan the Recluse puts it, "The descent of the mind into the heart by the way of breathing is suggested for the case of anyone who does not know where to hold his attention."[7] The problem of the restless mind is clearly recognized. St. Gregory of Sinai wrote, "You should know that no one can hold the mind by himself, if it be not held by the Spirit. For it cannot be held, not because of its mobile nature but because, through neglect, it has acquired the habit of turning and wandering hither and thither. . . . A mind thus inclined and withdrawn from God is led captive everywhere."[8] Breath is the instrument of what is called *theosis*, the Godward transformation of our very being. It is startling to those Christians who speak primarily of human sinfulness to recognize within the Christian tradition such powerful language of human transformation, divinization. As St. Athanasius puts it, "The Logos became man that we might become God."[9] Again, the Godward transformation is not only in the hour of prayer, but in all that we do, "that our life should become one with His life, our breathing with the Divine Breath that sustains the universe."[10]

Breath is always with us. Remembering the breath, returning to the breath, becomes a way, then, of remembering and returning to the present and to the presence of God. It is simply a matter of awareness, of shift in attention from the thousand thoughts and things that occupy the mind most of the time to the simple presence of the moment. Resting the mind on the breath for a sustained period of meditation or for a moment virtually any time of day is a vehicle for resting in the Spirit. It is a vehicle for returning attention to the moment and for returning attention to God. It is the Holy Spirit that continually turns and returns us to God.

Fire: The Power of the Spirit

Fire is one of the most ancient icons of the Divine. Before temples and images, names and incarnations, there was fire—vibrant, energetic, consuming, purifying. The burning bush, where God spoke to Moses. The fire of the ancient Zoroastrian tradition, symbol of truth and icon of the Supreme Lord of Wisdom, Ahura Mazda. The fire was and is an altar of sorts. It was into the campfire that we teenagers at church camp placed our sticks of wood, emblems of our commitment to Christ. It was around the tepee fire in Lame Deer that the Northern Cheyenne drummed and prayed all night for the soldiers in Vietnam. It did not surprise me a bit to discover in India that the fire altar was the most ancient place of worship. That fire widely symbolizes the Spirit of God, the Spirit of Truth, bearing witness to the Truth, enriches my sense of the Holy Spirit.

In ancient India three thousand years ago, before there were temples or images to dwell in the temples, the Aryans of the Vedic tradition made their offerings at carefully constructed fire altars built as circles, triangles, or squares. The fire was understood to carry the gifts offered to heaven. The ancients of India spoke of the divine fire as Agni—fire in heaven and on earth, as well as the messenger with flaming hair that streams between heaven and earth. The first hymn of the Rig Veda begins:

> I magnify God, the Divine Fire,
> the Priest, Minister of the sacrifice,
> the Offerer of oblation, supreme Giver of treasure.[11]

It is at the altars of Agni that many Hindu rites are performed even today—domestic rituals, weddings, and life-cycle rituals.

The most elaborate Vedic fire altar was built in the shape of a bird, laid out in a meadow beneath a temporary shelter of bamboo and thatching. The bricks of the fire altar represented the seasons and elements of the entire universe; the gifts offered into the fire through days and nights of chanting represented all that humankind could imaginably offer to the Divine. At the end of the rite, a rite almost inconceivably elaborate and intricate, the whole ritual arena—the bird-altar, the shelter, the implements—was set on fire and burned to ash.[12] Nothing material remained—no structure or image, no relic or reliquary—as if to underline the impossibility of fixing and containing the power of the Divine in the vessels of this earth. Insubstantial, yet all-powerful, fire easily conveys the meanings of the word Spirit.

In the Christian tradition, the language of the Holy Spirit is not only one of breath, attention, and presence, but also a language of energy and fire. The experience of the Spirit is not only the experience of calm insight, but also the experience of power and empowerment. The descent of the Spirit at the time of the baptism of Jesus, an event recorded in all four Gospels, was clearly an empowerment for his testing in the wilderness and then his public ministry. And the descent of the Holy Spirit at Pentecost is a story of the outpouring of heavenly power as fire, and it is also the story of the birth of the church.

As the Acts of the Apostles, recorded by Luke, begins, Christ speaks to the disciples at the time of his ascension into heaven, "You will receive power when the Holy Spirit has come upon you; and you will be my witnesses in Jerusalem, in all Judea and Samaria, and to the ends of the earth" (Acts 1:8). What would this receiving of power be like? The disciples returned to Jerusalem to wait, and they devoted themselves to prayer. They were surely uncertain about the future and uncertain about how to understand the past. Then, in Acts 2, Luke tells the mighty story of the outpouring of the Holy Spirit on the day of Pentecost. It was the culmination of the Feast of Weeks, fifty days after Passover, and Jews came from many countries on pilgrimage to Jerusalem. Luke tells us that there were devout Jews from every nation on earth living in Jerusalem, for in the Jewish liturgical calendar, the Feast of Weeks celebrated another outpouring of the Divine, the giving of the Torah on Sinai. It is not surprising that the Christian story of Divine empowerment is layered upon the story of the descent of divine power on Sinai.

"And suddenly from heaven there came a sound like the rush of a violent wind," Luke writes. "Divided tongues, as of fire, appeared among them, and a tongue rested on each of them. All of them were filled with the Holy Spirit and began to speak in other languages, as the Spirit gave them ability" (Acts 2:3–4). The people who had gathered in Jerusalem from Mesopotamia, Libya, Rome, and Egypt also heard this sound, this windrush. They listened, and they were amazed and said, "Are not all these who are speaking Galileans? And how is it that we hear, each of us, in our own native language?" Hearing about God's deeds of power, each in language they could understand, they said to one another, "What does this mean?" Peter spoke up and addressed the crowd, quoting the prophet Joel: "In the last days it will be, God declares, that I will pour out my Spirit upon all flesh, and your sons and your daughters shall prophesy, and your young men shall see visions, and your old men shall dream dreams." From that decisive event, a dozen discouraged, frightened men and women found the courage to launch a movement that would spread throughout the Roman world. This flaming shower of the Spirit did not lead simply to individual transformation, it gave birth to a community.

It is hard to ritualize Pentecost in the liturgical calendar of the church. As a time of the outpouring of sheer energy, it cannot be ritually repeated on schedule. It was an event that created what the anthropologist Victor Turner called "spontaneous *communitas*," a spiritual bonding of power and strength, mutuality and sacrifice, of what Buber calls the "essential We."[13] Such *communitas* must become routinized and ritualized in order to survive, though, and the church was no exception. Nonetheless, medieval churches were wonderfully imaginative in celebrating Pentecost as the "birthday of the church." When the great unruly day of Pentecost came in tenth-century Rome, for instance, the mystery of the Spirit was dramatized. There were "Holy Spirit holes" in the ceilings of the churches, opening them to the sky, dramatizing architecturally the openness of the church to God and the fabulous fact that the Spirit cannot be contained within the church. On Pentecost, doves were let loose through these holes to fly about in the church, bundles of rose petals were released to fall down upon the people like the tongues of fire, and choirboys were set to whooshing and drumming to call to mind the rush of the Spirit.

We need these Holy Spirit holes. Our churches need these skyward openings to the windrush of God, even the pentecostal churches that summon the Spirit every Sunday morning. Holy Spirit holes would be perpetual reminders to both the prophetic and the pentecostal movements in our churches that our knowledge of God is not complete. They would ceaselessly remind us that no image or icon, no petal or flame can domesticate God's Spirit. Its symbolic images, like the dove and the wildfire, are images of utter freedom.

The term *pentecostal* today calls up the image of pentecostal churches, with their emphasis on Spirit-filled prayer, including speaking in tongues, which certainly repeats in a way that first Pentecost. I want to reclaim quite another aspect of Pentecost, which is the experience of the worldwide Christian community of many languages, races, and cultures. At Pentecost, it is to the *community* that the Spirit is given, breathed, showered down like flames from on high. As Paul puts it, "For in the one Spirit we were all baptized into one body . . . and we were all made to drink of one Spirit" (1 Cor. 12:13). The living power of the Spirit, then, drives Christians today to discover the unity of the Holy Spirit and what it means to belong together as the church, not just within one small isolated community, but throughout the world.

I have felt what I would call Pentecostal energy in the experience of "church" that is most ecumenical—the great assemblies of the World Council of Churches (WCC), like those in Vancouver in 1983 and in Canberra in 1991. It is not surprising that when the World Council of Churches was formed in the wake of World War II, with Europe lying in shambles and the church painfully aware of the tragedy of its divisions, the opening sermon preached by the Sri Lankan churchman D. T. Niles focused on the text of the descent of the Spirit at Pentecost. The ecumenical movement became a new Pentecostal movement, gathering from a hundred countries, speaking dozens of languages, and miraculously experiencing the uniting energy of the Holy Spirit. The Lord's Prayer is prayed together simultaneously in every language. Worship includes the *Agios O Theos* of the Greek Orthodox church and the *Asithi Amen* of the churches of Africa. And in plenary discussions, an Anglican bishop from Kenya and a Baptist social worker from El Salvador will listen to one another through headsets and simultaneous translation and miraculously attempt to hear not just the words but the heart. This is what the modern Christian ecumenical movement is about—churches diverse in language and manifestation, yet straining to understand one another through the power of the Spirit. The ecumenical movement today, with its earphones and simultaneous translation, is a kind of modern-day electronic Pentecost, committed to the recognition of the go-between Spirit in a multiplicity of cultures and languages and contexts. The fire and energy of the Spirit is poured into community. The church is not just one gathered community, meeting in one church building; it is challenged by the Holy Spirit to be a much wider community.

After all, it was not unintelligible speech that those speakers-in-tongues spoke at the great Pentecost event. They spoke languages, all the languages of the earth. "We hear them speaking in our own tongues the wonderful works of God!" said the foreigners. The message of Pentecost is not of ecstatic utterance, but of the importance of hearing the Good News in every land, in every tongue. The love of God is not a family affair, nor is it in any way exclusive. It is translatable. It is news for everyone. In symbolic terms, Pentecost reverses the linguistic confusion of Babel. Those of various tongues can suddenly understand one another. And the gift of that understanding, whether among Christians who speak many languages and come from many cultures, or between Christians, Muslims, and Hindus, is the kind of miracle Christians can only refer to as a gift of the Spirit.

Understanding the Holy Spirit across cultures and churches is by no means easy. Indeed, a worldwide theological debate was touched off when the Seventh Assembly of the WCC met in Canberra in 1991 and it took as its theme "Come, Holy Spirit, Renew the Whole Creation." Two theologians were invited to speak about the Holy Spirit—a Greek Orthodox patriarch from Egypt and a young feminist Presbyterian theologian from Korea.[14] His Beatitude Parthenios, Patriarch of Alexandria and All Africa, spoke out of a tradition dating back to the first century. The Orthodox churches have always cherished and guarded the freedom of the Spirit in their traditions. He summed it up this way, "A wind, a breath that 'bloweth where it listeth,' a roaring sound, fire, a tongue of fire— these are the Holy Spirit." Wind, breath, sound, and fire are a challenging set of images. Yet when Chung Hyun Kyung entered the assembly hall to speak, the implications of the Spirit's freedom to "blow where it listeth" became quite visible. She led a troupe of dancers onto the stage—Korean dancers joined by an Australian Aboriginal. They moved to a rumbling drum. When she began to speak, Professor Chung spoke of the cries of the Spirit of God within the human spirit, invoking the remembrance of the spirit of Hagar, the Egyptian slave woman abandoned by Abraham and Sarah, the spirits of the babies killed by the soldiers of Herod, the spirit of Joan of Arc, of Mahatma Gandhi, of Steve Biko, the spirits of those who died in the crusades, in the gas chambers, in Hiroshima and Nagasaki. Having read the litany of the groanings of the Spirit of God in and through the human spirit, she lit the parchment on which their names were written and held the flames in her hand while it burned. Some who had just heard of the windrush and the fire from the patriarch of Alexandria were nonetheless outraged to see it enacted so dramatically by a feminist theologian in a new key that seemed to have overtones of Korean shamanism. The controversy sparked by her daring presentation of the Spirit raged through discussions of culture, gender, and theology. The word *syncretism* buzzed through the corridors.

Christians do not have a single, fixed story to tell about the Holy Spirit in the same way they have the story of the stable and the angels, Nazareth and the Sea of Galilee. The stories of the touch of the Spirit are as many as there are individuals and communities. The Holy Spirit perpetually reminds us of God's mystery and complexity. It is also a radical reminder of God's ineluctable freedom. Though we may glimpse God in the face of Jesus, we do not truly understand or comprehend God. Pentecost sets it all on fire.

The Dove: Comfort and Freedom

The image of the bird, the dove, is the most substantial icon of the Spirit. I remember clearly one of the dozens of candlelit icons at the cathedral church of Puhtica, a Russian Orthodox convent in rural Estonia, a Spirit-filled church, where the singing of the nuns seemed to lift the weariness of the farmers and pilgrims who crowded into the church for the daily liturgies. It was, no doubt, an icon of Christ, but what caught my eye was the dove sailing downward toward the earth with her wings outspread. The Methodist church in Bozeman would have been uneasy with all of these icons, gold and glittering, the icons that the "Hindu" in me has come to love in the Orthodox church. But this dove would have been right at home. In the pale purples and greens of the stained glass in the church in Bozeman, the dove is the only image there is. The wings of the Spirit-dove somehow span the cultural miles between Montana Methodism and Russian Orthodoxy.

Thinking again about the early church controversy over the "procession" of the Holy Spirit, one might find the audacity of the church's attempt to fix the route of the Spirit both astonishing and amusing. Can such matters really be brought to a council's vote? Isn't the freedom of God's Spirit, suggested by this ubiquitous dove, quite beyond the legislation of ecclesiastical councils? Surely councils of men, and most have indeed been of men alone, cannot settle by a vote, then or now, the pathways of the Holy Spirit. That which we Christians call the Spirit is as intimate and abiding as our breath, as elusive as the wind, as powerful and consuming as fire, and as surprising and mysterious as a sudden sense of presence.

Although that Spiritdove may seem tame enough, caught in midair in the icon or in the stained glass of a church, the Holy Spirit is not tame. She can hover protectively, and she also can soar. As one Spirit song put it, "She comes sailing on the wind, her wings flashing in the sun, on a journey just begun, she flies on."[15] The flight of a bird is the image of freedom, and the Spirit of God sails free. The bird is also an image of gentle comfort. The Psalmist who prays for shelter under the feathers of God's wings evokes the tender protection of the mother bird gathering her downy young under her wings. In William Blake's line drawing of the Holy Spirit, an immense bird stretches her wingspan over two figures, the Father doubled over and gathering up the crucified Christ. The hovering, encompassing presence has a wingspan that reaches out over and beyond suffering and death.

It is clear in the New Testament that the Spirit is a gift, not a reward. The descent of the Spirit upon Jesus during his baptism in the Jordan, often depicted as a dove with wings outspread sailing downward toward him, comes before his initiatory period of testing in the wilderness, not after. In most initiation sequences, one would expect the order to be reversed; after testing and trial, one is confirmed with a new cloak of blessing. But the empowerment of the Spirit is not earned, it is freely given. And so with the early church at Pentecost. It was not their courage or clarity that evoked the blessing of the Spirit, for they were vulnerable and confused. The Spirit is a gift, not a possession. The spirit inspires and gives the breath of life to the church, but the church does not encompass, contain, or own the Holy Spirit. The path of the Spirit certainly does not lead us only from church to church. For those of us who are Christians, we understand it to be the Holy Spirit that drives us beyond the comforts and certainties of what we know to the very boundaries where Christians and Hindus and Muslims meet.

The freedom made so clear in the winged flight of the Holy Spirit forces Christians to think about the mystery and power of spiritual life among people of every faith—Buddhist and Muslim, Hindu and Jewish. When we use the term *Holy Spirit* we mean the active, creative, energetic, mysterious, presence of the one we call God. The Spirit does not read the fine print of the prayer book or the creed. The Spirit, though she gave birth to the church, is not the possession of the church, let alone of its early church fathers or its modern theologians. The Pentecost experience reminds us that the Holy Spirit is, above all, a gift, a fullness, an outpouring. We cannot grasp it, we can only be attentive to it, awake to it and attest to its presence.

Emphasizing the freedom of the Spirit, however, does not mean that one part of God is cut loose from the Trinity to roam about the world while the other two are left at home in heaven or in the church. On the contrary, in emphasizing the freedom and mystery of the dove and the breath, Christians point to the freedom and mystery of the whole of what we mean by "God." In the ecumenical context of the World Council of Churches, it is the Orthodox theologians, one after another, who remind us of this. As Patriarch Ignatios IV of Antioch puts it,

> The Kingdom of the Spirit has no frontiers. It is present in the order and beauty of the world as well as in the revelation of history, to be fully revealed in the wind and fire of Pentecost. It impregnates Christ's whole being and springs forth from his pierced side, but if we know that it comes from the Father and leads to the Father, we also know that it blows wherever it pleases, and that our hands, our thoughts, can no more grasp it than they could clutch a stream of living water.[16]

It is a wonderfully Buddhist image—the vanity and futility of trying to stake out and claim a part of the river and clutch it for our own. But we cannot grasp it, just as we cannot grasp a stream of living water. Metropolitan Georges Khodr of Lebanon insists that it is the Holy Spirit that frees us, leads us, even drives us into the world and into serious dialogue with people of other faiths. "To ignore the questions and the answers that come from people of other faiths," he says, "would be a kind of disobedience to the Holy Spirit."[17] If we want to know what God has been up to in the world, the Spirit bids us keep our eyes and ears open to the witness of others.

At the Canberra assembly of the WCC in 1991, there were fourteen guests of other faiths. They did not speak of the Holy Spirit, but testifed to their faith and practice in their own terms. Their presence, however, enabled Christians to think about the language of the Holy Spirit in a wider way, without a sense of grasping and possession. Metropolitan Daniel of Moldavia said, "We cannot place limits to the work of the Holy Spirit outside the church. Like the wind, it blows where it wills."[18] He was speaking to one of the large sections of the WCC assembly, some four hundred people who spent a week discussing the unity of the Spirit. In the final report, the group wrote, "The Holy Spirit is at work in ways that pass human understanding: the freedom of the Spirit may challenge and surprise us as we enter into dialogue with people of other faiths. The Gospel of Jesus Christ has taught us the signs and fruit of the Holy Spirit—joy, peace, patience, and faithfulness (Gal. 5). Dialogue challenges us to discern the fruits of the Spirit in the way God deals with all humanity.[19] Another group of four hundred people spent the week discussing "spirituality," the transforming and sanctifying energy of the Spirit. They came up with a statement that included a remarkably similar affirmation. "The Holy Spirit is at work among all people and faiths, and throughout the universe. With the sovereign freedom which belongs to God, the Wind blows wherever it wants."[20]

The language is, of course, inclusivist. It is cast in the terms of Christian understanding and Christian vocabulary with which one would not expect the Buddhist or the Muslim to concur, but it nonetheless encourages Christians to be more bold in seeking dialogue with people of other faiths, for the Spirit which moved across the face of the deep on the first day of creation, the Spirit which Jesus likened to the wind, blowing where it will, the Spirit which poured out upon the Jews of Jerusalem and even upon the Gentiles in the house of the Roman Cornelius—this Spirit cannot be contained within the four walls of our churches. This Spirit cannot be contained even within our own Christian community. The Holy Spirit holes are everywhere.

Shakti: Energy for Life

In listening for the language of this energetic, fiery mystery of Spirit in the Hindu tradition, I have often been moved by what they call Shakti—divine energy, female energy. Remember that *ruach*, the generative breath that moved upon the waters at the dawn of creation, is a feminine noun. In the course of time, and no doubt in the interests of patriarchy, she became neuter in the Greek (*pneuma*) and eventually masculine in the Latin (*spiritus*). Some of the same church patriarchs who even today become indignant when the "He" language of the Father and Son is tampered with by feminists in the church are nonetheless unapologetic about the linguistic sleight of hand that changed the gender of the Holy Spirit. Of course, as we have seen, whether we use father or mother language in speaking of the Divine, we must be clear about the fact that it is *our* language. It is relational language, and it enables Christians to think analogically about our kinship with God. Like most theological language, it is more poetry than metaphysics.

I think of the energy of the Holy Spirit as feminine. She is what Krister Stendahl calls the "energy for life" which is creative, generative, and always at work awakening us to the mystery and presence of the Divine.[21] The divine energy is perceived by people of many traditions as somehow feminine; it is beneficent and life-giving energy, though not unambiguously so. The Spirit may be comforting, but she is also frightening; she may be gentle, but also restless; she may be the "sweet, sweet spirit in this place," as the old Gospel hymn has it, or a sense of seismic unsettling power.

Hindus speak of the divine, surging, mothering energy as Shakti, and the Hindu sense of Shakti has time and again steered me toward a larger understanding of the Holy Spirit. Shakti is the feminine aspect of God. The word *shakti* means literally "energy" or "power." It is not the power of the female in particular. It is *all* divine power and energy, and it is conventionally said to be an attribute of the Goddess. In Sanskrit and Hindi, the root of *shakti* is the helping verb which means "to be able." The energy to do anything is *shakti*. In the theological realm, when one speaks of the kinetic energy of God in the world, nourishing, enabling, kindling, breathing, moving in life and in death—this is Shakti. The famous hymn to the Goddess, the *Saundaryalahari*, begins, "If Shiva, the Auspicious One, is united with Shakti, He is able to create. If He is not, He is not even capable of stirring."[22] Put in popular language, "Without Shakti, Shiva is *shava*." The word *shava* means corpse. This is an example of the radical, pithy inversion of ideas with which the Hindu tradition so often confronts us: that God really is dead, or as good as dead, without this kindling kinetic energy which embues the whole creation.

God's transcendence and immanence, God's being and power, are not separable. Shiva and Shakti are inextricably one. It would not be quite right to say that they are God and Goddess, as if they were independent entities. The energy of Shakti's dance is grounded in Shiva. The indescribable transcendence of Shiva becomes describable and accessible in Shakti. The Hindu tradition does not shy away from giving image to these theological realities of inextricable interrelation. (The well-known Christian "image" of the Trinity, the Rublev icon of the three graceful youthful figures sitting quietly round a table, pales by comparison.) There is the image of Shakti standing on the inert body of Shiva, her wild dance held in balance only by union with him. And there is the divine androgyne, a single body, half woman and half man, wearing women's clothing on the left side and man's clothing on the right; or there is the non-anthropomorphic form, the *linga* of Shiva and the *yoni* of Shakti, the vertical shaft and the rounded base, male and female. However these are rendered, they are images not of two divine beings, but of one.

In India, I found not one, but a multitude of goddesses, linked by this sense of energy and power called Shakti. In Banaras, the Goddess has many temples and they are among the most popular temples in the city—the sanctuaries of Durga,

Annapurna, Sankata Devi. In the Vindhya Hills near Mirzapur, she is called Vindhyavasini, "Goddess of the Vindhyas." At the very tip of southern India, she is called Kanya Kumari, "The Virgin Goddess." In the Himalayan foothills, she is Jvalamukhi, "Flaming Mouth." She has many names and her particularities are important, but the sense of power and presence that abides in all these sanctuaries links them together. It is completely natural for Hindus to enter into a temple, press their palms together in respect and in prayer, and begin, "O Mother, . . . O Mother, . . ." Praying in mother language is a deep part of Hindu religious consciousness.

As we think about the reality and experience of the Holy Spirit, how does the Hindu experience of Shakti give us new insight? Is what Hindus mean by Shakti what Christians mean by Holy Spirit? That is not quite the way to pose the question, even though we could enumerate the ways in which both express divine energy and human empowerment. I do not claim they are the same, for each is meaningful only in the context of an entire worldview. I do know, however, that Hindu expressions of Shakti might push us toward a wider and more challenging understanding of the energy and power of the Holy Spirit. How might this be so?

First, under every name, Shakti is what Hindi speakers call *jagrita*, "wide awake," and her shrines are magnetic for that reason. They too are called *jagrita*. Shakti is immanent, present, near at hand. Her shrines are called *pithas*, "seats" or "benches," and they are located right in the midst of life, rooted in the earth of this shore, so to speak. Shakti is under the tree, on top of the hillock at the edge of town. Her shrines are ceaselessly visited with offerings and songs. She hears the cries of the poor, the concerns of the farmer, the prayers of the anxious or grieving. Hers are active shrines. They do indeed feel as if the Divine is "wide awake" there, although sometimes the noise and clutter of her shrines—the piles of garlands and the red *kumkum*; the shattered coconuts slammed to the pavement as offerings; the hundreds of hands reaching at once for a touch of her sanctified flame—make it difficult to be attuned to the Spirit if one is used to listening for what the prophet Elijah called "the sound of sheer silence."

When I think of the churches of Boston, indeed most churches I know in the United States, I would not call many of them *jagrita*. We do not gravitate to them after work or in the evening. If we did we would often find them locked. Many churches, especially Protestant churches, are closed most of the week and there is a sense of sleep that settles upon them. On Sunday mornings there is activity, perhaps there is even a service every weekday morning; on the whole, however, the sense of power and presence that one feels in a great sanctuary of Shakti is not there, except in a few very energetic churches. Of course, one could say that the church is not a building, that the church is the community carried into the world by the church members. Even so, there is something in us that yearns for the places, the sanctuaries, where people throng for a sense of God's wakeful presence.

The most *jagrita* place I know in North America is the Basilica of Our Lady of Guadalupe on the outskirts of Mexico City. Every day, all day, people come to this sanctuary. They come on pilgrimage from parishes all over Mexico, bringing their banners, their placards, their corn and candles, their dances, and their prayers. It is a place where one feels the life and vibrance of faith. Were my Hindu friends to visit the basilica, I have no doubt they would find this shrine to be *jagrita* and would not hesitate to speak of the Virgin of Guadalupe as Shakti. Indeed, Marian shrines throughout the world are filled with the "feel" of Shakti. So is the community of Taize in France; so are the parish church of Saint James Picadilly in London and the Cathedral of Saint John the Divine in New York; so too is Twelfth Baptist in Boston's Roxbury neighborhood. As a Christian, the wakeful shrines of Shakti help to pose the question: How do we understand the presence of this vigilant energy? How do we account for its absence in so much of religious life?

A second way in which the Hindu perception of Shakti might stretch our Spirit-consciousness is the linking of Shakti with nature. The River Ganges is the greatest example of this, for it is a river which Hindus everywhere in India speak of as "Mother" and consider to be a liquid form of Shakti. The power of dawn on the Ganges in Banaras is not simply the collective power of worship, but the seamless interpenetration of prayer, bathing, the river, and the sunrise. The great rivers of India have been called "mothers" from the time of the ancient Vedas, hymns sung as long as 3,500 years ago. The Ganges came to be seen as the holiest among them, a river of heaven that descended from heaven to earth because of her grace and compassion. She is said to have cascaded from heaven to bring the blessings of renewal to the weary and life to the dead. Pilgrims from all over India come to bathe in the Ganges, to sip the waters of the Ganges, to bring the ashes of the dead to the Ganges. Along the river, from its source near Gangotri in the Himalayas to its mouth in the Bay of Bengal, there are shrines containing anthropomorphic images of the Ganges as Goddess. And yet when the evening lamp-offerings called *arati* are made to her, the attention of the priest and the worshipers quickly turns from the representation of Shakti in the temple to the liquid Shakti of the river. The fire of the oil lamps is dipped time and again to touch the river itself.

A Hindu friend, a professor in a women's university in Delhi, once told me what it meant to her to bathe in the Ganges at Hardwar at the time she brought her father's ashes there for immersion. "I felt as if an electric shock passed through my body. I felt completely transformed," she said. "When I came up out of the water, I felt as if I could now bear the death of anyone, even those people I loved most, even my own."

The river powerfully attests to the Shakti that streams through the whole of nature. The earth is called Adi-Shakti, the "Primordial Shakti." The life-energy of trees has also been sensed as divine and generative. Special trees are wrapped round and round with the red and yellow threads of the Goddess, their branches laden with the twists of cloth and hope left by the faithful. The continuum of divine infusion in the universe is expressed by one of the Sanskrit words for "the whole creation," a single word which means "from Brahma to a blade of grass." It is a fully inclusive sense of life energy. As Rabindranath Tagore wrote in *Gitanjali*, the collection of poems for which he won the Nobel Prize,

> The same stream of life that runs through my veins
> night and day runs through the world and dances in
> rhythmic measures.
> It is the same life that shoots in joy through the dust
> of the earth in numberless blades of grass and breaks
> into tumultuous waves of leaves and flowers.[23]

In Montana, every mountain and river has a name, and our Montana culture speaks these names with familiarity and reverence—the Gallatin and Madison, the Bitterroot and Blackfoot. Nature does indeed reveal both the glory and terror of the Divine. But most of us in the Christian tradition have not let the icons of nature become a powerful part of our theological language. There is no part of nature that carries for Christians the cultural power and mythic energy of the Ganges, as much as I love the Madison, the Gallatin, and the Blackfoot rivers. Why not? Perhaps those of us in the Western prophetic traditions have been afraid that we will worship nature and not God. After all, the prophets of Israel embarked on a bold religious venture—to see the mighty power of God *not* in the mysteries of nature, as did their neighbors in the ancient world, but in the mystery of historical events. It was to human history that they looked for the expression of God's presence: the freeing of captives, the securing of justice for the poor and the oppressed.

But "nature" and "history" are not true opposites. Do we really need to choose one and not the other? Even though it may seem clear enough to the scholar or polemicist to contrast the cyclical time of "nature religion" with the linear time of "prophetic religion," most peoples, ancient and modern, have not lived their lives within the confines of one view of time. Both nature and history are revelatory. Both are infused with the energy and breath of God. If I can attest to the life of the Spirit in the daring history of the modern Christian ecumenical movement, I can also insist upon the presence of the Spirit in the cyclical renewal of nature.

The Bible provides ample evidence of the Spirit in nature—not opposed to nature, but integrated with nature. From the opening of Genesis through the Psalms to the final chapter of Revelation, all creation is infused with the breath of God. Standing on top of Haystack Mountain in Montana's Bob Marshall Wilderness Area, at the brink of the long escarpment of the Rocky Mountains called the Chinese Wall, I pulled the pocket book of Psalms from my saddlebags and read Psalm 104, the only *mahatmya* that could possibly match the vastness of rock and sky: "You are wrapped in light as with a garment. You stretch out the heavens like a tent, you set the beams of your chambers on the waters, you make the clouds your chariot, you ride on the wings of the wind. . . ." One cannot dismiss as pantheism the revelation of God in nature, the glimpse of nature streaming with the life of the Holy Spirit. Indeed, such a vision of nature is celebrated in the Divine Liturgy of the Orthodox churches with the exultant refrain "Let everything that has breath praise the Lord!"

There is still another way in which Shakti might push us toward a wider openness to the Spirit. It is more difficult to explore. The tremendous power of Shakti moves not only through the veins of life, as Tagore has so beautifully written, but into the presence of death. One particular name under which Shakti is widely known is Kali. I first met Kali in Calcutta, "at home," so to speak, in the city named for her temple by the banks of the Hooghli River at Kali Ghat. Her four-armed image is everywhere on the streets approaching the temple—black, with huge eyes and a lolling red tongue, her neck circled with a garland of skulls and covered with fresh offerings of red hibiscus, holding a cleaver in one hand and a severed head in another, yet somehow incongruously with her other hands gesturing not to be afraid and holding forth a lotus flower. Her worshipers are clearly not terrified of her. Indeed they come before her with folded hands, say-ing, "O Mother, Mother Kali," as if she were as life-bearing as the Ganges.

At first I found the image repulsive, especially the cleaver and the necklace of skulls. But it was clearly powerful and evocative for those who stood before her in worship, undaunted, and called her Mother. I could not simply dismiss this image of Shakti from my religious consciousness and put her on the shelf in my study as part of my "academic work." There was something in this seemingly vi-olent image that was profoundly true. It was the truth of divine power claiming the terrain of both life and death, difficult as it might be to look death in the face. Bearing the lotus in one hand and the cleaver in another, she clearly signals that the fullness of life includes both the flowering and the finality. The poet Ram-prasad ends one of his songs to Kali with the question "What will you do, bound by Death?" His signature line: "Ramprasad says: Call the Mother. She can han-dle Death."[24]

Is the Holy Spirit present only in life and absent in death? Present only in peaceful death, and absent in violent or untimely death? These are the questions that the formidable Kali poses as she stands there in her skulls. I do not know Kali personally, so to speak. I do not know the faith of the Hindu who stands be-fore her in the din of her inner sanctum in Calcutta. I do not really know the sense of assurance that a Hindu might feel standing before the Goddess in a cave at Vindhyavasini or at the shore of the sea at Kanya Kumari. But having been to these sanctuaries, I do know, as a Christian, that they have challenged me to be open to the presence and power of God in places where it is uncomfortable to be, in places that are frightening, in places where we confront the skulls.

Even the spiritually benumbed might sense God's presence in the sunrise, in the stillness of the cathedral with the plainsong of the choir rising heavenward. In such moments it is easy to sit still in the pure communion of the "Go-Between God," the Holy Spirit. It is harder to sit still and be in God's presence in the places where we confront death. Most of us in the modern West run away from such places. We do not linger at the deathbed, in the morgue, at the graveside or the crematorium to wonder if the Holy Spirit might be there as well. But if faith is to sustain us at all, we will finally have to be open to the hovering Spirit in those very places that frighten us and make us tremble, to face the horror and trust the presence of God.

My brother Laury was only forty-eight when he died a very painful death. He was beaten up in a jail in Juarez, just over the border from El Paso. He had been detained without charges, kicked and beaten in detention. He limped around for a few days with a rupturing spleen, and when it ruptured he was alone in a dingy hotel room, in agony. When he was finally taken to the Juarez General Hospital, he died within half an hour. My mother and Laury's son Bryan met me in El Paso. We spent days retracing his steps—the desk clerks, the cashiers, the doctor sitting at a card table in a parka, the streets of the poor among whom he had decided to live. And then the morgue. The American consul and Señor Sanchez from the funeral home took us in a big old Chevy through the muddy back streets into a parking lot. The medical examiner was there and described it all in the Spanish only Laury would have been able to understand. The blows, the ruptured organs. We would identify the body. As we entered the large cold room, the three of us did not know if we would be able to stay or would have to flee.

I saw nothing in the morgue but Laury. Six-foot-five, cold, wrapped in a large sheet and plastic. Completely peaceful. His face is imprinted clearly and forever in my memory. We had gone to graduate school at Harvard together in the fall of 1969, driving tandem in our Volkswagen Beetles from Montana to Boston. He was an attorney and a man of real Christian faith. He probably didn't really understand my keen interest in Hindu temples. He surely did not understand Kali. Neither do I. But I know I did not run away from that moment. As Mom and Bryan and I held fast to one another, I opened the Book of Common Prayer and read slowly and carefully the words of the Twenty-third Psalm and the prayers for the dead. "Even though I walk through the valley of the shadow of death, I will fear no evil, for Thou art with me . . ." I have no idea how long we stood there in the morgue, but it was a time in which the Holy Spirit hovered with immense wingspan over us.

CHAPTER 6

Attention to God

The Practice of Prayer and Meditation

ATTENTION! It is a word I associated for many years with the barking command of a military officer, a sports coach, or a school principal coming on over the loudspeaker. Attention. Pay attention. May I have your attention please. Attention, class. On my grade school report cards under the heads "Desirable Habits and Attitudes" there was a box for "Pays Attention" in which I always got an *S* for "Satisfactory."

I was well into my twenties, however, before I paid any attention to attention. It was an itinerant Zen teacher who came to Cambridge in the early 1970s who told the tale of the Japanese Zen master Ikkyu, an eccentric teacher who was approached by a serious student and asked about the main teachings of Zen Buddhism. Ikkyu took a brush and wrote out the Japanese word for "attention" on a paper and handed it over to the student. Thinking this to be a little brief for a profound teaching, the student asked if Ikkyu would add something to it. Again Ikkyu took his brush and he wrote, "Attention, Attention." When pressed by the student for something additional, he wrote with his brush, "Attention, Attention, Attention."

The itinerant Zen master had us all sitting on pillows in the enormous wood-paneled room of Memorial Hall, with its stained-glass images of the saints of Harvard. We tried out Ikkyu's instruction. Just pay attention to the breath, in and out, counting each breath to ten, not losing track of the count by sailing into the reveries and imaginings of inattention. Sounded easy enough, but I never once made it to ten that day. My mind was off and running. Thinking, How am I doing? Thinking, What's the use of counting to ten? Thinking, The guy next to me is breathing too loud. I lost the count. After a while I improvised and tried paying attention to the Lord's Prayer instead of the counting. Surely something meaningful would be easier to stick with than counting to ten. I took it a phrase at a time. I never once made it all the way to "forever and ever" without my mind drifting from the familiar sacred words into the eddies of extraneous thoughts. If the report cards on desirable habits and attitudes had been sent home with us, I would never have gotten an *S* for paying attention. But from that day on, the importance of this word *attention* began to grow on me, or within me. Just being awake, alert, attentive is no easy matter. I think it is the greatest spiritual challenge we face. Finally, I think, it is the only one.

Just as I was finishing my doctoral thesis, one of my friends who had been plugging along the same track of Ph.D. studies for nearly five years was diagnosed as having brain cancer. Karen had taught at Princeton for a short while and had just returned to Cambridge to complete her thesis work. The doctor's post-operative prognosis was that she would die within a few weeks. In her room at Massachusetts General Hospital a small circle of her friends, professors, and family kept up a steady rotation of visits. At first there was a week of good and deep conversation, then the conversation became more one-sided. We read to her, sat with her, told her news and stories. She became weaker, and even listening seemed to exhaust her. She would respond to our presence, however, by a squeeze of the hand. Then, in the last week of her life, there was no response at all. It was Wednesday night of Holy Week that she died. It was my night on in the hospital and I was supposed to be preparing a chapel talk for the next morning's prayers at Appleton Chapel in the university. Fighting sleep in the corridor, armed with a cup of coffee from the vending machine, my eyes fell upon the familiar Maundy Thursday story with a revelatory sense of comprehension.

"Wait here and watch with me," Jesus told his disciples in the garden of Gethsemane on the last night of his life. Jesus is described in the Gospel of Matthew as sorrowful and troubled. He told his friends, "My soul is very sorrowful, even to death." Before going apart to pray, he asked them to keep watch nearby. They tried, but they fell asleep. Staying awake and keeping watch is a serious and difficult spiritual discipline, especially for people of action. "Could you not

watch with me one hour?" asked Jesus. "Watch and pray that you may not enter
into temptation; the spirit indeed is willing, but the flesh is weak."

In Gethsemane, we see Jesus in his most human hour—in anguish and probably afraid. When Jesus asked his disciples to keep watch, he was not asking
them to stand guard in order to warn him when Judas came. He was not about
to run away. He was asking them to watch *with* him—to wait and be awake
with him in the hour of crisis. Twice he asked them, and twice he returned to
find them sleeping. In Gethsemane the disciples Peter, James, and John are also
fully human—falling away by falling asleep. If Jesus had asked them to flee
with him, to bring arms, to rally supporters and protectors, these three disciples
would surely have found it in themselves to stay awake and work tirelessly
through the whole night. But he was not calling them to heroic action; he was not
asking them to "do" anything at all. He was calling them to simple attention,
watchfulness, and that was infinitely more difficult.

Keeping watch is one of the hardest things. Watching *with* someone who is
troubled, grieving, or perhaps dying requires that we be wakeful, present, and
engaged, but it does not permit us the exercise of our restless, goal-oriented in-
stinct to *do* something. In the weeks before Karen's death, it was clear to us and
to her that she was dying. No radical action, no heroics, could alter that fact. We
were all "doers," but there was nothing any of us could do. No act, no word, no
prayer seemed adequate in this day-by-day encounter with death. All that was
possible was vigilance, and we, like Peter, James, and John, discovered how difficult and exhausting the alert stillness of the watch can be. Especially at the end,
when Karen seemed buried in the mass of tubing, stillness and presence were all
we could bring. I, at least, was unpracticed at that kind of vigilance: the watchful
stillness of the vigil, the passive activity of just being there, sitting still in the
presence of dying. Most of us have not practiced the arts of simple attention and
watchfulness, and in the times of the soul's deepest anguish, these are the arts we
need in order to be faithful.

When we keep watch we do not busy ourselves changing the course of events.
We are not able to use our cleverness, our strength, our connections, to alter the
circumstances, for moments of fear and grief are often unalterable. How many
are the times we fail one another, not by intentional or malicious actions, but simply by our ineptitude at watching with, at being with, at being vigilant. We want
to do something about the suffering of a friend, the grief or the fear or the dying
of a loved one. There are, of course, times when we can and must act. But Geth-

semane reminds us of those times when what we are asked to do is something more simple and more difficult than springing into action: keeping watch, staying awake. I knew from my taste of meditation practice that the ones who are really good at staying awake are the Buddhists.

Action and Stillness

"Could you not watch with me one hour?" Years later, I still hear the personal challenge of these words as I rise from the meditation cushion in my study, having struggled to keep watch for only twenty minutes. The seeds planted by that itinerant Zen master have somehow sprouted over the years and continued to grow. The meditation instructions of the resident teacher at the Cambridge Insight Meditation Center, a Buddhist center down the street, seem easy enough: Let the attention rest on the breath, in and out, rising and falling. Watch the breath. Focus the mind on the sensation of the breath in the nostrils, in the chest, or in the abdomen. When the mind wanders, as it surely will within a few minutes, bring it back to the breath. It is not that the breath is so inherently fascinating, but the breath is always with us. As a focus of meditation, it is indeed a portable, invisible icon of the Spirit. Returning attention to the breath in meditation practice is a way of learning, slowly, to stabilize one's attention.

Most of the time the mind is quite unstable, its attention moving from one thing to another on the free wind of association. Hindus compare it to a pack of monkeys, tumbling through our consciousness, yanking in one thought after another. As we have seen, Eastern Orthodox mystics like Gregory of Sinai speak of the mind's "habit of turning and wandering hither and thither."[1] Joseph Goldstein, an American Buddhist teacher, says, "The mind has no shame. It will hop on the train of association and will allow itself to be taken almost anywhere." How true it is; whether in meditation or in the daily round of activity, the mind often has a way of going about its business quite independently. Thinking judging, meandering through the past, imagining the future, swinging like a pendulum between past and future without resting in the present.

Developing the capacity for stable attention is the most important of spiritual arts. As a nineteenth-century Russian Orthodox teacher put it, "Without attention there is no prayer."[2] Attention can be cultivated by repeating words or brief prayers or by focusing on an image or object. The mantras of Hindus and Buddhists, the Jesus Prayer of the Eastern church, and the *dhikr* of the Muslim tradi-

tion are all ways in which attention is focused, united, stabilized. Many traditions of meditation, like insight or *vipassana* meditation, focus attention on the
breath. This appeals to me as a Christian because, as we have seen, the breath
leads naturally into the domain of the Holy Spirit; gently returning attention to
the breath, over and over, brings the mind back to the recognition of the presence
of the Spirit—right here and right now. One can practice such wakefulness on
the cushion, but as Buddhists well know, attention to the Spirit must gently be
awakened in all our living and doing.

Contemplative traditions, whether Hindu, Buddhist, or Christian, explore
the meaning of wakefulness. These traditions have refined that type of action
which is stillness. They have practiced the art of being awake—and it is an art.
Indeed, the Hindu and Buddhist traditions have not seen our human problem in
terms of "original sin," but rather in terms of our proneness to distraction and to
sleep. Sleep is one term that well describes our human condition. It is not only
that we fall asleep when we ought to be awake, but that we sleep even when we
are awake. Our minds drift from the present, swept down lanes of memory or
tumbling out the window into the imagination of the future. We are somewhere
else. Clear, wakeful presence is rare. The practice of meditation, beginning with
attention to the breath, allows us to gain insight into the nature of our minds.
One of the first things we notice is that the mind will not stay with the breath. We
can see for ourselves how it runs away, how it dozes off. Thomas Merton wrote,
"The spiritual life is, then, first of all a matter of keeping awake."[3]

The Buddha, literally the "one who is truly awake," was, according to the
most ancient Buddhist tradition, fully human, a man who through disciplined
meditation saw into the heart of reality and woke up. It is said that after his enlightenment the Buddha's face shone and he was stopped on the road and
asked, "Are you a god or a magician?" He answered, "No, I am not a god nor am
I a magician. I am awake."[4] The clear implication is that most of us, most of
the time, are not fully awake. The purpose of meditation is not to remove us from
the space and time of the world into some otherworldly abstraction. Rather, it is
the practice of wakefulness, of mindfulness. Through the practice of meditation, the rambling mind is gradually enabled to pay attention. It is not a doctrine
but a practice—cultivating the ability to be fully present, not only in hours of sitting, or meditation, or prayer, but in working and acting. And to be fully wakeful in those times when we are called not to action but to presence.

In the Bhagavad Gita, Lord Krishna speaks to Arjuna of the meaning of wakefulness. He is urging the hero and warrior Arjuna to action, and yet it is action which is a form of meditation. He puts it provocatively: "One who sees inaction in action and action in inaction has understanding and is disciplined in all action he performs."[5] As for inaction in action, even the most vigorous involvement in the world can be done in a spirit of nonattachment, giving up one's personal claims to glory and one's own sufferings in loss. Action done in such a spirit does not stick to us, as water drops do not stick to a waxy lotus leaf. But in order to act in this way, stable attention is fundamental. And stable attention is developed by meditation. Meditation might be seen as "action in inaction." The yogi is the one whose body and mind are brought to perfect stillness and one-pointedness, "like a lamp unflickering in a windless place." And yet this seeming inaction, this stillness, is a form of action. It is not "doing nothing." It is sitting with the stillness and the alertness of a tiger. This quality of mind can be brought into the world of action.

The ideal of Krishna's teaching in the Gita is to plunge into the world of action, but with the selflessness, stability, and spaciousness of mind that does not seek acquisition or profit from the results of those actions. The disciples in Gethsemane were not called to action in the usual sense, but to the action of inaction, to attentive presence. Thomas Merton's book *Contemplation in a World of Action* addresses the meaning of prayer in a world oriented toward "getting things done."[6] The person who plunges into the world of action, even self-sacrificing action, without deepening his or her self-understanding and cultivating nonattachment, will have nothing to give.

I first encountered Thomas Merton, a Trappist contemplative monk, when I returned from my first stay in India for my senior year at Smith College. That year Amiya Chakravarty, a Bengali philosopher who had been the literary secretary for Rabindranath Tagore, was a visiting professor at Smith. He knew Merton and gathered a small group of us at Smith to read some of Merton's essays together. Several of us wrote to Merton and he responded, asking, as apparently he often did, for photographs of us. In March of 1967, he wrote:

> I do really have the feeling that you have all understood and shared quite
> perfectly, that you have seen something that I see to be most precious—
> and most available too. The reality that is present to us and in us: call it Be-
> ing, call it Atman, call it Pneuma . . . or Silence. And the simple fact that by
> being attentive, by learning to listen (or recovering the natural capacity to

listen which cannot be learned any more than breathing), we can find our-
self engulfed in such happiness that it cannot be explained: the happiness
of being at one with everything in that hidden ground of Love for which
there can be no explanations.[7]

I did not understand or "share quite perfectly" this insight into the "hidden
ground of Love" as a twenty-one-year-old. But I continued to read Merton's
works and to write to him.

In the fall of 1968, Merton travelled to South Asia, eager to meet in person
those Buddhist and Hindu contemplatives whose way of spiritual discipline
seemed so like his own, eager for what he called "the dialogue with those who
have kept their silences." His notes for a talk given in Calcutta in October 1968,
recorded in his *Asian Journals*, tell us, "I think we have now reached a stage of
(long-overdue) religious maturity at which it may be possible for someone to remain perfectly faithful to a Christian and Western monastic commitment, and
yet to learn in depth from, say, a Buddhist or Hindu discipline and experience. I
believe that some of us need to do this in order to improve the quality of our own
monastic life."[8] As is well known, Merton died on that trip to Asia, accidentally
electrocuted in his guestroom in Bangkok. I remember just where I stood on
Massachusetts Avenue in Harvard Square when I read the news. He was an important spiritual interlocutor and guide, and he had not yet written the reflections I was eager to read.

The Dawn of "Spirituality"

Spirituality is a term much in use in the 1990s. For many, the word *religion* is too
thing-ish, too static, too exterior and institutional in its present connotations.
The term *spirituality* has come to the rescue, designating the vibrant "inner
dimension of the person called by certain traditions 'the spirit.' "[9] Clearly, for
many people "spirituality" has a more positive connotation than "religion."
Spirituality as the inner dimension of religiousness has always been an integral
part of Christian life, and indeed of all religious life in virtually every tradition.
In the past decade, however, the use of the term has mushroomed and has taken
over much of the verbal domain of the term *religion*. I am quite sure that Brother
Van in frontier Montana did not use the word *spirituality* and would have associated it with spiritualism, seances, and the occult. Today, however, the term seems
to connote "real religiousness" or "religion that really means something." The
popular fascination with this term is an important fact of our time.

At one end of the spectrum of meanings of the terms *ruach*, *pneuma*, and *spirit* is the "human spirit," that inner dimension that is said by the Jewish and Christian traditions to be God-given. As we have seen, it is not "a spirit" incarcerated in the body, but rather the dimension of a human being that opens into the Spirit of God as one comes to awareness of God's presence. Spirituality might be said to be the cultivation of that awareness. When I use the term spirituality, I mean the disciplined nurturing of inner spiritual life. Spirituality has an outward dimension too, so much so that the phrase "spirituality for combat" has come into use in liberation discourse to speak of discipleship in the struggle for human liberation. But as Thomas Merton made clear, the outward dimension is integrally related to the inward. All spirituality requires a journey inward. Without it, action or "combat" leads quickly to burnout.

In 1952, Heinrich Zimmer introduced his book *The Philosophies of India* with the following words: "We of the occident are about to arrive at the crossroads reached by the thinkers of India some seven hundred years before Christ."[10] At that crossroads there is a road that leads inward. Zimmer seems to have seen that the limits of "outer" exploration were being stretched in every direction. There is no question that many in the West, in this last part of the twentieth century, are embarked now on the inward journey. Our cultures are thirsty for whatever it is that is named with the word *spirituality*. Our lives are busy. Our days hurtle by with a roar. Our rooms are piled with books to read, filled with the sound of televised news reports, with minute-by-minute coverage of baseball games and national and international disasters, filled with music as we like. There is so much to keep up with that stopping for periods of real stillness is increasingly difficult. We have practiced the routes of having, doing, going, making, getting, and keeping so frequently that we know the terrain by heart. The ways of watchfulness and attention will take both learning and unlearning.

Even a century ago, the alarm was sounded that the West had lost its spiritual bearings in the midst of the rapid development of science, industry, and technology. Religion in an institutional sense was flourishing. Christian mission was expanding, as with John R. Mott's call in the early 1900s for the "evangelization of the world in this generation." But the spiritual foundations were probed and found to be increasingly weak. Those who discerned this were not only the critics in the West, but also Asians who had been the very "objects" of Christian mission. When Vivekananda came to the World's Parliament of Religions in 1893, he toured America and was deeply upset by what seemed to him to be spiritual emptiness. He felt that it was the responsibility of Hindus to help. While Protestant missions to India and China were in high gear, Vivekananda announced that America was in need of mission. His call to mission had the urgency and passion of any church mission society:

> Spirituality must conquer the West. Slowly they are finding out that what they want is spirituality to preserve them as nations. They are waiting for it. They are eager for it. Where is the supply to come from? Where are the men ready to go out to every country in the world with the message of the great sages of India? Where are the men who are ready to sacrifice everything, so that this message shall reach every corner of this world? Such heroic souls are wanted to help the spread of truth. Such heroic workers are wanted to go abroad and help to disseminate the great truths of the Vedanta. The world wants it; without it the world will be destroyed.[11]

As Vivekananda launched the Ramakrishna Mission to help revitalize and reform Hindu society in India, he also launched the Vedanta society to bring Hindu teachers to America to teach the wisdom of Vedanta. While in India his Ramakrishna Mission took on social, educational, and health projects, it seems to have been Vivekananda's view that the social and humanitarian dimension of religiousness was well developed in the United States. What was needed was the depth dimension, the spiritual nurturance that the East could offer. When he delivered an address to the Graduate Philosophical Society at Harvard in 1896, he was introduced by Professor C. C. Everett as "a missionary from India to America."[12]

Vivekananda's perception that the crying need of the West was something he called "spirituality" has been borne out in the one hundred years since the Parliament. Especially in the past twenty years, teachers with a rainbow of spiritual methods and messages have come from India, Southeast Asia, Korea, and Japan. Like religious teachers everywhere, some have been genuine spiritual leaders and others spiritual hucksters. But all of their movements have spoken to the question of spirituality. Transcendental Meditation, Zen, yoga, Tibetan meditation, mantra, and *asana* have come into our common vocabulary. Even people who have little interest in deepening their spiritual life may practice yoga as a physical discipline to tone and balance the body, or may be taught meditation as a means of lowering blood pressure and decreasing the occurrence of stress-related illness. In medical terms, the hypometabolic state produced by meditation for twenty minutes is deeply restful to the body, like sleep, and yet is a state of wakefulness.

The Spirit Blows East

The Cambridge Insight Meditation Center is an old Victorian house surrounded by a simple Japanese fence and a peaceful garden of shrubs and flag-
stone. Every day in the early morning and evening people gather in the tran-
quility of the large meditation hall and sit for an hour together on the rows of
forest-green *zafus* and *zabutons*. At the front of the room the golden image of
the Buddha is also seated in meditation and is clearly more the model for sitting
than the focus of devotion. Those who come to the center practice the discipline
of attentiveness, presence, awakeness called *vipassana* meditation. The Tuesday
evening introductory courses, open to the public, are usually well attended by
twenty or thirty people from all walks of life. The Wednesday night "sitting"
sessions, followed by informal "Dharma talks" on the Buddhist path, are
packed. Not long ago, the resident teacher let it be known that he would offer the
opportunity for those who had long been practicing to "take refuge"—to place
themselves intentionally on the Buddhist path. More than 150 regulars, mostly
Cambridge and Boston professional people, came that evening, and after a session of sitting and a brief Dharma talk, took the vows: "I take refuge in the Buddha. I take refuge in the Dharma, the Teaching. I take refuge in the Sangha, the
Community." They also pledged themselves, in English and in Pali, to the simple moral precepts at the basis of any spiritual life: to refrain from harming others, from taking anything not freely given, from speaking in harmful ways, from
misusing sexual energy, and from alcohol and drugs.

There are three other major Buddhist meditation centers within a five-mile
radius of Harvard Square. Some of the hundreds of people who frequent these
centers would call themselves Buddhists, but I am quite certain that many more
are Episcopalians, Methodists, Catholics, and Jews. There are also seekers who
do not wish to attach any label to their seeking. This serious "crossing over" into
the spiritual terrain of an Eastern religious tradition is one of the most important spiritual movements of today. Indeed, Buddhist meditation is becoming an
important strand of Christian spirituality. On a Tuesday evening there is no
church among the dozen in Harvard Square that is packed with seekers who
want to deepen their life of prayer; no church even opens its door for such an offering. Those who are serious about spiritual practice go to the Buddhists.

What does it mean that there is such a keen interest in a spiritual discipline as
demanding as meditation? It is surely more than perfunctory attendance at a
weekly religious gathering. There is real seeking here for a form of practical

guidance that apparently is not being offered in the life of Christian churches. Where "spiritual direction" is offered in the churches, it is often in a hierarchical, patriarchal, or monastic context not quite accessible to most of the women and men who take their seats on the green cushions at the Insight Meditation Center. One certainly can point to Western disciplines of prayer, and many who explore the spirituality of the East eventually find their way to these traditions back home: the Eastern Orthodox *Philokalia*, with its emphasis on breath as a way of directing the heart to God; the Benedictine Rule; the spiritual exercises of St. Ignatius; the contemplative prayer of Thomas Merton; and the "centering prayer" of Basil Pennington. But at least on a Tuesday night in Cambridge, there are no introductory courses in these matters for all those seekers who don't know where to begin but who are yearning for a stillness of mind and heart before God—or, for those who have lost touch with God, simply a stillness of mind and heart.

A Methodist minister, speaking frankly to me about this state of affairs at a recent conference of women clergy at Boston University, said, "Nowhere in my seminary education did I have a professor speak about listening for the guidance of the Spirit." "Did anyone speak about prayer?" I asked her. "Well, come to think of it, no. But we were supposed to do it." The truth is, many Christians who feel they are supposed to pray are still not very successful at it.

In 1929 or 1930, the British lay theologian Evelyn Underhill wrote an open letter to the Archbishop of Canterbury about the matter of prayer and spiritual depth. It was a plea for spiritual renewal among both clergy and laity; the laity were ready for the interior journey, but the clergy seemed not to be. She wrote:

> I do not underrate the importance of the intellectual side of religion, but all who do personal religious work know that the real hunger among the laity is not for halting attempts to reconcile theology and physical science, but for the deep things of the Spirit. . . . We look to the clergy to help and direct our spiritual growth. We are seldom satisfied, because with a few noble exceptions, they are so lacking in spiritual realism, so ignorant of the laws and experiences of the life of prayer. Their Christianity as a whole is humanitarian rather than theocentric. . . . God is the interesting thing about religion, and people are hungry for God.[13]

Hunger for God requires the cultivation of silence. Even in the midst of engagement, crisis, and activity, we need to seek the inner space where we may be sustained and renewed. We need to cultivate "the sound of sheer silence" in order to learn to listen. The prophet Elijah was told to go out and stand on the mountain, for God was about to pass by. "Now there was a great wind, so strong that it was splitting mountains and breaking rocks in pieces before the Lord, but the Lord was not in the wind; and after the wind an earthquake, but the Lord was not in the earthquake; and after the earthquake a fire, but the Lord was not in the fire; and after the fire a sound of sheer silence" (1 Kings 19). When Elijah "heard" the sound of sheer silence, he wrapped his head in his mantle, we are told, to listen to what God would say.

"The Practice"

After an hour's sitting at the Cambridge Insight Meditation Center, the medita-tors stretch their legs. Knees creak, backs arch, and shoulders roll. Settling onto the green cushions again, they raise questions to the teacher, Larry Rosenberg. The questions have nothing to do with belief or doctrine. They speak only of what they call "the practice"—the practice of mindfulness in breathing, sitting, walking. They ask about the restlessness of the mind. The playback of a recur-rent argument at home. The pain in the knees. The annoying chatterbox ob-server who seems to sit invisibly on one's shoulder, commenting, cheering, con-gratulating, distracting.

Spirituality is not simply a matter of belief or a warm feeling of intention. It is a "practice," a "how," a "technique," a "way," a spiritual *discipline*. It is experi-mental. "Come and see" was the invitation of the Buddha. Don't believe in me or in what I have to say, but try it out for yourself. The experimental nature of the practice has appealed to many in the West. In one of the early scriptures of the Pali Canon, the Buddha tells his followers not to accept what he says, or what anyone else says, because it is claimed to be revelation, or because it is logical, or because it conforms with one's preconceptions, or because of the prestige of the teacher. Only when they see for themselves that something is true should they ac-cept it.[14] The path of insight begins not with a dogma, but with an invitation to test one's own experience.

For most of us, especially those of us who are Protestant, prayer is not seen as an experimental discipline and the "hows" of prayer are not addressed. When the disciples asked Jesus to teach them to pray, he taught them forms of praise, penitence, and intercession, but he did not teach them the wakeful, watchful, at-tention of, say, a Buddhist meditator. Peter, James, and John could not keep watch for one hour. Neither can we, most of us, be watchful before God for one

hour. Indeed if we are asked to sit still for five minutes, we will find after a min-
ute has passed that our minds are chasing off after one thought and then another
and that our bodies begin to experience this and that discomfort.

The Christian tradition of prayer speaks of prayer as a "gift of the spirit."
Paul speaks for us all when he says in Romans, "Likewise the Spirit helps us in
our weakness; for we do not know how to pray as we ought, but the Spirit inter-
cedes for us, with sighs too deep for words" (Rom. 8:26). It is comforting to imagine that our wordless sighs are indeed a form of prayer and an attestation of the
presence of the Spirit, and yet many would like to lift the veil on the mystery of
prayer just a bit.

The anonymous medieval author of *The Cloud of Unknowing*, one of the
great mystical texts of the Christian tradition, emphasizes the importance of the
prayer of the heart before God. It would be misleading to say it contains no instructions in prayer, for the author does recommend focusing the mind upon a
word, what Hindus call a mantra. "A word like 'GOD' or 'LOVE'. Choose
which you like, or perhaps some other, so long as it is of one syllable. And fix this
word fast to your heart, so that it is always there come what may."[15] This word-
prayer then becomes "the sharp dart of longing love" that the heart uses to batter
and pierce "the cloud of unknowing" and to push the wanderings, imaginings,
and grousings of the mind beneath "the cloud of forgetting." *The Cloud of Unknowing* is a mystical essay and for this reason it may be somewhat inaccessible
to the ordinary person wanting a deeper life of prayer. How is one to begin this
practice? The author admits, "If you ask me *how* you are to begin, I must pray
Almighty God, of his grace and courtesy, to tell you himself."[16] We know on the
one hand that prayer is the gift of the Spirit, and on the other hand that the life of
prayer, as our monastic traditions have emphasized, must be cultivated and nurtured. Many ordinary Christian lay people would profit from instruction in
daily spiritual practice, and would welcome it.

There is Western religious literature, especially from the Orthodox traditions, that is more explicit about practice. For example, the Russian Orthodox
classic *The Way of a Pilgrim* speaks of prayer as "the practice of the presence
of God." It takes practice to be present to God. The "pilgrim" receives instruction from the *Philokalia*: "Sit down alone and in silence; bow your head and
close your eyes; relax your breathing and with your imagination look into your
heart; direct your thoughts from your head to your heart. And while inhaling
say, 'Lord Jesus Christ have mercy on me,' either softly with your lips or in your
mind. Say it moving your lips gently, or simply say it in your mind. Endeavor

to fight distractions but be patient and peaceful and repeat this process frequently."[17]

If prayer practice were taught by the heirs of the Eastern Orthodox tradition, it would no doubt attract many spiritual seekers. The great new spiritual fact of our Western culture, however, is that many of those most serious about the discipline of the spirit have "turned East," not with the faddism of the 1970s but with the sustained discipline of the 1990s. The three-month silent retreat at the rural Insight Meditation Society in Barre, an hour west of Boston, is booked months in advance. Nearly two hundred people somehow manage to arrange their lives, jobs, and family responsibilities in such a way as to be there in Barre for three months, meditating from five o'clock in the morning until ten in the evening, living all day, every day, in silence. No stack of books in the room. No journal to write in. No buzz groups to discuss one's experience. Total silence.

Traditions of yoga and meditation have not been so diffident about the "how." Spiritual guides, Hindu and Buddhist alike, are not afraid of saying "First of all, sit down and sit still. Sit as comfortably and stably as you can. Be still for an hour, or for just ten minutes. See if you can let your mind rest in the breath and come to stillness." When the body learns stillness, the mind is enabled to be still. When the mind is truly still, like a still pond, one can see deeply. The still mind is the prerequisite for insight. The path of such spiritual discipline is experimental and experiential. Try sitting this way, try breathing this way, feel your breath as it rises and falls, try counting your outbreaths one to ten. Focus on these words as a mantra to reign in your thoughts. Spirituality is not a vague luminous glow, it is a very specific practice. It requires the daily discipline and attention that playing the piano requires: it requires practice. One does not wait until one is inspired to pray in some glorious or desperate moment. To learn to pray one must practice.

One might well ask, What are we practicing *for*? The goal of this "practice" is not to get to some other place, some lofty dazzling experience, but truly to recognize the place where we already are. In Buddhist terminology it is to wake up, and the Buddha was that pathfinder who saw clearly the nature of our frantic grasping at life, who saw the painful way in which we try to stop the clock, to have permanence in a world of perpetual change. "Stopping the mind" may seem an odd goal for most of us, at least until we begin to look at the unruly nature of the mind as it goes about its business. Concentration is difficult, whether on the breath in meditation, or on conversation, or on a book. There is another sense, however, in which all of us experience complete concentration, what yogis call "one-pointedness" of mind: in sports, in arts, in listening to music. The mind is fully present. We can recognize, from experience, that the focus of attention is essential to concentration. We cannot play tennis while thinking about something else. To cultivate that quality of alert attention is the point of meditation. "We see the Buddha sitting in meditation," says Larry Rosenberg, assuming for a moment an exaggeratedly serious meditational pose, his hands just so, the tips of his thumbs touching in his lap. He relaxes and a broad smile comes over his face. "But the quality of mindfulness practiced in meditation has to be carried over into the rest of life. We don't have images of the Buddha with a vacuum cleaner or a carrot peeler, but we should have. The meditating Buddha is simply a reminder of that mindfulness."

Attention is key to the disciplines of the spirit. Attention can turn any activity to prayer. What is the difference between sitting on a cushion and sitting on a cushion in meditation? What is the difference between breathing and breathing as part of meditation? What is the difference between vacuuming and vacuuming mindfully? It is attention alone: bringing the mind consciously to what one is doing. As spiritual practitioners the world over have found, the whole of life can be transformed by the practice of such intended effort. It is not at all a matter of "checking out," but of being truly capable of checking in to life. The Vietnamese teacher Thich Nhat Hanh has written books, meditations, and poems that illumine the art of ordinary mindfulness. It is this quality of mind that enables us to settle into the present, spacious, and vivid moment, rather than letting it roll by unnoticed as a merely instrumental moment. Waking up, setting one's feet upon the floor, opening the window, looking in the mirror, running the tap water—all become occasions for awareness. It is intention, paying attention, that transforms the ordinary moment.

Pilgrimage in the Spirit

Many Christians have trouble praying. We may say prayers, but don't feel we really pray. We may "listen in" on the minister's prayer, if we ever go to church, and yet feel we could not put so many words together ourselves. Praying is for the experts, whether ministers or monks. Or we may, perhaps, find even the minister's prayers artificial, stilted, and boring. And we may discover that even ministers and priests have trouble praying. As Bishop John A. T. Robinson put it, speaking for himself and many Anglican priests in *Honest to God*, the theological classic of the early sixties, "We are not the 'praying type.' And so we carry on with an unacknowledged sense of failure and guilt."[18]

Prayer is seen by many as turning *away* from the activities of daily life to be with God, as disengagement and withdrawal. No doubt there are times when withdrawal is necessary and nourishing, like those three months of silence at the Insight Meditation Society in Massachusetts. But most of us don't have three months to spare for silence, or at least we think we don't. It is no wonder that prayer seems discouraging if we are continually trying to fit it into the interstices and gaps of life or if we are waiting for that perfect moment of silence. Most of us are unlikely to become desert monks or forest-dwelling renouncers. We need a practice we can live with where we are—in the world. When the phone rings or when we stop at a red light, we can either see these as interruptions on our path to somewhere else, or as occasions for mindfulness, occasions to practice the presence of God. The Buddha with the vacuum cleaner would be a good fellow traveler with the carpenter from Nazareth. Both take their prayer and practice onto the road and into the world.

What does it mean to be a Christian who practices some "Hindu" or "Buddhist" form of meditation? This was not a question that troubled Saint Paul, Augustine, Luther, or even Barth. It is really a new question. The terrain is new and the experience of the explorers is just beginning to be gathered. There is much to be learned from Christians who have pursued such spiritual paths as part of their pilgrimage of faith. William Johnston is a Jesuit who has lived long in Japan and whose book *The Still Point* contains his own reflections on Zen and Christian practice. In 1970 he wrote,

> The fact is that not only Zen but all forms of Buddhism are going to make an enormous impact on the Christianity of the coming century. If there has been a Hellenized Christianity, there is every likelihood that the future will see the rise of an Oriental Christianity in which the role of Buddhism will be incalculably profound. Indeed, this process has already begun. . . . Now certain forms of Zen meditation have found their way into Japanese Christianity; they have put down roots; and no one yet knows the richness of the fruit that may well be gathered from the transplanted vine.[19]

There is no dearth of guidebooks for the pilgrimage. Anthony de Mello, an Indian Jesuit, has written a book called *Sadhana: A Way to God*, taking the title from the Sanskrit word from spiritual practice. It is a guide to awareness—mindfulness—that is written in Christian language for Christians, but begins with exercises straight out of the Hindu and Buddhist traditions.[20] There are the books of John Main, a Benedictine who learned meditation in India and taught meditation for years in Montreal. He begins each of his books of talks with the same simple lesson: "Sit down. Sit still and upright. Close your eyes lightly. Sit relaxed but alert. Silently, interiorly, begin to say a single word. We recommend the prayer-phrase *maranatha*. Recite it as four syllables of equal length. Listen to it as you say it, gently but continuously. Do not think or imagine anything—spiritual or otherwise. If thoughts and images come . . . keep returning to simply saying the word. Meditate each morning and evening for between twenty and thirty minutes."[21]

What motiviates a spiritual journey into the disciplines of another tradition? What are the conflicts that one might encounter along the way? What insights and perspectives have been gained by these spiritual pilgrims? As we have seen, in the late twentieth century these are not questions that can be answered in the abstract, as matters of doctrine or theology. They can only be addressed by real people, and there are many of them, whose spiritual lives as Christians have been shaped by their encounter with the seekers and the spirituality of another tradition. In 1987, the group I worked with in the World Council of Churches brought a number of these people together to see what their journeys had been like. We met in a contemplative Christian study center in Kyoto. It was an extraordinary congregation.

"'Taste the Lord, and see that He is good!' I had known these words of the Psalmist," said Michael, "but it was only in the months of sitting at Hosshinji that I had a taste."[22] Michael Como, a Harvard undergraduate, had grown up as a Methodist in Chicago and had gone when he was scarcely twenty, with a year of intensive Japanese under his belt, to a Zen monastery in Japan. The very week he arrived, the monastery launched a week of intensive sitting (called a *sesshin*) for which he was hardly prepared. "I can still recall how terrified I was and how sore my legs were after the first couple of days. . . . Day after day I sat with the monks in the meditation hall and, after bowing to my cushion, stared at the partition in front of me. It was beautifully, terrifyingly simple. I didn't have to move or even think; all I had to do was focus on my breathing. For the first time in my life I was asked to do something with my whole self."[23] For Michael, the meaning of a phrase like "Taste the Lord, and see that He is good" gradually became a reality. The Lord was not only to be affirmed in creeds, discussed in theologies, but also to be tasted, experienced through the aching, back-breaking struggle to be still.

A Catholic nun from Taiwan, Sister Agnes Lee is a Chinese convert to Christianity, but was attracted to the meditation practice of her Buddhist heritage, which did not seem to have a counterpart in the monastic discipline of the convent. She began the discipline of sitting. At first she had to move against the strong tide of her order to gain permission and time to do this. Now her order in Taiwan has a meditation room and many sisters have taken up sitting as part of their spiritual discipline. Novices are not required to sit, but sitting practice is introduced to them as an option. Through years of meditation, Sister Agnes has rediscovered something of the Buddhist tradition from which she had originally come. Reflecting on her early life as a Christian, a sister of the Order of the Sacred Heart, she said, "There were so many 'oughts' and 'shoulds' without providing concrete prescriptions to actualize the 'oughts' and 'shoulds.'" Worship was too wordy and too busy. There was no silence and no way into silence. Sitting and working through the breath, one is moved deep down, in the very core. "If the message of Christ doesn't get into my breath," she said, "it remains skin deep."

Sister Pascaline Coff, a Benedictine, was called to be director of novices in her own community and found herself without the resources for the responsibility. "People thought they would be taught to pray. They expected this. But I asked myself, *How* does one teach them to pray? In looking for spiritual guidance it was clear to me that more depth and method must be available somewhere." Sister Pascaline's own spiritual search led to the Christian ashram of Father Bede Griffith in southern India, and gradually into other forms of meditation practice and spiritual dialogue. Today her Benedictine community in Oklahoma is called the Osage Monastery and Ashram, where there is continual monastic exchange between East and West, including exchange visits with Tibetan Buddhist nuns. This phenomenon of inter-monastic exchange is so pervasive in the world of Catholic religious orders today that there is a regular *Bulletin of the North American Board for East-West Dialogue* filled with news of such exchange programs and retreats.[24] A recent issue announced, for example, a contemplative retreat in Portland, Oregon, led by an accredited Catholic Zen master, the Reverend Pat Hawk of Amarillo, Texas; the fourth annual Silence and Awareness Retreat in Mankato, Minnesota, featuring the Carmelite spirituality of Saint John of the Cross and Buddhist *vipassana* meditation; and a retreat at the Zen Mountain Monastery in Mt. Tremper, New York, led by a

Catholic priest, Ruben Habito, who studied Zen under Yamada Koun Roshi in Japan.

Murray Rogers is an Anglican priest who has spent over forty years in Asia. In northern India, in Jerusalem, and now in Hong Kong he has founded communities engaged in interreligious and spiritual dialogue. "Being blessed with friends from these 'other' spiritual paths, I have grown to know that there are no 'other faiths,' except in the most external and sociological terms," he told us. "Being allowed myself, by God's grace, to rejoice in and live 'by faith,' that is, by trust in God as He is made real to me day by day through Christ in the gospel and in the eucharist, I discover as brother, as sister, any person living 'by faith,' whether a follower of the [Hindu] Sanatana Dharma, of Islam, or of the Buddhist, Jewish, or Taoist way."[25] He spoke of his gratefulness to God and to his Hindu and Buddhist friends for the understanding of *sadhana* as daily spiritual practice, enabling the Holy Spirit to take hold of one in bodily, spiritual, and mental transformation. Speaking of his fellow pilgrims in the Hindu, Zen, and Taoist traditions, Murray Rogers said, "I gladly share, without fear of disloyalty to Christ, their treasures of experience, their perceptions of the Mystery, their ways of breathing the Reality beyond all name and form. 'I' and 'they' have almost disappeared and in their place it is 'we.' No longer am I driven to fight crusades to bring 'them' over to 'my' side, as if Christ were on 'my' side. Fanaticism, including Christian fanaticism, is seen to be what in fact it always is, an appalling insult to the Divine Mystery lying beyond and within creation."[26]

All of these Christians have found through disciplines of meditation a deeper life of prayer described not simply as the prayer of words, but as the ability of the heart to pay attention. The Reverend Yves Raguin, a Jesuit, has studied and taught Buddhism and Chinese religions for years as the director of the Ricci Institute for Chinese Studies in Taipei. He said, "From Zen practice I learned not to search for a God on high, a transcendent God, but I turned towards my inner being, facing my human nature. Since my human nature is God's image, I simply wait for this image to manifest itself to me." The discipline of Zen meditation had helped him "to stay in pure attentiveness before my inner mystery."[27]

Prayer is just this "attention of the heart," what *The Cloud of Unknowing* speaks of as standing upon the cloud of forgetting—putting aside concepts, thoughts, judgments, simply to *attend*. An Indian Christian, Swami Amaldas, spoke of hatha yoga, the physical discipline of yoga popular in the West, as immensely valuable in deepening the attention which is prayer. The *asanas*, or postures, he said, enable one to be still. One morning as we gathered for prayer, he stood at relaxed attention, ready to begin the phases of the yogic Salute to the Sun, reciting slowly a psalm: "Stand quietly before God. Wait patiently for his coming." Later he explained, "Doing the *asanas* well, slowly, prayerfully, teaches me to move graciously, doing only one movement or action at a time. This helps one during the day to practice the wisdom of mindfulness—keeping my consciousness fully in the present moment, in the here and now."

Yves Raguin reflected on the issue of "method" and Christian prayer. "Many people object to these kinds of practices," he said. "They tell us that Zen method cannot be separated from Buddhism, and that Taoist ways of contemplation cannot be Christianized. They forget that Christianity never had any method of its own because Christ never taught any method." For Raguin, then, the Zen method is not contradictory to some other "Christian" method of prayer, for there is none. But the aim of Zen practice, simple undivided attention, is completely consonant with the attention needed for prayer. The stillness nurtured by a practice of meditation truly restores the soul. The proof is in the practice.

And what about Christ? In letting go of labels and words, is there a danger one lets go of Christ? Again, this is not a question that can be answered in theory by theologians or wary sceptics; it can be answered only in the crucible of experience in spiritual practice. Speaking of his own practice, Yves Raguin said,

> No thinking could make me realize this inner mystery of mine. I could not rely on any thought, any desire, to reach this presence of God in me. When I was told not to think, not to rely on anything, I was a little disturbed. I was not allowed to think of Christ. Then I realized, after some years, that the last step of the Gospel was not to follow Christ or to imitate him. These are necessary steps, but the last step of the Gospel is taken when Christ says: 'It is good for you that I go.' . . . In fact it is the practice of Zen which helped me to understand that the final step is not to follow Christ or to imitate him, but to be animated by him, because he lives in us.[28]

The labels "Christian," "Buddhist," or "Hindu" are not relevant to spiritual discipline. Sitting, breathing, the attention of mind and heart is not Christian or Buddhist. The practice of *vipassana* "mindfulness" meditation or of *zazan* "sitting" might enable one to be still, to be truly present to the Spirit, to cease clinging to concepts and images of Jesus, and to realize the living presence of God within.

Bettina Bäumer, an Austrian Catholic, had been my neighbor in Banaras and had lived many years by the banks of the Ganges. She was not so sure about "adopting" practices from other religious traditions as if they were not part of a total context of meaning. She said in Kyoto, "My attitude at the beginning . . . was certainly one of openness, wanting to learn and being ready to receive inspiration from Indian spirituality for my own inner life as a Christian. But I was not conscious of the full implications of entering into another spiritual world. . . . I can still feel this attitude in many of my good Christian friends. We could compare it to somebody wanting to bathe in a river without getting wet!"[29] Bettina began to feel that appropriating or utilizing spiritual practices quite outside their context might be seen as a kind of spiritual theft, as if Hindus started celebrating the Mass without understanding the whole context of which it is a part.

Having accepted the wider implications of a Hindu discipline, the empowerment for spiritual practice by a guru and the unfolding of that practice, the next question is, How can one belong to two spiritual traditions at the same time; does it not lead to either schizophrenia or dishonesty? Bettina Bäumer answered, "It is precisely here that I am completely naked and exposed and depend on nothing but divine grace." For Bettina, the journey is really on two wheels— the Christian and the Hindu traditions. She points to other pioneers on the path, such as Swami Abhishiktananda, the Dominican monk who came to India in 1948 and explored boldly the spirituality of the Hindu tradition. "But I have to tread the way myself in all sincerity, in spite of the tremendous encouragement received from him and others. My conviction is that only such an experience can really build bridges between the old and still persisting misunderstandings among the diverse spiritual traditions."[30]

Crossing over into the spiritual life of another tradition opens the possibility, for some people the risk, of real change and transformation. This is not a journey on which one embarks for quick answers or spiritual souvenirs. There will be no souvenirs, and one will not return unchanged. "I could have easily said that what I learned from Hinduism was a way of meditation," said Bettina, "but in fact this meditation leads to a transformation of life itself, of one's experience of oneself, of others, of nature, of God. Meditation is not a particular yoga technique or a Zen way of 'sitting,' taken out of their context. If one allows it to unfold with all its implications, one may be surprised at the transformation that is taking place."[31]

Letting go of the safe confines and containers of Christianity has enabled Bettina and many others to discover a spacious world of the spirit that finally cannot be divided. "Are we Christians not too much concerned with labels instead of contents?" she asked. "A spiritual dialogue should precisely be beyond labels, enabling us to discover that perhaps the unknown pilgrim on the dusty and hot Indian road, in whose presence we feel 'our hearts burning,' is in reality He, the Risen One."[32]

The life of a learner is by nature a life of outer and inner dialogue, dialogue with others and within ourselves. The dialogue of learning *about* another religious tradition through study of its ways—its holy books, its appropriation of the crises of the life cycle—gives us another place to stand and think about our own tradition. And becoming self-conscious of the questions and presuppositions of our own tradition, in turn, helps us to see how we might understand or misunderstand another. Dialogue, both with others and within ourselves, could be said to be a simple pedagogical principle of learning for those who would come to some intellectual grasp of another religious tradition.

What about in the spiritual journey? Does the dialogue which so sharpens, tests, and refines our understanding in the intellectual realm suddenly become questionable or dangerous in the spiritual realm? Spiritual journeys like those of Yves Raguin and Bettina Bäumer have taken them through many years. Indeed, the dialogue has been built into their inner lives. Dialogue of this sort requires both faith and openness. It requires the real risk of pilgrimage. One cannot know at the outset just what one will find or how one may be changed. When a stone is dropped in a pool there are rings of repercussions. Some are felt immediately and others will gradually make their presence felt on the shore.

"Is Our God Listening?"

Exclusivism, Inclusivism, and Pluralism

I N CHAIM Potok's novel *The Book of Lights*, a young rabbi from Brooklyn, on leave from his post in Korea during the Korean War, travels for
the first time in Japan. One afternoon he stands with a Jewish friend before
what is perhaps a Shinto shrine with a clear mirror in the sanctum or perhaps a
Buddhist shrine with an image of the Bodhisattva of Compassion. We are not
told which, and it really does not matter. The altar is lit by the soft light of a tall
lamp. Sunlight streams in the door. The two young men observe with fascination a man standing before the altar, his hands pressed together before him, his
eyes closed. He is rocking slightly. He is clearly engaged in what we would call
prayer. The rabbi turns to his companion and says,

> "Do you think our God is listening to him, John?"
> "I don't know, chappy. I never thought of it."
> "Neither did I until now. If He's not listening, why not? If He is lis-
> tening, then—well, what are we all about, John?"[1]

Is "our God" listening to the prayers of people of other faiths? If not, why not?
What kind of God would that be? Would the one we Christians and Jews speak
of as maker of heaven and earth not give ear to the prayer of a man so earnestly,
so deeply in prayer? On the other hand, if God is listening, what are *we* all
about? Who are we as a people who cherish our own special relationship with
God? If we conclude that "our God" is not listening, then we had better ask how

we are to speak of God at all as people of faith in a world of many faiths. But if we suspect that "our God" is listening, then how are we to speak of ourselves as people of faith among other peoples of faith?

Is our God listening? It is a disarmingly simple question, a Sunday school question, not the sort most proper academic theologians would care to pursue. But this simple question leads us into the most profound theological, social, and political issues of our time. We all know that this is not solely a question about God's ears, the capacity of God to listen, or the destiny of our prayers. It is a question about the destiny of our human community and our capacity to listen with openness and empathy to people of faith very different from ourselves. It is a question about how we, whoever we are, understand the religious faith of others.

The question of religious difference elicits a variety of responses. A collection of Gandhi's writings on religion is published under the title *All Religions are True*, and that assertion is certainly one way of responding to difference. At the other end of the spectrum, there are those that assert that all religions are false and are fundamentally misguided—look at the wars and violence, the atrocities perpetrated in the name of God. A third option is to insist that one religion is true and the rest are false. Or one might claim that one religion is true and the others are partially true. Most of us have operative ideas about the diversity of religious traditions that fall somewhere along this spectrum. We carry these ideas along with us as we encounter people whose religious faith is different from ours. Even those who consider themselves quite secular employ some such set of evaluative ideas about religions in order to interpret the meaning of religion and of religious difference. We also carry with us notions of what it means for something to be true—literally true, metaphorically true, true for us, universally true.

While the interpretation of religious difference and plurality has long been a question, the close proximity of people of many races, cultures, and religions in urban environments has decisively shaped our response to this question today. In 1965, Harvey Cox began *The Secular City* with the observation that "the rise of urban civilization and the collapse of traditional religion are the two main hallmarks of our era and are closely related."[2] In the urban environment from which the gods have fled, he argued, secularism was the dominant worldview, relativizing and bypassing religion, rendering it irrelevant and a private affair. In 1985, Harvey Cox noted "the return of religion" with *Religion in the Secular City*. The demise of religion had been prematurely announced. Sud-

denly there were Jerry Falwell and the Moral Majority; one in five adults in the
United States weighed in with the Gallup Poll as an evangelical or pentecostal
Christian.

In the "secular city" of the 1990s, we would have to report the rise of *religions*,
in the plural. We just might be tempted to turn Cox's sentence wholly around
and postulate that today the collapse of urban civilization and the rise of traditional religions are the two main hallmarks of our era. It is not that secularism is now no longer an issue, for the privatization and relativization of religion is still a reality to contend with. The challenge today, however, is not so
much secularism, but pluralism. If one of the great issues of the secular city was
anonymity, the great issue of the multicultural city is identity—ethnic, racial,
and religious identity, African-American, Caucasian, Asian, Hispanic, Buddhist, Muslim.

In both the urban and global contexts we rub up against the new textures of
religious diversity with increasing frequency. The question Is our God listening? poses in a blunt way the challenge of our encounter with real difference.
Responses to this question take theological, social, and political forms. There are
many types of responses, but we will explore just three possibilities, indicative of
the range of interpretation within almost every religious tradition.

First, there is the exclusivist response: Our own community, our tradition,
our understanding of reality, our encounter with God, is the one and only truth,
excluding all others. Second, there is the inclusivist response: There are, indeed,
many communities, traditions, and truths, but our own way of seeing things is
the culmination of the others, superior to the others, or at least wide enough to
include the others under our universal canopy and in our own terms. A third response is that of the pluralist: Truth is not the exclusive or inclusive possession of
any one tradition or community. Therefore the diversity of communities, traditions, understandings of the truth, and visions of God is not an obstacle for us to
overcome, but an opportunity for our energetic engagement and dialogue with
one another. It does not mean giving up our commitments; rather, it means
opening up those commitments to the give-and-take of mutual discovery, understanding, and, indeed, transformation.

Put in terms of our question, in the view of the exclusivist "our God" is not
listening to those of other faiths. For the inclusivist, "our God" is indeed listening, but it is our God as *we* understand God who does the listening. The pluralist might say "our God" is listening, but he or she would also say that God is

not ours, God is our way of speaking of a Reality that cannot be encompassed by any one religious tradition, including our own.

The most significant difference between the inclusivist and the pluralist is the self-consciousness of one's understanding of the world and God. If we are inclusivists, we include others into a worldview we already know and on the terms we have already set. If we are pluralists, we recognize the limits of the world we already know and we seek to understand others in their own terms, not just in ours. In the final chapter, I will suggest that pluralists go beyond this, however, for the terms of "the other" are no more sacrosanct than our own and the point of our encounter is to bring the terms in which we understand the world into dialogue with one another—even into the dialogue of mutual truth-seeking critique.

Mere plurality—diversity—is not pluralism, though often the two words are used as if they were interchangeable. We can interpret diversity as exclusivists, as inclusivists, or as pluralists. One might argue that the greatest religious tensions in the world in the late twentieth century are not found between the Western and the Eastern traditions, between the prophetic and the mystical traditions, or indeed between any one religion and another; they are the tensions that stretch between those at opposite ends of the spectrum in each and every religious tradition. Exclusivists and pluralists, fundamentalists and liberals, wall-builders and bridge-builders—are there in a variety of forms in every religious tradition. *Intra*-religious tension is today as powerful as *inter*-religious tension. Very often the religious conflicts that flare up have less to do with *what* one believes than with *how* one believes what one believes.

The last few years have seen a burst of Christian theological discussion of exclusivism, inclusivism, and pluralism. This is important work because it amply demonstrates the tremendous diversity within Christian thinking. There is no one Christian view of other faiths. Even in the statements of today's churches there is a wide range of Christian interpretation. For example, the 1970 Frankfurt Declaration of the Evangelical Church of Germany explicitly rejected "the false teaching that nonchristian religions and worldviews are also ways of salvation similar to belief in Christ."[3] This declaration is clearly an exclusivist statement. At the other end of the spectrum, members of the United Church of Canada meeting in Naramata, British Columbia, in 1985 crafted a clearly pluralist statement, insisting, "If there is no salvation outside the church, we reject such a salvation for ourselves. We come to this notion of the salvation of others through being loved by Christ. We would be diminished without the others as others."[4]

Since there are many theologians who have laid out typologies of the various Christian theological positions of exclusivism, inclusivism, and pluralism, I will not do that here in anything but a skeletal and suggestive form. My point is a wider one: that these three ways of thinking about the problem of diversity and difference are not simply Christian theological positions, but are recognizable in the thinking of people of other religious traditions and in the thinking of nonreligious people. All of us—Christians, Muslims, Hindus, and others—struggle to interpret the experienced facts of diversity to ourselves and to our communities, and our interpretations have social and political reverberations. Theology is not isolated from its context. If "our God" has no regard for our Muslim neighbors, why should we? Or, put the other way around, if we have no regard for our Muslim neighbors, why should God?

While we may be interested in exclusivism, inclusivism, and pluralism as theological viewpoints, it is all too clear that they are also social and political responses to diversity. We can recognize them in our churches, in our communities, and in our world. And while we speak of exclusivists, inclusivists, and pluralists as if they were entirely different groups of people, let us remember that these ways of thinking about diversity may well be part of the ongoing dialogue within ourselves. Since they represent attitudes, ways of thinking, the move from one position to another is often more of a sliding step than a giant leap. One of the continual challenges and dilemmas in my own writing and thinking is recognizing the ways in which I move back and forth along this attitudinal continuum, coming from a context of Hindu-Christian dialogue, understanding myself basically as a pluralist, and yet using what some will see as inclusivist language as I widen and stretch my understanding of God, Christ, and the Holy Spirit to speak of my Christian faith in a new way. I cannot solve this dilemma, but I can warmly issue an invitation to join me in thinking about it.

"In No Other Name . . ."

Every time I speak to a church group about religious diversity, someone inevitably raises a hand to confront me with a passage mined from the New Testament to illustrate the exclusivity of Christianity. If she were there, Grandma Eck would certainly have her hand up, too. "It says in the Bible, 'There is salvation in no one else, for there is no other name under heaven given among mortals by which we must be saved.' So how can you speak of the Buddha?" The statement quoted is that of Peter in Acts 4:12. It is true that it says "no other name." In those remarkable days following Pentecost, when the energy of the Holy Spirit made Peter bold in his faith, he healed a man lame from birth, saying, "I have no silver or gold, but what I have I give you; in the name of Jesus Christ of Nazareth, stand up and walk." Peter was asked by the elders and scribes of the temple, "By what power or by what name did you do this?" He was unambiguous. It was not in his own name he had healed the man, nor was it in the name of a foreign god, as the council of elders perhaps suspected. It was in no other name than that of Jesus Christ.

Krister Stendahl has often remarked that phrases such as this one "grow legs and walk around out of context." The words "no other name," despite the spirit of affirmation in which Peter must have uttered them, became words of condemnation: only those who call upon the name of Christ are saved and all others perish and suffer eternal punishment. Actually, Christians have disagreed through the ages on the meaning of "no other name." From the time of Origen in the third century, to John Wesley in the eighteenth century, to C. S. Lewis and Paul Tillich in the twentieth, there have been those who have insisted upon the universality of God's grace and the omnipotence of God to restore all creatures to Godself. And there have likewise been those such as Augustine in the fourth century, John Calvin in the sixteenth century, and the fundamentalists of the twentieth century who have insisted upon the eternal damnation and punishment of unbelievers. In the past few years two books have been published that attempt to summarize the range of meanings implicit in these words. In *No Other Name?* Paul Knitter sets forth the array of Christian interpretations of other religions across the Protestant, evangelical, and Catholic spectrums, questions the adequacy of exclusivism as a response to the religious plurality of today, and develops his own pluralistic position.[5] John Sanders's *No Other Name* retains the phrase as a declarative, not a question; it is what the author calls "an investigation into the destiny of the unevangelized," and it also presents a full range of Christian views on the subject.[6]

In the decades and centuries following Jesus' death, many Christians gradually transferred their Spirit-filled affirmations about Christ to affirmations of allegiance to "Christianity" and "the church." Over time, their positive affirmations about Christ somehow became sharply negative judgements about any religious community other than the church. By the time of Cyprian, in the third century, we have the famous dictum *"Extra ecclesiam nulla salus"*—"Outside the church there is no salvation." This church-centered exclusivism dominated Christian thinking for many centuries. In the sixth century, for example, we hear, "There is no doubt that not only all heathens, but also all Jews and all heretics and schismatics who die outside the church will go to that everlasting fire prepared for the devil and his angels."[7] In the early fourteenth century we hear Pope Boniface VIII insist even more strongly on church-centered salvation: "We are required by faith to believe and hold that there is one holy, catholic and apostolic Church; we firmly believe it and unreservedly profess it; outside it there is neither salvation nor remission of sins."[8]

As a Methodist, it is always somewhat disquieting to recall that with the Protestant Reformation, Protestants were also numbered among those who would die outside the Church and be plunged into the fires of hell. Gradually the official papal view on the salvation of Protestants began to change, but as late as the 1950s a notorious Catholic chaplain at Harvard, Father Leonard J. Feeney, fulminated in Harvard Square against both Jews and Protestants in boldly exclusivist terms. "Outside the *Catholic* church there is no salvation" meant just that. Finally, after months of heated controversy, Pope Pius XII confirmed in a papal encyclical that Feeney had gone too far, contravening the papal view that those who belong to the church "with implicit desire" might also be eligible for salvation. Father Feeney, unwilling to change his views, was excommunicated in 1953.[9]

Protestants have also had their share of exclusivism. Luther returned the condemnation of the Roman Catholic church with his own brand of exclusivism. He insisted that all worship apart from Christ is idolatry and that "those who remain outside Christianity, be they heathens, Turks, Jews or false Christians although they believe in only one true God, yet remain in eternal wrath and perdition."[10] The "false Christians" were Roman Catholics.

The great twentieth-century Protestant theologian Karl Barth takes a different starting point, insisting that "religion is unbelief. It is a concern, indeed, we must say that it is the one great concern, of godless man."[11] Religion is here opposed to revelation, and revelation is God's initiative; it is Christ alone. All the world's religions are human attempts to grasp at God, to understand God and are set in radical distinction from God's self-offering and self-manifestation. According to Barth, the truth of the Christian message has nothing to do with its structures of "religion," it is the gift of revelation. Barth did not know much of other religious traditions, or of Buddhist, Hindu, and Islamic claims to the gift and the grace of divine revelation. When asked by the Asian theologian D. T.

Niles how he knew for certain that Hinduism is "unbelief," given the fact that he had never met a Hindu, Barth is said to have responded, *"A priori"*—it is a given; it derives from revelation, not experience.[12] The Dutch theologian Hendrik Kraemer followed Barth, writing forcefully of the "radical discontinuity" between the Gospel and all other religions. In the influential book *The Christian Message in a Non-Christian World*, which Kraemer prepared for the meeting of the International Missionary Council in Tambaram, India, in 1938, he speaks of other religions as but "human attempts to apprehend the totality of existence."[13] He poses two alternative ways of thinking about religious diversity. "The first maintains the continuity between the essential tendencies and aspirations to be found in the ethnic religions and the essential gift of the Christian religion. . . . The second position stresses the discontinuity, and takes this as the starting point of its thinking."[14] Kraemer finds the second position "inescapable" and Christian revelation the "sole standard of reference."[15]

Of course, Christianity is not the only religion with an exclusivist streak of interpretation. Not surprisingly, however, the exclusivist position has been most extensively developed by the monotheistic Jewish, Christian, and Muslim traditions, each with its "sole standard of reference." These prophetic Western traditions have uncompromisingly emphasized the oneness of God, the oneness of truth, and the exclusivity of the way to truth and the community of truth.

The idea that the human apprehension of truth is multi-sided, a view developed so extensively in the traditions originating in India, is quite alien to the monotheistic consciousness of the West. "I am the Lord, and there is no other!" rings like a refrain through the biblical books of Deuteronomy and Isaiah. The Psalmist, too, addresses God in exclusive terms: "You alone are God" (Ps. 86:10), "You alone are the Most High over all the earth" (Ps. 83:18). The exclusivity is reciprocal. God says to Israel, "You alone have I chosen of all the nations on earth!" (Amos 3:2). Even though Jews also affirm the universality of God's covenant with Noah and through him with all humanity, Israel's chosenness and covenant with God through Abraham is finally an exclusive covenant.

Christians pick up on this chosenness, this covenant, transforming the language of the old covenant into a "new covenant" made with humanity through the life, death, and resurrection of Christ. The new covenant is also held to be exclusive: Christ is *the* way, the truth, and the life. Similarly, Muslims affirm the finality of the One God's revelation to the Prophet Muhammad. The *shahadah*, or "testimony" of faith, is a clarion affirmation with an exclusivist ring about it: "There is no God but God and Muhammad is God's messenger." There is nothing that can be likened to or compared to God—no image, no icon, no partner, no incarnation. The human response to this message of God is "the straight path"—Islam. And since the One God is universal, so is the path of human righteousness.

It is important to realize, however, that these religious foundations of Western monotheism are not in themselves exclusivist, for they have also been the religious foundations for inclusivists and pluralists. The emphasis on God's oneness, for example, can also lead to a sense of the wideness of God's mercy that undergirds both the inclusivist and the pluralist position. Even so, it is clear that monotheism has often produced the kind of monolithic mindset and dogmatic language that has readily lent itself to exclusivist interpretations. One God alone, one Son of God, one Seal of the Prophets—and none other. And along with the oneness goes onlyness, the sense of surety about God's will that can be seen in groups like the Christian Embassy in Israel, the Gush Emunim, and the Islamic Jihad. Even outside the monotheistic traditions of the West, however, there are strains of exclusivism. In Japan in the thirteenth century, for example, the sectarian Buddhist teacher Nichiren insisted that *only* the name of the Lotus Sutra was salvific. Sheer faith in the name of the Lotus Sutra alone, exclusive of all others, would lead to salvation.

Oneness and *onlyness* are the language of identity. The exclusivist affirms identity in a complex world of plurality by a return to the firm foundations of his or her own tradition and an emphasis on the distinctive identity provided by that tradition. This identity is in part what social theorists call an "oppositional identity," built up over against who we are *not*. Exclusivism is more than simply a conviction about the transformative power of the particular vision one has; it is a conviction about its finality and its absolute priority over competing views. Exclusivism may therefore be the ideological foundation for isolationism. The exclusivist response to diversity, whether theological, social, or political, is to mark ever more clearly the boundaries and borders separating "us" from "them." It is little wonder that exclusion has been one of the tools of racism and ethnocentrism. The series of Asian exclusion acts that erected walls around a Eurocentric idea of America were an attempt to define an American identity, as were the 1920s Supreme Court discussions of the meaning of "Caucasian" or "white person" as qualifications for U.S. citizenship. The language of interrelatedness and interdependence that has come increasingly to the fore as nations and peoples struggle with issues of plurality is experienced by the exclusivist as compromising and threatening to identity and to faith.

The very fact of choice can precipitate a sense of threat to identity. My own grandmothers and great-grandmothers made many pioneering choices. Anna Eck pulled up stakes in Sweden. Hilda Fritz left her windswept farm in Iowa for a homestead in the Pacific Northwest. Ida Hokanson Fritz set out for college, the first in her family to do so, and landed a teaching job in the lumber camps of Washington State. But for all the choices they made out of necessity and creativity, they did not have to choose whether to be Christian or Buddhist. They did not even have the opportunity to think about it. At most they chose to be more or less actively Christian. For many people, this is still the case today; for our society as a whole it is not. We *do* have to choose our religious affiliation more actively than those who lived a generation ago. Most of us have some opportunity to know other ways of faith and to see them for what they are—powerful life-changing and world-ordering responses to the Transcendent. I see this opportunity as a positive thing. It is clear, however, that many people experience the fact of difference as a failure of the church's mission to the "lost" and "unreached," and experience choice as threatening. The crisis of belief generated by the plurality of religions and the problems of secular culture has made the certainties of Christian exclusivism, indeed of any kind of exclusivism, more attractive.

Today's exclusivism, with its variety of fundamentalist and chauvinist movements both ethnic and political, may be seen as a widespread revolt against the relativism and secularism of modernity. This does not mean that all "fundamentalists" are conservative or traditional in rejecting the modern world. But they have not made peace with modernity or made themselves at home within it.[16] The Enlightenment heritage of modernity—the inquiry into the sources of scripture; the critical academic study of society, culture, and religion; the historical comparison of truth claims; the evolutionary claims of science—is by and large rejected by fundamentalists. Religious truth is "a given" and is plain, simple, and clear.

In America, the burst of Christian fundamentalism in the 1970s and 1980s grew amidst the threat of burgeoning plurality and choice in virtually every arena of life, including sexuality and religion. Nothing could be taken for granted as a given. One could choose a hometown, an occupation, a "lifestyle," a worldview, and even a religious tradition—choices people in traditional societies do not confront as individuals. In *The Heretical Imperative*, sociologist of religion Peter Berger has pointed out that the word *heresy* has its root in the Greek word for choosing on one's own, apart from the community. Today such individual choice in matters of religion, formerly "heretical," has become the modern imperative. Individual choosing is expected and necessary—even in matters of religion.

A new wave of exclusivism is cresting around the world today. Expressed in social and political life, exclusivism becomes ethnic or religious chauvinism, described in South Asia as communalism. Religious or ethnic identity is the basis on which a group campaigns for its own interests against those others with whom it shares the wider community of a city, state, or nation. As we have observed, identity-based politics is on the rise because it is found to be a successful way of arousing political energy, as was clear with the rise, however brief, of the Moral Majority in the United States, the rise of the Soka Gakkai in Japan, and the Bharatiya Janata Party (B.J.P.) in India.

The new Muslim resurgence has somewhat different roots. The affirmation of Islamic culture against the tide of Western capitalist, materialist culture finds its voice in the new sometimes strident assertiveness of Islamic identity. It is little wonder that the old colonial West and its new heir, the United States, are cast in a negative light. Over forty countries with substantial Muslim populations have gained independence since World War II and in various ways have found Islam to be the foundation of nation building. And yet the postcolonial era has left social and political problems, and sometimes chaos, that are quite dissonant with the Islamic vision of society. This too stimulates the call to a reassertion of Islamic fundamentals. For most interpreters, these fundamentals do not permit the bifurcation of the world into the "secular" and the "religious," for the *shari'a*, the Muslim "way," is a whole comprehensive worldview which creates a transnational community and challenges that community to a life of obedience, a life aligned with the truth God has revealed in the Qur'an.

Exclusivism often arises among minorities, or those who have a minority consciousness even if they are not numerical minorities. While some minorities are content to be minorities and to experience themselves as the salt or the leaven that improves the whole, it is nonetheless often the case that the sense of fear and threat that are especially powerful among minorities gives rise to fundamentalist or exclusivist movements. The sense of being pitted against a dominant and engulfing "other" that threatens one's identity leads to the assertion of self over or against the "other" as a form of self-protection. The exclusivism of the early church, the beloved community of which the author of the Gospel of John writes, is a good example of the way in which minority consciousness engenders a very clear sense of boundaries and some strongly exclusivist language.

There are many places where such an exclusivist, fundamentalist, or communalist position is enacted by minorities in public affairs. The sense on the part of Sikhs of being gradually engulfed in a dominant and increasingly secular Indian culture has surely contributed to the anti-Hindu rhetoric of militant Sikhs and the demand for a separate Sikh state of "Khalistan." The militant Jewish leadership of the late Rabbi Kahane and of the Gush Emunim often takes the form of anti-Arab Zionist chauvinism, gaining strength from the sense among Israelis of being under seige in an engulfing Arab world. In both cases, minority consciousness gives rise to an unbending exclusivism. This is even more the case with smaller and less powerful minorities than Jews or Sikhs. In South India and Thailand, for example, the minority Christian churches are often extremely fundamentalist theologically and exclusivist socially, in part because Christians feel they are too few to permit an attitude of openness and interrelatedness without being submerged by the majority culture.

Minority consciousness is not entirely a rational matter of numbers, however. In Sri Lanka, for example, the Buddhist Sinhalese majority has a minority consciousness. Even though the Tamils are a small minority in Sri Lanka itself, the southern Indian state of Tamilnadu, a short distance across the straits, presents a large Tamil population and a wide context of Tamil culture and influence. In India, the recent rise of Hindu chauvinism is fueled by the sense that Hindus, though they are the majority numerically, have no power in their own land because of the proliferation of special privileges and reservations given to minorities. A new exclusive sense of Hindu identity is in the process of formation.

It is important to note, however, that some numerical minorities do not have an exclusivist consciousness at all. The native peoples of the Americas, for example, while being protective of their rites and lifeways, also see the truth in other ways and paths. Over forty years ago, Chief White Calf of the Blackfeet of Montana offered a critique of Christian exclusivism that was very expressive of Native American attitudes. As an old man, in the summer of 1958 he told the story of creation to one Richard Lancaster, whom he called his son.

I am Chief White Calf of the Blackfeet, and I am one hundred and one years old, and I give you this story that I got from my father, Last Gun, who got it from the old men of the tribe. . . . You are my son and I give it to you.

Only once before I tried to give this story. There was a missionary and I called him son and gave him a name and tried to give him this story but he would not take it because he said that this is not the way things were in the beginning. But I was not proud to have him for my son because he says there is only one path through the forest and he knows the right path, but I say there are many paths and how can you know the best path unless you have walked them all. He walked too long on one path and he does not know there are other paths. And I am one hundred and one, and I know that sometimes many paths go to the same place.[17]

Deep conviction about one's own path need not be exclusivist. It might be simply the evangelical or neo-orthodox enthusiasm for one's own roots, one's own people, or one's own tradition. Traditions and people of faith are continually revitalized by the return to roots and energy of new revival movements. But exclusivism is not just ardent enthusiasm for one's own tradition. It is coupled with a highly negative attitude toward other traditions. Like the missionary who would not even listen to White Calf's story, the exclusivist does not participate in dialogue, does not listen openly to the testimony of others. Exclusivism has to do not only with how we hold our own convictions, but also with how we regard the convictions of our neighbor. In a world of close neighbors, the exclusivist has a real problem—one will likely meet those neighbors. One might discover they are not anathema after all. Or one might discover that they are equally ardent exclusivists.

Is "our God" listening? The exclusivist, whether Christian, Jewish, or Muslim, feels no qualms in speaking about "our God" or speaking about "the truth." The use of the possessive with reference to God does not seem peculiar. Nor is there reticence in saying that "our God" does not listen, at least appreciatively, to the prayers of others; as Bailey Smith, the president of the Southern Baptist Convention, put it bluntly in 1978, "God Almighty does not hear the prayers of the Jew." The Christian exclusivist insists that the truth of Christ excludes all others: *Extra ecclesiam nulla salus*—outside the church, no salvation. This voice has sounded long and loud in the churches—so much so that many imagine it is the only way Christians think about the matter.

"One Great Fellowship of Love"

While the exclusivist response may be the most loudly expressed, most Christians are probably inclusivists. The evangelical message of Christianity is not exclusive, they would argue. No indeed—the invitation is open and the tent of Christ is wide enough for all. As the words of an early-twentieth-century Protestant hymn put it, paraphrasing Galatians 3:28, "In Christ there is no east or west, in him no south or north, but one great fellowship of love, throughout the whole wide earth." The hymn was written for an exhibit of the London Mission Society in 1908. At least one strong stream of the mission movement was fed not by an exclusivist theology that deemed all non-Christians to be lost heathen, but by an inclusivist "fulfillment theology" that held non-Christians to be genuine seekers of a truth found fully in Christ. That is, other religious traditions are not so much evil or wrong-headed as incomplete, needing the fulfillment of Christ. In some ways other religious traditions have prepared the way for the Good News of Christ. While not wholly false, they are but partially true. All people of faith are seekers, and Christ, finally, is what they seek. All can be included in the great fellowship of love.

In such a view, the plurality of religions is not experienced as a threat, and "others" are not seen as opponents. Rather, the diversity of peoples and traditions is included in a single worldview that embraces, explains, and supersedes them all. For Christians, inclusivism at its best may mean articulating a sense of the mysterious workings of God and of Christ among people of other faiths. Such a view, however, often hides within it a hierarchical acceptance of plurality, with one's own view of things on top. It is also a hierarchical view that goes, often unreflectively, with power. Everyone is invited in, and we are the ones who put up the tent. Others are gathered in, but on our terms, within our framework, under our canopy, as part of our system.

Is "our God" listening? C. S. Lewis, a Christian inclusivist, would say, "I think that every prayer which is sincerely made even to a false god . . . is accepted by the true God and that Christ saves many who do not think they know him."[18] The inclusivist attitude is, of course, much more open than the exclusivist, but the presupposition is that in the end ours is the truth wide enough to include all. Ours are the terms in which truth is stated.

Recall for a moment how, at the close of the World's Parliament of Religions in 1893, John Henry Barrows expressed great satisfaction that each day of the Parliament included the "universal" prayer of Jesus, the Lord's Prayer. J. N. Farquhar, a missionary in India, studied the Hindu tradition with respect, but concluded in his book *The Crown of Hinduism*, published in 1913, that Christ is the fulfillment of the highest aspirations and aims of Hinduism. Not surprisingly, such inclusivism is a way of thinking that is common to people of faith in virtually every tradition. Many a Hindu would surely think of Vedanta as the culmination and crown, not only of Christianity, but of all religious paths. And it is common to hear Muslims say, as did a Muslim taxi driver who took me from downtown Washington, D.C., to the mosque on Massachusetts Avenue, "To be a good Muslim, you first have to be a good Jew and a good Christian. Islam includes everything that is there in Judaism and Christianity."

There is a dilemma here, for to some extent all religious people are inclusivists insofar as we use our own particular religious language—God, Jesus Christ, the Holy Spirit, the Buddha, Vishnu—and struggle with the limits and meaning of that language. As long as we hold the religious insights of our particular traditions, cast in our particular languages, to be in some sense universal, we cannot avoid speaking at times in an inclusivist way. It is important to recognize this. For instance, my Buddhist friends at the Cambridge Insight Meditation Center do not perceive their understanding of the nature of human suffering and the potential of human freedom as a peculiarly Buddhist truth, but as a truth about the human condition which is universal and accessible to all who would look clearly at their own experience. "*Ehi passika*," "Come and see," was the invitation of the Buddha. Wake up and see for yourself. For Muslims, the revelation of the Qur'an in the "night of power" is not a parochial revelation meant for the ears of Muslims alone, but a revelation to all people, before which the proper response is *islam*, literally "obedience." For Muslims, aligning one's life with the truth God has revealed, which is what Islam means, makes all believers *muslims* with a small "m." Similarly, when Hindus quote the words of the Rig Veda, "*Ekam sat vipraha bahudha vadanti*"—"Truth is one, but the wise call it by many names"—they are not claiming this to be the case only for Hindus, but to be universally true. Similarly, Christians who speak of the Christ event do not speak of a private disclosure of God to Christians alone but of the sanctification of humanity by God, a gift to be claimed by all who will but open their eyes to see it. In the words of Charles Wesley, "The arms of love that circle me would all mankind embrace!"

In the West, inclusivism has taken the particular form of theological supersessionism, as we see clearly in the progression of the prophetic monotheistic traditions from Judaism to Christianity to Islam. We not only come from the same stock, we are perpetually interpreting one another. The Christian tradition contains within its scriptures and traditions an interpretation of Judaism. For a long period, Christian theological orthodoxy held that the Christian community supersedes the Jewish community in a "new covenant" with God. The Muslim tradition, acknowledging the validity and prophecy of the Jewish and

Christian traditions, claims to have superseded both of them as the final revelation of God, clarifying the distorted vision of both with the corrective lens of the Qur'an. My Muslim cab driver in Washington was right, in a sense, about Islam including an understanding of the Jewish and Christian traditions. He would no doubt object, however, to the further revelation claimed by Baha' Ullah in Iran in the mid-nineteenth century, just as Christians would reject the postbiblical revelation claimed by the Reverend Sun Myung Moon. No one wants to be superseded.

In my own Methodist tradition, the theological foundation of inclusivism is John Wesley's conviction that universal love is the heartline of the Christian message. No one could say, according to Wesley, that the "heathen and Mahometan" would suffer damnation. Far better to leave this matter to God, "who is the God of the Heathens as well as the Christians, and who hateth nothing that he hath made."[19] And who is this God? Charles Wesley's famous hymn "O Come Thou Traveller Unknown," written on the theme of Jacob wrestling with the unknown God, exclaims, "Pure Universal Love thou art!" The refrain repeats throughout the hymn—"Thy Nature, and thy name, is Love."

On the Catholic side, exclusivism has gradually yielded to an inclusivist view, seeking ways to include in God's salvation those "outside the church." It perhaps began with the discovery of what was called the New World, but which was clearly new only to the newcomers. The indigenous peoples had been there for many centuries and had never heard so much as a whisper of the name of Jesus. How was the church to think of the destiny of their immortal souls? Could a merciful God, whose providence extends throughout all creation, have condemned to hell all these who died outside the church but had never even heard of Christ? Finally, in 1854, the Vatican launched the doctrine that would later be the nemesis of Father Feeney, the doctrine of salvation to those individuals of godly faith handicapped by what was termed "invincible ignorance." "Although juridically speaking they are 'outside' (*extra*) the Catholic church and formally not its members, yet in a vital sense they are 'inside' (*intra*) . . . invisible members of the Catholic church."[20]

With closer acquaintance, however, it became clear—often through the missionaries who knew them best—that the wisdom of native peoples, Hindu philosophers, and Buddhist monks could not simply be classified as the "invincible ignorance" of those who did not have the opportunity to know Christ. Even when they did have the opportunity to be acquainted with Jesus through the Gospel and the sometimes unappealing witness of the church, they were often suaded to cast off their own traditions of wisdom or spirituality. Indeed, missionaries themselves sometimes glimpsed the wisdom of the Hindus or Buddhists among whom they worked and began to raise questions. The new attitude took a long while to ripen. It was really with the fresh air of Pope John XXIII and the Second Vatican Council (1962–1965) that a new strain of inclusive thinking was born. The council drew up a statement, "The Relation of the Church to Non-Christian Religions," known by its first two words as *Nostra Aetate*.[21] It begins, "In this age of ours, when men are drawing more closely together and the bonds of friendship between different peoples are being strengthened, the Church examines with greater care the relation which she has to non-Christian religions." This remarkable document starts with the affirmation that all people "form but one community," citing the reference of Acts 17 that God made from one stock all the peoples of the earth, in order that they should seek after God and find God. The statement allows that God's "providence, evident goodness, and saving designs extend to all men."

Nostra Aetate is an appreciative statement of the depth of various traditions. Hindus, it affirms, "explore the divine mystery and express it both in the limitless riches of myth and the accurately defined insights of philosophy." Buddhism "testifies to the essential inadequacy of this changing world" and proposes a way of life which leads to liberation. Muslims "highly esteem an upright life and worship God, especially by way of prayer, alms-deeds and fasting." Jews and Christians especially "have a common spiritual heritage," and Jews "remain very dear to God, for the sake of the patriarchs, since God does not take back the gifts he bestowed or the choice he made."

The most quoted paragraph of the document sums up the inclusivist position:

> The Catholic church rejects nothing of what is true and holy in these religions. She has a high regard for the manner of life and conduct, the precepts and doctrines which, although differing in many ways from her own teaching, nevertheless often reflect a ray of that truth which enlightens all men. Yet she proclaims and is in duty bound to proclaim without fail, Christ who is the way, the truth, and the life (John 14:6). In him, in whom God reconciled all things to himself (2 Cor. 5:18–19), men find the fulness of their religious life.

Nostra Aetate goes on to affirm that the suffering of Christ was not just for Christians, but for all people, and the cross of Christ is "the sign of God's universal love and the source of all grace." The document says, "We cannot truly pray to God the Father of all if we treat any people in other than brotherly fashion, for all men are created in God's image." The Catholic theologians of Vatican II do not propose that there is salvation outside the church, but do affirm God's "saving designs" and the universality of "general revelation" through which grace is made available to all. Yet in and through all such revelation, it is the cross of Christ that is both "the sign of God's universal love and the source of all grace."

The Catholic theologian Karl Rahner went a step beyond Vatican II in his inclusivism. Like John Wesley, he takes as his starting point the central message of the Gospel: God's universal love, the gift of God's grace, and God's desire to save all humankind. Rahner uses a splendid word, *heilsoptimismus*, "holy optimism," inviting us to "think optimistically" about the possibilities of salvation outside the church. Among the channels of God's grace, according to Rahner, are the great religions. They are "positively included in God's plan of salvation."[22] Rahner's most famous phrase is "anonymous Christians," by which he means faithful people of non-Christian religions who do not "name the name" of Christ, but who are nonetheless saved by his power and grace, even though they do not know it. Christ is the "constitutive cause" of salvation, and wherever God's saving grace abounds in the world, Christ is present, whether in name or not.

Inclusivism is an appealing way of looking at things and there is much to appreciate in inclusivist viewpoints. Whether it is Christian, Hindu, or Muslim inclusivism, this bent of mind is mostly benign toward other traditions or faiths. The inclusivist does not exclude or condemn others, is not usually chauvinistic, defensive, or self-aggrandizing. Granted, an inclusivist uses his or her own language and conception—God's universal love, for the Christian, or perhaps Krishna's omnipresence and omnipotence, for the Hindu— as a way of understanding the other, but would insist that, realistically, we can only understand the world in and through the language and the symbols we have inherited from our own traditions. So in Rahner's inclusivist scheme my Hindu friends are baptized "anonymous Christians" and Muslims are saved by the mediation and grace of Christ, even though this certainly violates their self-understanding. And yet, to be fair, Rahner states explicitly that the term "anonymous Christians" is not intended for dialogue with others, but only for what we might call internal use as Christians set their own understanding aright.[23]

There is still something unsettling here. While it preserves the integrity of

my own self-understanding, inclusivism often dodges the question of real difference by reducing everything finally to my own terms. The problem with inclusivism is precisely that it uses *one* language—the religious language of one's
own tradition—to make definitive claims about the whole of reality. What
about the self-understanding of the Muslim? What about her testimony of
faith? What about the Jews who do not speak of being "saved" at all and would
object strenuously to the notion of being saved by Christ behind their backs,
making them anonymous Christians whether they like it or not? What about
the Hindus who would find it an extraordinary theological sleight of hand to attribute all grace to Christ? Mr. Gangadaran, my Hindu friend from South India, is a Shaiva Siddhantin. His life is infused with a sense of God's love and
grace, as conveyed in the hymns of the Tamil saints, which he sings with as much
gusto as any Methodist sings those of Charles Wesley. But the voices of people
like Gangadaran do not really count in the Christian inclusivist frame of reference. The inclusivist viewpoint would be challenged by the independent voices
of other people of faith, people who do not wish to be obliterated by being included in someone else's scheme and on someone else's terms without being
heard in their own right.

The inclusivist viewpoint would also be challenged by the encounter with
other inclusivisms. The Muslim, for example, who would argue that all who
bow their heads and bend their wills to the one God are *muslims*, with a small
"m," is an inclusivist. So is the Buddhist abbot of Mount Hiei in Japan, who,
when he met Pope John Paul II, included him in the Buddhist family by pro-
nouncing him a reincarnation of the Buddhist monk Saicho. So was my Hindu
friend in Banaras who was certain that I had been a Hindu in my past life, which
explained my affinity for the holy city. So is the Vaishnava Hindu who sees all
truth and all paths as leading up to Krishna. In the Song of God, the Bhagavad
Gita, Krishna vows to receive all prayers offered, to whatever god, in whatever
name, for he is the recipient and lord of all worship.

> I am the way, sustainer, lord,
> witness, shelter, refuge, friend,
> source, dissolution, stability,
> treasure, and unchanging seed.

For those on the receiving end of the inclusivist's zeal, it often feels like a form
of theological imperialism to have their beliefs or prayers swept into the interpretive schema of another tradition. The inclusivist, however, is often not aware

of how it feels to be "included" in someone else's scheme. Inclusivists often simply assume, either in innocence or in confidence, that their worldview ultimately explains the whole. From each inclusivist point of view, it does. Mission, in its positive sense, whether Christian, Buddhist, or Muslim, is an outgrowth of such inclusivism—the "other" is not so much dangerous as immature and in need of further enlightenment. It was this way of thinking that lay behind Kipling's sense of "the white man's burden" to be the bearer of civilization. It was also this thinking that lay behind Swami Vivekananda's mission to bring spiritual growth to the immature and materialistic West.

Those of us who are English-speaking women readily recognize inclusivist strategies through our own experience of language. We are said to be included in terms and locutions that do not mention our name, like the "brotherhood of man." Women learned the rule of thumb men provided to cope with this problem: "men," of course, means "men and women," except in those instances in which it does not mean "men and women." The problem with inclusivism is clear. Inclusivism is a "majority consciousness," not necessarily in terms of numbers, but in terms of power. And the consciousness of the majority is typically "unconscious" because it is not tested and challenged by dialogue with dissenting voices. The danger of inclusivism is that it does not hear such voices at all.

The inclusivist, wittingly or unwittingly, thinks of himself or herself as the norm and uses words that reduce the other to that which is different: non-Christians, non-whites, non-Western. The economic inclusivist speaks of "developing" countries, as if all will be well when they are "developed" like us. The hierarchies built into inclusivism enable the inclusivist to assume uncritically that racial minorities, or "third-world" peoples, or women will come someday to share in "the system," and that the system will not change when they do. Inclusivists want to be inclusive—but only in the house that we ourselves have built. Such inclusivism can easily become the "communalism of the majority." Its presuppositions are unchallenged by alternatives. When the inclusivist really begins to listen to the voices of others, speaking in their own terms, the whole context of theological thought begins to change along the continuum toward pluralism.

Is "our God" listening? Of course, "our God" listens to the prayers of all people of faith, but it is "our" God who does the listening in the inclusivist view. We, after all, know perfectly well who God is, and if God is going to listen to the prayers of the Hindu uttered before the granite image of Vishnu, it is the God *we* know.

"There's a Wideness in God's Mercy"

For the Christian pluralist, there is no such God as "our" God. Humility or simple honesty before God requires that we not limit God to the God we know or to the particular language and image through which we know God. As Wilfred Cantwell Smith has repeatedly put it, God transcends our idea of God. We sing the hymn "There's a wideness in God's mercy, like the wideness of the sea. . . ." But what does it really mean to take seriously the wideness of God's mercy?

Religiously, the move to pluralism begins for Christians the moment we imagine that the one we call God is greater than our knowledge or understanding of God. It begins the moment we suspect that the God we know in Christ "listens," if we wish to put it that way, to the earnest prayers of people whose religious language and whose God we do not even understand. It is our understanding of the wideness of God's mercy that provides the theological impulse toward pluralism. And, as we shall see, it is also our confidence in Jesus, the Christ, who was open to all people regardless of religion or status, that pushes Christians into the wider world of faith.

For Christians, to stress God's transcendence does not take away the precious particularity of the Christian tradition, but it does take away our ability to claim the comprehensive, exhaustive universality of our own tradition. There are "other sheep," as Christ himself affirms, who are not of this fold (John 10:16). There are faces of the Divine that must lie beyond what we ourselves have glimpsed from our own sheepfold. It is God's transcendence which drives us to find out what others have known of God, seeking truly to know, as it was put at the Parliament, "how God has revealed himself in the other." It is God's transcendence which drives us to inquire more deeply into the insights of those Buddhists who do not speak of God at all.

In a Christian pluralist perspective, we do not need to build walls to exclude the view of the other, nor do we need to erect a universal canopy capable of gathering all the diverse tribes together under our own roof. We do not need to speak of "anonymous Christians." From a Christian pluralist standpoint, the multiplicity of religious ways is a concomitant of the ultimacy and many-sidedness of God, the one who cannot be limited or encircled by any one tradition. Therefore, the boundaries of our various traditions need not be the places where we halt and contend over our differences, but might well be the places where we meet and catch a glimpse of glory as seen by another.

This does not mean we cease speaking in our own language and adopt some neutral terminology, but it does mean that we cease speaking only to ourselves and in the terms of our own internal Christian conversation. We will speak in the context of interreligious dialogue. For example, as a Christian, I will continue to speak of God, of Christ, and of the Holy Spirit. I may speak of the "wideness of God's mercy," even though the Buddhist will see this as a particularly Christian or theistic way of understanding the grounds for pluralism. The Buddhist will continue to speak of the Buddha and the Dharma, the teachings of the Buddha. And some Buddhists may insist that the "positionless position" of a nondogmatic Buddhism is what clears the ground for pluralism. But my primary concern will not be to "include" the Buddhist in my terms, but to understand the Buddhist in his or her own terms, to test and broaden my own self-understanding in light of that encounter. Neither of us will speak as if the other did not exist or were not listening or could be absorbed into our own religious worldviews. And each of us will begin to understand our own traditions afresh in light of what we have learned from the other.

In the Christian pluralist perspective, the plurality of religions is not interpreted as a "problem" to be overcome. It is a fact of our world. And it is one we must encounter creatively if we are to make sense of the world. People have always and everywhere responded to what Christians would call "God's presence" among them. Perhaps this great human movement of seeking, and of finding, is part of what we speak of as "the providence of God." Saint Paul reminded those to whom he preached in Athens that "from one ancestor God made all nations to inhabit the whole earth, and he allotted the times of their existence and the boundaries of the places where they would live, so that they would search for God and perhaps grope for him and find him—though he is not far from each one of us. For 'In him we live and move and have our being,' as even some of your own poets have said, 'For we too are his offspring' " (Acts 17:26–28).

Despite Paul, there are many Christians who are happy to see people of other faiths as "searching and groping" for God, but are not so sure about the finding. In 1983, at the Vancouver General Assembly of the World Council of Churches, there was a heated debate over a single sentence in a report which recognized "the work of God in the lives of people of other faiths." Is God really at work in the lives and faith of others? Many delegates were not sure. A dozen substitute formulations were offered. There was scarcely time to consider the matter fully at the end of a steamy week in August. Finally, the assembly settled for a watered-down recognition of "God's creative work in the *seeking* for religious truth among people of other faiths."[24] In the confusion of plenary debate, delegates were finally uncertain about the "finding." But the apostle Paul was not uncertain. He did not leave others groping after the Divine. He acknowledged the finding as well as the seeking. How many Christian missionaries, like Paul, have thought to "bring God" to some part of Africa or Asia, only to find that the one they called God was already there. So if there is a "finding," is it not the imperative of the Godward heart to inquire after what has been found?

In January of 1990, the World Council of Churches called a theological consultation in the little village of Baar in Switzerland to address the theological confusion among Christians about what it means to speak of God's presence among people of other faiths. Protestant, Catholic, and Orthodox theologians formulated a statement of current thinking on the matter, beginning with an understanding of creation and the implications of affirming God as the creator of heaven and earth.

> We see the plurality of religious traditions as both the result of the manifold ways in which God has related to peoples and nations as well as a manifestation of the richness and diversity of humankind. We affirm that God has been present in their seeking and finding, that where there is truth and wisdom in their teachings, and love and holiness in their living, this, like any wisdom, insight, knowledge, understanding, love and holiness that is found among us, is the gift of the Holy Spirit. . . .
>
> This conviction that God as creator of all is present and active in the plurality of religions makes it inconceivable to us that God's saving activity could be confined to any one continent, cultural type, or group of peoples. A refusal to take seriously the many and diverse religious testimonies to be found among the nations and peoples of the whole world amounts to disowning the biblical testimony to God as creator of all things and father of all humankind.[25]

In some ways it is not so unlike the Catholic language of *Nostra Aetate*. There is much that is necessarily inclusivist in such a recasting of Christian language. And yet there is an important point of departure here. For if Christians acknowledge—as do those of us who forged this language at Baar—not only the "seeking" but the "finding" of God by people of other faiths, then the encounter with the Hindu or Muslim is truly an opportunity to deepen our knowledge and understanding of the one we call God. It is an occasion for truth-seeking dialogue—to offer our own testimony, to hear the testimonies of others in their own terms, to wrestle with the meaning of one another's terms, and to risk mutual transformation.

Within each tradition there are particular religious resources for the move toward the active, truth-seeking engagement with others that is the distinguishing mark of pluralism. And there are people in each religious tradition attempting to think afresh about their own identity within the context of interreligious dialogue. I speak of what I call "Christian pluralism," exploring the wider world of faith as a Christian. Jews who seek a context for pluralistic thinking often speak of God's ancient and unbroken covenant with the whole of humanity—the covenant with Noah signaled by the rainbow and spanning the earth as the sign of God's universal promise. Muslims also begin with the sovereignty of God, the creator of the universe, the sole judge in matters of truth, and the one who challenges the diverse religious communities to "compete in righteousness." As the Qur'an puts it, "If God had so willed, He would have made all of you one community, but He has not done so that He may test you in what He has given you; so compete in goodness. To God shall you all return and He will tell you the Truth about what you have been disputing" (5:48). Buddhists often refer to the Buddha's teaching of the interdependence of all things and remind us of the Buddha's simple statement about the raft of *dharma*, of religious practice, as a way of crossing the river; it is a vehicle, not an end in itself. Only the fool would reach the far shore and then, out of loyalty to the raft, pack it along with him. Hindus begin with the oneness and transcendence of what they call Sat—the Real, Truth. It is that which becomes known to human beings through many names and forms. It is that which human beings can no more comprehend as a whole than the blind men of the parable can comprehend the entirety of the elephant.

The aim of all this religious thinking is not to find the lowest common denominator or the most neutral religious language. Far from it. The aim is to find those particular places within each tradition that provide the open space where we may meet one another in mutual respect and develop, through dialogue, new ways of speaking and listening. The aim is not only mutual understanding, but mutual self-understanding and mutual transformation. As the Jewish scholar Jean Halperin put it at an interreligious consultation held in Mauritius in 1983, "We not only need to understand one another, we need one another to understand ourselves."[26]

The British philosopher and theologian John Hick has been a pioneer in pluralist thinking. He speaks of pluralism as the "Copernican revolution" in

ary theology. From a "Ptolemaic" Christian inclusivist position in
her traditions of wisdom or devotion were understood to revolve
the sun of the Christian tradition, their validity measured by their dis-
from the center, the Christian pluralist makes a radical move, insisting that
a e become aware of the traditions of Buddhists or Muslims, we must begin
to see that it is God or Ultimate Reality around which our human religious traditions revolve—not any one tradition or way of salvation. As Hick puts it,
"We have to realize that the universe of faiths centres upon God, and not upon
Christianity or upon any other religion. [God] is the sun, the originative source
of light and life, whom all the religions reflect in their own different ways."[27] For
Christians this means that others cannot simply move into our own orbit, but
must be seen and appreciated on their own terms, moving, as we ourselves do,
around that center which cannot be fully owned or claimed by any one tradition alone.

The World House:
Toward a Practical Understanding of Pluralism

The Copernican revolution is a good image for dramatizing the revolution in religious understanding that we are now experiencing. It is as dramatic as Coper-
nicus's discovery that what we thought was at the center of our universe turned
out not to be. God always transcends what we humans can apprehend or understand. No tradition can claim the Holy or the Truth as its private property. As
Gandhi put it so succinctly, "Revelation is the exclusive property of no nation,
no tribe."[28]

Every image has its limitations, however, and that of the Copernican revolution and the new solar cosmos is no exception. We know today, for example,
that ours is but one of a number of solar systems, so even the heliocentric universe has its limits. Anyway, the paradigm of all the great religions sailing
around the center on their own particular orbits is not entirely satisfactory. It
lacks the dynamic interaction of the world in which we live. Our worlds and our
worldviews are not on separate orbits, but bump up against one another all the
time, even collide. People of different religious traditions do not live apart, but
are in constant interaction and need, if anything, to be in more intentional interrelation. A theocentricity patterned after the solar system will not carry us far as
an image for our new world, for our problem is not only our understanding of

Truth, but our relationship to one another. We need a more interactive way of thinking.

If the move toward pluralism begins theologically in the places where people of different traditions find an openness—and even an imperative—toward encounter with one another, it begins historically and culturally with the plain fact of our religious diversity, our cultural proximity to one another, and our human interdependence. In very practical terms, how are we all to live with one another in a climate of mutuality and understanding? Is it even possible? Those who live according to an exclusivist paradigm frankly do not wish to live closely with people of other faiths and would prefer to shut them out—which is increasingly impossible—or to convert others to their own view of the world. Those who appropriate differences, as do the inclusivists, assume that the worldview of others looks very much like their own, and the ground rules are presumed to be "ours." But those who think about life together as pluralists recognize the need for radical new forms of living together and communicating with one another.

What, then, is pluralism? The word has been used so widely and freely as a virtual synonym for such terms as *relativism, subjectivism, multiculturalism,* and *globalism* that we need to stop for a moment and think clearly about what it does and does not mean. Pluralism is but one of several responses to diversity and to modernity. It is an interpretation of plurality, an evaluation of religious and cultural diversity. And finally it is the ability to make a home for oneself and one's neighbors in that multifaceted reality.

First, pluralism is not the sheer fact of plurality alone, but is active engagement with plurality. Pluralism and plurality are sometimes used as if they were synonymous. But plurality is just diversity, plain and simple—splendid, colorful, maybe even threatening. Diversity does not, however, have to affect me. I can observe it. I can even celebrate diversity, as the cliche goes. But I have to *participate* in pluralism. I can't just stand by and watch.

Religious and cultural diversity can be found just about everywhere—in Britain and Brazil, in the ethnic enclaves of the former Eastern bloc, in New Delhi and in Denver, in the workplace and in schools. Pluralist models for successfully engaging diverse peoples in an energetic community, however, are relatively rare. In the Elmhurst area of Queens, for example, a *New York Times* reporter found people from eleven countries on a single floor of an apartment building on Justice Avenue. There were immigrants from Korea, Haiti, Vietnam, Nigeria, and India—all living in isolation and fear—each certain that they were the only immigrants there.[29] Diversity to be sure, but not pluralism.

Mere cosmopolitanism should also not be mistaken for pluralism. In Cambridge, Massachusetts—which, like Queens, is highly cosmopolitan—Muslims, Christians, Jews, and Buddhists live along with many people who have no active or passive identification with any religious faith at all. The whole world seems to live in this small city. There is cultural diversity and diversity of style; anyone sitting in the sidewalk cafés of Harvard Square will observe the parade of Cambridge life. But again, the mere presence of wide-ranging religious diversity is not itself pluralism. Religious pluralism requires active positive engagement with the claims of religion and the facts of religious diversity. It involves not the mere recognition of the different religious traditions and the insuring of their legitimate rights, but the active effort to understand difference and commonality through dialogue.

Second, pluralism is not simply tolerance, but also the seeking of understanding. Tolerance is a deceptive virtue. I do not wish to belittle tolerance, but simply to recognize that it is not a real response to the challenging facts of difference. Tolerance can enable coexistence, but it is certainly no way to be good neighbors. In fact, tolerance often stands in the way of engagement. If as a Christian I tolerate my Muslim neighbor, I am not therefore required to understand her, to seek out what she has to say, to hear about her hopes and dreams, to hear what it meant to her when the words "In the name of Allah, the Merciful, the Compassionate" were whispered into the ear of her newborn child.

Tolerance does not take us far with ideas that challenge our own. For a majority people, tolerance is simply another expression of privilege. As the philosopher Elizabeth Spelman puts it, "If one is in a position to allow someone else to do something, one is also in a position to keep that person from doing it. To tolerate your speaking is to refrain from exercising the power I have to keep you from speaking. . . . And of course I don't have to listen to what you have to say. . . . Tolerance is easy if those who are asked to express it needn't change a whit."[30]

Tolerance is, of course, a set forward from active hostility. When the mosque in Quincy was set ablaze by arson, when a mosque in Houston was fire-bombed at the time of a Middle East airplane hijacking, when the Hindu-Jain temple in Pittsburgh was vandalized and the images of the deities smashed, and when a group of youngsters soaped swastikas on windows and cars in Wellesley, people called for tolerance—an unquestionable virtue under the circumstances. There are many places in the world where the emergence of a culture of tolerance would be a step forward—when religious, racial, and ethnic rivalries flash into violence in Northern Ireland, in India, in the Sudan or Nigeria, or in Los Angeles or Miami. But tolerance is a long way from pluralism.

As a style of living together, tolerance is too minimal an expectation. Indeed, it may be a passive form of hostility. Christians can tolerate their Jewish neighbors and protect their civil liberties without having to know anything about them and without having to reconsider some of the roots of Christian anti-Semitism. Tolerance alone does nothing to remove our ignorance of one another by building bridges of exchange and dialogue. It does not require us to know anything new, it does not even entertain the fact that we ourselves might change in the process. Tolerance might sustain a temporary and shaky truce, but it will never bring forth a new creation.

Third, pluralism is not simply relativism, but assumes real commitment. In a world of religious pluralism, commitments are not checked at the door. This is a critical point to see plainly, because through a cynical intellectual sleight of hand some critics have linked pluralism with a valueless relativism—an undiscriminating twilight in which "all cats are gray," all perspectives equally viable, and as a result, equally uncompelling. In saying that pluralism is not simply relativism, I do not wish to side with today's slippery critics of relativism, such as Allan Bloom, who stigmatize openness and cultural relativism as new academic dogmas. My main points is to distinguish pluralism from certain kinds of relativism. While there are similarities between pluralism and relativism, the difference between the two is important: Relativism assumes a stance of openness; pluralism assumes both openness *and* commitment.

Relativism, like pluralism, is an interpretation of diversity. It is also a word with many meanings. On the whole, relativism simply means that what we know of the world and of truth we can only know through a particular framework. In this, the pluralist would agree—what we speak of as truth is relative to our cultural and historical standpoint as well as the frame of reference through which we see it. What is true is always "true *for*" someone, for there is always a point of view—conditioned in multiple ways by whether one is Christian or Muslim, American or Asian, male or female, rich or poor, a prosperous farmer or a homeless refugee. Matters of truth and value are relative to our conceptual framework and worldview, even those matters of truth that we speak of as divinely ordained.

Relativism, then, to a certain extent is a commonsense interpretation of di-

versity. It is clear that what I hold as truth is historically relative. If I had lived
in the fourteenth century, I would likely have held the world to be flat. What I
hold as truth is also culturally and religiously relative. As a Christian, I know that
the Muslim who speaks of justice and human community appeals to the authority of the Qur'an as energetically as I appeal to the authority of Jesus or
the Bible. It is indisputable that certain "facts" of my childhood learning, such
as "Columbus discovered America," were accurate only from a European
point of view. From the standpoint of the native peoples of this continent, "the
discovery" was perhaps more accurately an invasion. And as for morality, it is
clear that in some frames of reference, the Hindu or Jain for instance, any willful
taking of life, including animal life, is rejected; vegetarianism is religiously en-
joined and culturally presupposed. Through other frames of reference, including ours in most of the Christian West, there is little religious debate about
the moral dimensions of what we should eat. But when it comes to the taking of
human life—through war, capital punishment, or abortion—there are religious people lined up on both sides of every argument with evidence to support
their views.

A thoughtful relativist is able to point out the many ways in which our cogni-
tive and moral understandings are relative to our historical, cultural, and ideological contexts. So far, the pluralist would be a close cousin. But there are two
shades of relativism that are antithetical to pluralism. The first is nihilistic relativism, which denies the very heart of religious truth. One of the common strategies for diffusing the challenge of religious and ideological difference is to insist
that there is no ultimate centering value, no one life-compelling truth. For the
nihilistic relativist, the impossibility of universalizing any one truth claim suggests the emptiness of all truth claims. According to Spelman, the nihilist says,
"If I can't maintain my position of privilege by being the sole arbiter of truth, I
at least can insist that no one is."[31] If all religions say different things, this only
proves that all of them are false. As we well know, nihilistic relativism is not the
property of any one culture or continent today. It is a truly worldwide phenomenon, just as religious exclusivism and secular materialism are worldwide phenomena. As Abraham Joshua Heschel puts it, "We must choose between interfaith and inter-nihilism."[32]

The second shade of relativism that must clearly be distinguished from pluralism is a relativism that lacks commitment. There are relativists who are committed Jews, Christians, and Hindus who speak of commitment to "relative

absolutes," recognizing the relativity of those symbols we hold as "absolute." There are many more, however, who are completely uncommitted, which is why relativism is equated by some critics with laissez-faire plurality. Mind you, the uncommitted certainly have a place in the dialogue of a pluralistic world, but the heart of the issue with which we struggle is the difficult, potentially explosive, and potentially vibrant encounter of people with strong and very different commitments. Pluralism can only generate a strong social fabric through the interweaving of commitments. If people perceive pluralism as entailing the relinquishing of their particular religious commitments they are not interested. Neither am I.

Relativism for me and for many others becomes a problem when it means the lack of commitment to any particular community or faith. If everything is more or less true, I do not give my heart to anything in particular. There is no beloved community, no home in the context of which values are tested, no dream of the ongoing transformation of that community. Thus the relativist can remain uncommitted, a perpetual shopper or seeker, set apart from a community of faith, suffering from spiritual ennui. Indeed relativism as a view in itself is often identified with secularism and the disavowal of any religious faith.

The pluralist, on the other hand, stands in a particular community and is willing to be committed to the struggles of that community, even as restless critic. I would argue that there is no such thing as a generic pluralist. There are Christian pluralists, Hindu pluralists, and even avowedly humanistic pluralists—all daring to be themselves, not in isolation from but in relation to one another. Pluralists recognize that others also have communities and commitments. They are unafraid to encounter one another and realize that they must all live with each other's particularities. The challenge for the pluralist is commitment without dogmatism and community without communalism. The theological task, and the task of a pluralist society, is to create the space and the means for the encounter of commitments, not to neutralize all commitment.

The word *credo*, so important in the Christian tradition, does not mean "I believe" in the sense of intellectual assent to this and that proposition. It means "I give my heart to this." It is an expression of my heart's commitment and my life's orientation. Relativism may be an appropriate intellectual answer to the problem of religious diversity—all traditions are relative to history and culture. But it cannot be an adequate answer for most religious people—not for me, nor for my Muslim neighbor who fasts and prays more regularly than I do, nor for my

Hindu colleague whose world is made vivid by the presence of Krishna. We live our lives and die our deaths in terms of cherished commitments. We are not relatively committed.

Pluralism is not, then, the kind of radical openness to anything and everything that drains meaning from particularity. It is, however, radical openness to Truth—to God—that seeks to enlarge understanding through dialogue. Pluralism is the complex and unavoidable encounter, difficult as it might be, with the multiple religions and cultures that are the very stuff of our world, some of which may challenge the very ground on which we stand. Unless all of us can encounter one another's religious visions and cultural forms and understand them through dialogue, both critically and self-critically, we cannot begin to live with maturity and integrity in the world house.

Fourth, pluralism is not syncretism, but is based on respect for differences Syncretism is the creation of a new religion by the fusing of diverse elements of different traditions. There have been many syncretistic religions in history. In the fourth century B.C.E., the Ptolemaic kings fused Greek and Egyptian elements in the cult of Serapis to aid in the consolidation of empire. In the third century, Mani interwove strands from the Zoroastrian, Buddhist, and Christian traditions to create Manichaeism. The Mughal emperor Akbar's Din-i-Ilahi ("Divine Faith") brought together Hindu and Jain philosophy, Muslim mysticism, and Zoroastrian fire sacrifice in sixteenth-century India. To a certain extent what goes by the name of New Age religion today is an informal religious syncretism, piecing together a package of spiritual aids from Native American ritual, Hindu yoga and Ayurvedic medicine, Buddhist meditation, and Sufi and Christian mysticism. Of course it goes without saying that there is a process of adaptation and enculturation that is part and parcel of every tradition as it enters into the life of new peoples and new cultural contexts. The discussion of whether this is or is not "syncretism" is a long one and hinges too much on terminology to detain us here.

There are some critics who imagine, however, that pluralism is aimed at generating a new syncretistic religion knit together from the most universal or most interesting elements of various world religions. Or that pluralism is a kind of global shopping mall where each individual puts together a basket of appealing religious ideas. Or that pluralism will reduce each tradition to the bland unity of the lowest common denominator. So it is important to say, once again, that pluralism, while not plurality, is based on plurality. A pluralist culture will not flatten out differences, but has respect for differences and the encounter of differences. Its aim is quite the opposite of syncretism. While common language will be crafted out of the give-and-take of dialogue, there is no attempt to make up a common language, to produce a kind of religious esperanto that all would speak.

There are religious traditions that have an open and somewhat syncretistic flavor today. The Unitarian Universalists, for example, who hold a humanitarian view of Jesus and a wide respect for other religious teachers, often include the prayers and scriptures of many traditions in their worship. The ecclecticism of some Unitarian congregations today includes neopagan and neo-Hindu influences as well as a strong Christian universalism. The Baha'is build a similar appreciative stance toward religious diversity into their various temples. In New Delhi, for example, there is a splendid new Baha'i temple built in the shape of a lotus and housing a number of shrines around its central sanctuary, one for each of the religious traditions, all brought together under one roof.

The aim of pluralism, however, is quite different. It is not to create a world-wide temple of all faiths. It is rather to find ways to be distinctively ourselves and yet be in relation to one another. No doubt there is common ground to be discovered along the way; no doubt there are common aspirations to be articulated. But joining together in a new "world religion" based on the lowest common denominator or pieced together from several religious traditions is not the goal of pluralism. In some ways, it is the very antithesis of pluralism.

Fifth, pluralism is based on interreligious dialogue. The isolation or dogmatism of the exclusivist is not open to dialogue. The inclusivist, while open to dialogue, does not really hear the self-understanding of the other. The truth seeking of the pluralist, however, can be built on no other foundation than the give-and-take of dialogue. There is something we must know—both about the other and about ourselves—that can be found in no other way.

We do not enter into dialogue with the dreamy hope that we will all agree, for the truth is we probably will not. We do not enter into dialogue to produce an agreement, but to produce real relationship, even friendship, which is premised upon mutual understanding, not upon agreement. Christians and Muslims, for example, may find we agree on many things. We share prophets like Abraham and foundational values like justice. But a clear understanding of differences is as precious as the affirmation of similarities.

The language of dialogue is the two-way language of real encounter and it is for this reason that dialogue is the very basis of pluralism. There must be constant communication—meeting, exchange, traffic, criticism, reflection, reparation, renewal. Without dialogue, the diversity of religious traditions, of cultures and ethnic groups, becomes an array of isolated encampments, each with a different flag, meeting only occasionally for formalities or for battle. The swamis, monks, rabbis, and archbishops may meet for an interfaith prayer breakfast, but without real dialogue they become simply icons of diversity, not instruments of relationship. Without dialogue, when violence flares—in Queens or Los Angeles, Southall or New Delhi—there are no bridges of relationship, and as the floodwaters rise it is too late to build them.

A second aim of dialogue is to understand ourselves and *our* faith more clearly. Dialogue is not a debate between two positions, but a truth-seeking encounter. If Muslims assume that the taking and giving of interest on loans is morally wrong and Christians embedded in a capitalist framework never thought to question the matter, what can we learn from one another? If Buddhists describe the deepest reality without reference to God and Christians cannot imagine religiousness without God, what will each of us learn that is quite new, through the give-and-take of dialogue? The theologian John Cobb has used the phrase "mutual transformation" to describe the way in which dialogue necessarily goes beyond mutual understanding to a new level of mutual self-understanding.

The Sri Lankan Christian theologian Wesley Ariarajah has spoken of dialogue as the "encounter of commitments." When dialogue was first discussed broadly and ecumenically by the Christian churches at the assembly of the World Council of Churches in Nairobi in 1975, there was much heated discussion. A bishop of the Church of Norway led the attack, calling dialogue a betrayal of Christian mission. The church should be engaged in proclaiming the Gospel to the ends of the earth and making disciples of all nations, not in interreligious dialogue, he said. There were many, then and now, who saw dialogue as a sign of weakness of faith. Ariarajah and many others have insisted that quite the opposite is true. What kind of faith refuses to be tested by real encounter with others? What kind of faith grows by speaking and proclaiming without having to listen, perhaps even be challenged, by the voices of others?

Discovering one's own faith is inherently part of the human pilgrimage. What motivates us deeply, what orients us in the world, what nourishes our growth and gives rise to our most cherished values? Every human being must cope with these questions or suffer the anxious drift of avoiding them. But our challenges on the human pilgrimage are not solved once and for all by the unfolding discovery of our own faith, for we encounter other pilgrims of other

faiths. Dialogue means taking a vibrant interest in what motivates thes
pilgrims, what orients them in the world, what nourishes their growth a...
rise to their most cherished values. To live together we need to know these things
about one another and to risk the changes of heart and mind that may well come
when we do.

There is a third aim of dialogue. Mutual understanding and mutual transformation are important, but in the world in which we live, the cooperative
transformation of our global and local cultures is essential. It is surely one of the
most challenging tasks of our time. Buddhists and Hindus, Muslims and Jews,
Maoris and Christians have urgent work to do that can only be done together. As
Wilfred Cantwell Smith so succinctly put it, "Our vision and our loyalties, as
well as our aircraft, must circle the globe."[33]

Supernatural
Extrovertisan

CHAPTER 8

The Imagined Community

Spiritual Interdependence and a Wider Sense of "We"

AT THE closing session of the World's Parliament of Religions in 1893, its president and one of the chief visionaries of the Parliament, Charles Bonney, declared, "Henceforth the religions of the world will make war not on each other, but on the giant evils that afflict mankind!"[1] None of us can read these words without a sigh of sadness and perhaps a tinge of cynicism. The past one hundred years have scarcely borne out Bonney's vision. Interfaith cooperation has gotten a good start, but interfaith violence has kept pace. The world's religious traditions still manage to provide fuel for the world's strife. The giant evils that afflict humankind have grown as rapidly as our dreams; the chasms between the cultural, racial, and religious families of humankind have opened as quickly as the bridges we have built to span them. Each day's newspapers remind us that Sikhs and Hindus struggle with one another in India, Christians and Muslims in the Philippines and Nigeria, Jews and African-American Muslims in the United States, Catholics and Protestants in Northern Ireland. These struggles are not wholly religious in origin, but they are made more difficult and complex by the extensive use of religious language and symbolism. The encounter of people of differing faiths in the world today, for better and for worse, is one of the most important facts of our time.

There are many ways of describing the world scene in the late twentieth century. There are alarming statistics on population growth and the growth of dire poverty and illiteracy. There are statistics on the growth of carbon dioxide emissions, on the pollution of the seas, the stripping of the forests, the extinction of species of plant and animal life. There are statistics on the high rate of infant mortality, on disease and death in children, on prostitution and the sexual enslavement of women, on the worldwide growth of vast populations of refugees. Above all, there is the growing recognition that these problems are all interrelated. The one word which increasingly describes the complexity and relatedness of the world is *interdependent*. The problems cannot be isolated one from the other and neither can the people who hope to solve them.

The 1987 publication of *Our Common Future*, the report of the United Nations World Commission on Environment and Development, makes clear the ecological interdependence of the world—the transnational consequences of acid rain, deforestation, nuclear testing, flooding, and desertification. The overuse of land, the creation of vast deserts, and the cycles of famine are not just Africa's problem; the erosion of the ozone layer above the Antarctic is not just Antarctica's problem; the effects of the nuclear disaster at Chernobyl are not just Russia's problem. More than any single issue, the environmental crisis has enabled a much more nuanced understanding of what this word *interdependence* means. It means we as a whole suffer the consequences of the part, and as a whole we must address the solution. None of us can "go it alone" as peoples or nations to solve these problems. A glimpse of Earth, "the blue planet," beamed back from space should be enough to convince us that there is no longer any such thing as "alone" in this interdependent world.

In a set of lectures given in the late 1930s, the Indian philosopher Radhakrishnan, then at Oxford University, saw the beginnings of the world's interdependence and raised the question of its implications:

> For the first time in the history of our planet its inhabitants have become one whole, each and every part of which is affected by the fortunes of every other. Science and technology, without aiming at this result, have achieved the unity. Economic and political phenomena are increasingly imposing on us the obligation to treat the world as a unit. Currencies are linked, commerce is international, political fortunes are interdependent. And yet the sense that mankind must become a community is still a casual whim, a vague aspiration, not generally accepted as a conscious ideal or an urgent practical necessity moving us to feel the dignity of a common citizenship and the call of a common duty.[2]

Radhakrishnan spoke of the "ferment of restlessness" created by modernity. "The world has found itself as one body," he said. "But physical unity and economic interdependence are not by themselves sufficient to create a universal human community. . . . The cause of the present tension and disorder is the lack of adjustment between the process of life, which is one of increasing interdependence, and the 'ideology' of life, the integrating habits of mind, loyalties, and affections embodied in our laws and institutions. . . . The supreme task of our generation is to give a soul to the growing world consciousness."[3]

Interdependence describes not only the inextricable relatedness of nations and economies, but also that of peoples, religious traditions, and cultures. Religious interdependence is a reality of our world and interreligious dialogue a necessity, an instrument of our common work to transform the world in which we live. Interreligious dialogue is a basic communication network and it has an extensive ethical and practical agenda. Terms like "peace" and "justice" will become nothing but the well-intentioned yet meaningless slogans of our separate tribes if they are not understood to involve a serious commitment toward working in partnership with people of other faiths.

The phrase "global village" has become a common way of referring to the ever-smaller world in which we live. But what does it mean in human terms? If our world were a village of a thousand people, who would *we* be? The World Development Forum tells us that there would be 329 Christians, 174 Muslims, 131 Hindus, 61 Buddhists, 52 Animists, 3 Jews, 34 members of other religions, such as Sikhs, Jains, Zoroastrians, and Baha'is, and 216 would be without any religion. In this village, there would be 564 Asians, 210 Europeans, 86 Africans, 80 South Americans, and 60 North Americans. And in this same village, 60 persons would have half the income, 500 would be hungry, 600 would live in shantytowns, and 700 would be illiterate.[4]

For North American Christians, most of whom would be among the sixty in the world with half the income, it is a sobering reality. We like to think that we would not tolerate such economic inequity in our own village, so how is it that we tolerate it in the world? We are not simply evil or uncaring. The answer to such a question has to do with a single word—the word *we*. The casual *we* for most of us does not include the 50 percent hungry, the 60 percent in shantytowns, and the 70 percent illiterate. Most of us construct our *we* without including *them*. Thinking of the world close up, as if it were a village of one thousand people, forces us to confront what we mean when we say 'we.' As Wilfred Cantwell Smith used to say, the meaning of that word *we* constitutes one of the most important facts about any people.[5] Is it we Christians, we Protestants, we Americans, we scholars, we human beings? Our *we* will include different people at different times and we need to signal this in our writing and speaking. Sometimes in these pages I have meant we Christians, sometimes we people of religious faith, sometimes we human beings whether or not we are explicitly involved in a religious tradition.

Here I ask of all of us, how often does our *we* come to include people of other faiths, other nations, other races? How often does our *we* link rather than divide? Our relation with the "other" may move, as Smith puts it, through a number of phases. First we talk *about* them—an objective "other." Then perhaps we talk *to* them, or more personally, we talk to you. Developing a real dialogue, we talk *with* you. And finally, we all talk with one another about us, all of us. This is the crucial stage to which our interreligious dialogue must take us if we are to be up to the task of creating communication adequate for an interdependent world.[6]

There is *we* language in every religious tradition, for the *we* issue is not simply a sociological matter but a theological issue, inextricably related to our deepest religious values. Hindus speak of the whole world as a single family—*vasudhaiva kutumbakam*. Buddhists speak of the *sangha* of the four directions; Muslims find ways of interpreting the *umma*, the Muslim community, in a broader and more open sense to include all people who have aligned their lives toward God. Jews speak of God's covenant with Noah as a covenant with all who keep basic moral precepts. There may be isolationists and survivalists who see the future in terms of the widening of the distance between *we* and *them*. But in every tradition there are also these currents of thinking that are attempts to steer toward a wider *we*, a *we* that links rather than divides.

In the Christian tradition, there is the language of the *oikos*, the household. The Gospel of John speaks of the household of God in which there are many rooms, many mansions. From this term *oikos* comes the word *oikoumene* (or *ecumene*), which means the household of the "whole inhabited earth." It is not surprising that the Christian ecumenical movement found this term expressive of the worldwide reach of the church, a worldwide household. And yet clearly the "whole inhabited earth" is not Christian. In the Office on Interreligious Relations at the WCC headquarters in Geneva, a poster bears the reminder "*Oikoumene* is the whole inhabited earth—Not just the Christian part of it."

The word *ecumenical* is also related to those other household words *economics* and *ecology*. Both are reminders of the household dynamics that hold the whole world together. Economy is the management of a household or of a society ordered after the manner of a household. In a household, if 6 percent of the people had half the wealth, that 6 percent would not be seen as successful, but as un-just. Ecology is concerned with understanding the interrelated household of liv-ing and non-living beings. Even the most seemingly insignificant or humble being is critical to the balance of the larger whole. To think ecumenically, ecologi-cally, and economically is to think about the world and its interrelations with the same loyalty and care that one brings to the consideration of one's own household.

Here again, India has cast up a teacher who has pointed the way to a larger sense of *we* for me and for many Christians—M. K. Gandhi. As we have glimpsed in earlier chapters, Gandhi's life is a good example of the potential meanings of pluralism. He was both committed to his own Hindu tradition and open to dialogue with others. The dialogue went beyond mutual understanding to real mutual transformation. In relation to Christians especially, he both taught and learned a great deal. His reverence for the way of Christ became part of who he was as a Hindu, but he did not become a Christian. He not only sought to recast and enlarge the *we*, he sought to create communities on the basis of that larger *we* and to commit their energies to the transformation of society.

Gandhi's Re-creation of the We

For years I acquiesced in the commonly held notion that there was nothing left of Gandhi in India but his name and his portrait, much revered and much for-gotten. During the early years of my work in Banaras, I lived among Hindus in the most old-fashioned of Hindu cities. There were times when I imagined that I could have been living in the seventeenth century. When I finished my book on Banaras, I took a deep breath of twentieth-century Indian air, spent more time in Delhi, and began meeting people who were more my own contemporaries and counterparts—intellectuals, activists, and feminists. To my surprise, I dis-covered that many of these people thought of themselves as Gandhians.

There was Devaki Jain, an economist and feminist who had established a net-work of support for hundreds of grass-roots agencies all over India that address themselves to the needs of women, who are the poorest of the poor. There was her husband, Lakshmi, who for years had been head of the All-India Handi-crafts Board, generating cottage industry at the village level. They were con-scious daily of what it meant to be consumers; they did not wear or buy anything, if they could help it, that was not produced or sold by the poor. Then there was Ela Bhatt, founder of the Self-Employed Women's Association in Ahmedabad, which organized self-employed women into cooperatives, occupational networks, and credit unions. "Self-employed" meant street vendors, paper scavengers, kerosene vendors, home spinners, cigarette rollers—all women who had previously had nothing and no one to rely on as social and financial support in times of crisis, sickness, or indebtedness. There was the formidable and venerable Kamaladevi Chattopadhyaya, who had been one of the first women to join Gandhi on the Salt March and who was one of the founders of the modern women's movement in India. And there was Radha Bhatt, who headed a Gandhian ashram in the Kumaon areas of the Himalayas, a productive community of girls and women dedicated to basic education, self-sufficiency, and environmental education. In the next valley over, the environmentalist Sundarlal Bahuguna helped to launch the Chipko movement, which has effectively stopped the widespread deforestation and erosion by the lumber companies, using the only power the villagers had at their disposal—fearlessness. They embraced the trees, saying, "Let the axes fall first upon our backs."

I began to realize that the Gandhian movement in India was perhaps small, but it was active and very much alive. While some were concerned with electoral politics, most were involved with what Gandhi had called "constructive work," meaning work for real change at the village level. Like Gandhi, they were concerned with the transformation of society, not simply with replacing the names and faces in government offices, so to those who look only at what governments do they were relatively invisible. I recalled that it was Gandhi, more than any one else in the Indian freedom movement, who insisted that India's freedom could not be brought about simply by changing who was in power. Gandhi had always been critical of what he called "British rule without the British"; freedom could only come by deep-seated change within the Indian people themselves. In 1914 Gandhi wrote, "The English have not taken India, we have given it to them. They are not in India because of their strength, but because we keep them."[7] He believed that India would be free in the most important sense the moment people began to think of themselves as free and to act as free.

In reconstituting the *we*, Gandhi was ahead of his time in speaking of solidarity with the poor and oppressed. He was the advance guard of what would later be liberation theology, with its "preferential option for the poor." It is little wonder that he has been read and studied by those who have directed their lives to human liberation—Howard Thurman, Martin Luther King, Jr., Adolfo Perez Esquivel, Ernesto Cardenal, Nelson Mandela. At the Gandhi *samadhi* in

Delhi, the place of Gandhi's cremation and last rites, there is an inscription known as "Gandhi's talisman" chiselled in the marble. "I will give you a talisman. Whenever you are in doubt or when the self becomes too much with you, try the following expedient: Recall the face of the poorest and the most helpless person whom you may have seen and ask yourself if the step you contemplate is going to be of any use to him."

What attracted me to Gandhi was the fact that he took seriously and personally the teachings of the Sermon on the Mount, which he thought should "revolutionize the whole of life," but which most Christians praise and do not practice: identifying with the poor, loving one's enemies, absorbing insults and returning love. Gandhi said, "If, then, I had to face only the Sermon on the Mount and my own interpretation of it, I should not hesitate to say: 'Oh yes, I am a Christian.' . . . But I can tell you that, in my humble opinion, much of what passes as Christianity is a negation of the Sermon on the Mount."[8] Gandhi considered himself a follower of Jesus, but he did not respect the dogmatism he saw in much of the Christian tradition. He did not like the preachers who had stood in his native town of Rajkot pouring abuse on the Hindu gods; he did not like the arrogance of some forms of Christian mission, holding Truth tight-fistedly as if it were an exclusive possession, and a club at that. For Gandhi, Truth, or God, cannot be the exclusive possession of any one people, but is the very transcendence of ourselves that calls us into relationship with others. Gandhi also did not like the materialism he saw in Christian culture, nor the violence. And he did not think all of this was worthy of the teachings of Christ.

In re-creating the *we*, Gandhi began at the household level or with the village of one thousand people; his vision was to extend the ethics, the care, and the common sense of the household to the whole of humankind. He began with the symbols of the domestic, the immediate, the near at hand. In religion, this means that the locus of religious life is not to be sought afar, by leaving home and society to journey to the far shore, the horizon, the frontier. The proper arena for religious life is not the Himalayas or the hermitage—not out there, but right here in the interrelatedness and struggles of the household and the village, on the "frontiers of encounter." This is where the *we* must be reconstituted: in how one behaves as well as in what one believes. Gandhi's favorite Christian hymn was "Lead Kindly Light," which includes the words "Guide Thou my feet . . . I do not ask to see . . . the distant scene . . . one step enough for me." That last line, "one step enough for me," became something of a slogan for Gandhi's distinctive style of leadership; he saw each step of the process to be as important as the horizon toward which it was aimed, for each step of the process creates the result.

Gandhi's *we* included the poor and the oppressed. In Gandhi's world this included, among others, the indentured laborers of South Africa, the landless farmers of rural northern India, and the "untouchables," whom he called Harijans, "children of God." "It is a mystery to me how anyone can feel himself honored by the humiliation of a fellow being," he said. Gandhian thinking about the deeply rooted sense of purity and pollution that produced untouchability in Hindu India was revolutionary. He did not simply protest. There was no march on Delhi to eliminate untouchability. He did something far more radical: he cleaned the latrines himself, he volunteered in the hospital and emptied bedpans, he took on the work of untouchables. He invited others to do the same. He publicly ate with untouchables. He adopted an untouchable girl as his own and insisted that an untouchable family become part of the Sabarmati Ashram. He spoke of himself as "touchable by birth, and untouchable by choice."

Similarly, when it came to the life-and-death issue of food and clothing, Gandhi did not speak of charity, but of the transformation of the life of the rich to identify with the basic needs of the poor. Many think of Gandhi's personal austerity, including his food and dress, as one of his idiosyncrasies. For Gandhi, however, what one eats and what one wears are the very first political decisions one makes. The "personal" is the "political." In Gandhi's view there is no point in speaking of the oppression of the poor or of economic injustice as a matter of public policy if all of us continue to support the status quo through the personal choices we make every day. He chose to eat little and simply—no more than five articles of food a day. He chose to dress simply—in the cotton *dhoti* and sandals of villagers.

His book *Hind Swaraj* ("Indian Home Rule") sets out many of the themes of Gandhi's political and economic thought. For Gandhi, home rule truly begins at home. It is not "British rule without the British." It begins the moment we set our own house in order, clean up our own latrines, spin our own cloth, and free ourselves of the oppression that is within us. When Gandhi came to leadership in the Indian National Congress in the early 1920s, it was a movement of English-educated Indians in suits and bowler hats, looking very much like their British counterparts. How could most of village India, poor as it was, participate in such a movement? They could participate only if the English-educated lawyers would give up their suits made of cloth spun in Lancashire and take up the hand spinning and hand weaving that had been destroyed by the British Raj. Gandhi did not launch a verbal or legislative campaign against the imported cotton goods that had decimated the Indian handloom industry. From the rural women of Gujarat he learned hand spinning with the simplest of spinning wheels. From 1925 on, membership dues in the Indian National Congress were to be paid not in cash, but in homespun yarn made and worn by every member. Spinning became the declaration of India's freedom as well as the evidence of the freedom movement's solidarity with the poor.

Gandhi redefined the inclusive *we* not just in theory, but in practice. The ashram communities he created—Phoenix Farm and Tolstoy Farm in South Africa, Sabarmati and Sevagram ashrams in India—were attempts to expand radically the meaning of "family" and to extend the ethics of the family to a larger community inclusive of caste, religion, and race. In the ashrams everyone shared domestic duties—cooking, sweeping, cleaning latrines, and emptying chamberpots. The *we* included women and men, Hindus and Muslims, Christians and Jews, Brahmins and untouchables. "Distinctions of caste were not observed," he wrote. "Untouchability had not only no place in Ashram, but its eradication from Hindu society was one of our principal objectives. Emancipation of women from some customary bonds was insisted upon from the first. Therefore women in the Ashram enjoy full freedom. Then again, it was an Ashram rule that persons following a particular faith should have the same feeling for followers of other faiths as for their co-religionists."[9]

Gandhi saw the ashram as a religious community. But for him the ashram was not a "retreat" from the world, as the teaching ashrams of ancient India had been, but rather a microcosm and crucible for a new world. Gandhi used to say that everywhere religious devotees and tillers of the soil get up early. "Four a.m. is not early," he said in his instructions to his community, "but the latest time when we must be up and doing."[10] Getting "up and doing" included a foundation of daily prayer, which began and ended each day's schedule in the ashram. Gandhi's daily prayer meetings, usually held in the open air, attracted hundreds of people. Since people from many religious traditions were part of the ashram communities, the prayer meetings included readings from the Qur'an, the Gita, and the Bible; they included Christian hymns and Sikh *bhajans*. This tradition is still very much a part of the Gandhian way. At the headquarters of the Self-Employed Women's Association in Ahmedabad, I joined in the women's daily morning prayer, which included both Hindu and Muslim readings. At

Lakshmi Ashram in the Himalayas, I was up in the half-light of a Himalayan dawn and made my way down the trail to the community room where the girls assembled for *prarthana*, daily prayers, their "morning watch." There was song as well as prayer before breakfast. The little girls discovered that I knew "Lead Kindly Light" and insisted that I sing it each day as my contribution to the service.

Finally, for Gandhi the *we* had to include one's enemies and opponents. This was the basis of his nonviolence, or *ahimsa*. Gandhi was not one to avoid a nonviolent fight, but he never cast a fight in terms of the humiliation and defeat of the opponent. He saw clearly that if conflict is cast in terms of winning or losing, of *us* prevailing over *them*, then there will be no way forward toward a transformed community. Even if one wins absolutely, one still has a defeated enemy. The next round of the conflict is only postponed. In Gandhi's evolving philosophy of nonviolence, this is a crucial point. Gandhi refused to concede that the adversary—whether the opponent in a legal case, the opponent in a political battle, or the opponent in combat—would forever remain polarized as the "other." If the polarization is not broken, then what we call "winning" is still losing, for we are still left with an opponent, an enemy. The supposed triumph of the victor and the defeat of the vanquished are illusory in the village of one thousand people. The vanquished do not disappear. Violence in a village claims everyone as its victims, winners and losers alike, as the urban unrest of American cities has so vividly shown.

Breaking the cycle of violence requires re-creating the *we*. Gandhi never forgot that there was a person on the other side of a given conflict. When Gandhi was imprisoned by Jan Smuts in South Africa, he made Smuts a pair of leather sandals with his own hands during his time in prison and presented them as a gift when he was released. In India, when Gandhi was about to undertake the Salt March in defiance of the tax on salt, a tax which he knew fell more heavily on the poor, he wrote a striking letter to Lord Irwin, begging him to repeal the tax, reminding the viceroy of the tremendous inequities between the British administration and the villagers it taxed.

Take your own salary. It is over 21,000 rupees [about $7,000] per month . . . against India's average income of less than two annas [four cents] per day. Thus you are getting over five thousand times India's average income. On bended knee, I ask you to ponder over this phenomenon. I have taken a personal illustration to drive home a painful truth. I have too great a regard for you as a man to wish to hurt your feelings. I know that you do not need the salary you get. Probably the whole of your salary goes for charity. But a system that provides for such an arrangement deserves to be summarily scrapped. . . . My ambition is no less than to convert the British people through non-violence, and make them see the wrong they have done India. I do not seek to harm your people. I want to serve them even as I want to serve my own. . . . [signed] Your sincere friend, M. K. Gandhi.[11]

Gandhi refused to demonize his opponent as a person, even when he was in profound disagreement with everything the opponent stood for. For him, only in the give and take of relationship would it be possible to construct a world which both could affirm.

Across the road from the Gandhi *samadhi* in New Delhi is a museum containing an assortment of exhibits. There is a photograph of his cremation, the day the crowd roared, "*Gandhi amar ho gaye*"—"Gandhi has become immortal!" There is a photograph of his niece Manu, who, like others, called this immortal Gandhi "Bapu," meaning not "father," but the familiar, "daddy." Like many, she found his qualities strikingly maternal and she titled her book *Bapu, My Mother*. In addition to the photographs, there are exhibits in glass cases: "*He Ram*. These Bloodstained Clothes were worn by Bapu-ji on his Last Day, 30-1-1948," "One of the Three Fatal Bullets that took away Bapu-ji from us." In one case the items Gandhi owned at the time of his death are collected: his glasses, his spare dhoti and shawl, his sandals, a pocket watch, a pincushion, and a pen. In viewing this exhibit, I was not at all amused by the old joke about how much money it took to keep Gandhi in poverty. There was a leanness here that was truly sacred. It is this same leanness and economy that was truly universal and has spoken to people widely separated in culture, language, and religion.

Above the door of the room of exhibits is a reminder of the pluralism that Gandhi so energetically fostered: "I do not want my house to be walled in on all sides and my windows to be shut. I want the cultures of all lands to be blown about my house as freely as possible. Mine is not the religion of the prison house." The tragedy of India's partition and the ongoing communal competition and violence in India do not diminish the credibility of Gandhi's vision, but rather make the need for such a wider sense of *we* all the more plain.

Interrelated Traditions and Lives

Were I asked to describe the religious situation of the world today, in the late twentieth century, it would be virtually impossible to do so by focusing on each tradition as a separate entity, for the histories of all of the religious traditions are intertwined despite the fact that they are often treated as separate chapters in books on "world religions." Korean Christians both distance themselves from and are shaped by the shamanistic and Buddhist traditions of Korea. In Japan, Christians struggle with how to venerate ancestors, a matter of such critical importance that the Roman Catholic church has prepared guidelines on the veneration of ancestors for Japanese Catholics. Hindus in India are undergoing a new period of self-definition in relation to Muslims and Sikhs. Muslims in North America are developing a new form of religiousness shaped by the denominational structure so typical of American Protestant, Catholic, and Jewish religious life. Native American people struggle with the appropriation of Native American symbols, rituals, and language in the context of Christian churches and in the context of the New Age movement. Buddhism is developing distinctive forms and lineages in North America, with many of its teachers women and many Jewish in origin. The rivers of our religious traditions roll on. Our religions are not complete, not finished, not able to pass on a finished "product" to the next generation. Our traditions are not isolated, but interrelated and interdependent. Both the interreligious dialogue and the interreligious conflict of the world today make us keenly aware of our constant and close interaction.

Individually we participate in one another's history as well. Gandhi is again a good example. He was very much influenced by his sojourn as a law student in England, where he read the Bible from cover to cover and was especially attracted to the Gospels, where he first read the Bhagavad Gita in the English translation by Edwin Arnold. In England he first met Christians who impressed him far more than the missionaries who had stood on the street corner in his native Rajkot, in Gujarat, insulting the Hindu tradition. Some Christians tried to convert him, impressed by Gandhi's eagerness to learn as much as he could about Christianity. He was honest. He could appreciate the centrality of Jesus as the distinctive testimony of Christians, but not as an objective fact that would deny his own experience as a Hindu. And yet to many Christians who met him, Gandhi as a Hindu revealed something of the true message of Christ. As the missionary E. Stanley Jones put it, "Never in human history has so much light been shed on the Cross, as has been through this one man, and that man not even called a Christian."[12]

Reciprocally, African-American church delegates Howard and Sue Thurman and Edward Carroll visited Gandhi in India in 1935 and discussed Gandhi's use of direct nonviolent action. They brought what they learned of Gandhian campaigns like the Salt March back to the African-American church community in the United States. In 1936, Benjamin E. Mays, later to be a mentor of Martin Luther King, Jr., visited with Gandhi in India. While King's acquaintance with Gandhi is usually traced to a lecture he heard in 1950 by Mordecai Johnson, then president of Howard University, it is clear that the African-American community's acquaintance with Gandhi and their knowledge of the potential power of nonviolence was already decades old by that time.[13] As King put it at the time of the Montgomery bus boycott, "Christ furnished the spirit and the motivation, while Gandhi furnished the method."[14] Just as the Christian tradition participated in the development of Gandhi's ideas, so did Gandhi's Hindu tradition participate in the formation of King's style of leadership and in the civil rights movement as a whole.

The process of interparticipation continues in countless ways. There are many religious exchanges, like the intermonastic exchanges of today—Zen teachers teaching Catholic monks and Catholic monks leading sessions in Zen monasteries. There are student exchanges: a twenty-year-old Jewish woman lives with a Muslim family in Banaras; a Nigerian Muslim law student studies at Harvard Law School. There are scholarly exchanges and academic studies that begin to reshape religious understanding on both sides. When I first met Yves Raguin, who had lived in Taiwan since 1934, he told me, "Chinese Buddhism and Christianity have met in me. The Gospel cannot help but take on new dimensions as it encounters each culture. In teaching Christianity and Buddhism to students in Chinese, I know that when I take a Chinese word to express what we mean by 'God' it will still carry the overtones and undertones of its own cultural heritage and long history." In my own case, there is no doubt that by writing an interpretive study of the city of Banaras I have participated as a Christian, in a small way, in the history of the Hindu tradition. It is also true that my Hindu friends and teachers have participated in the history of the Christian tradition through their influence on me and my thinking. The point is not difficult to grasp, but very important: our religious traditions already intersect and interpenetrate through the lives of countless men and women.[15] As the Reverend

Murray Rogers so clearly put it, speaking of his experience with people of other faiths in Hong Kong, Jerusalem, and North India, "the 'I' and 'they' have almost disappeared, and in their place it is 'we.'"[16]

The Interreligious Movement: Going It Together

Clearly interdependence is a fact of our global life. Even so, the world is not yet interrelated in the sense of actively and intentionally creating the international, intercultural, and interreligious relationships that will sustain a world in which we depend upon one another as much as we do. We share our communities and our world with men and women who worship in various ways, who base their judgments on differing authorities, who recognize differing revelations, who speak of God in strikingly different ways or do not speak of God at all. Our task is to learn to collaborate with one another on issues that none of us can solve alone.[17] The challenge could not have been stated more clearly than it was by the Jewish philosopher Abraham Joshua Heschel: "In the world of economics, science, and technology, cooperation exists and continues to grow. Even political states, though different in culture and competing with one another, maintain diplomatic relations and strive for coexistence. Only religions are not on speaking terms."[18]

At the closing session of the World's Parliament of Religions in 1893, the suggestion was made by one of the Unitarian conveners that the representatives of the world's traditions meet again in 1900 "on the banks of the Ganges in the ancient city of Benares."[19] But following the Parliament, at the turn of the century, the momentum to sustain a movement toward dialogue had not yet gathered. The whole idea of intentionally bringing people of various religious traditions together for colloquy was truly something new under the sun. Even Akbar, the broad-minded sixteenth-century Indian Mughal emperor who had convened men of various faiths for discussion in his private audience hall, had used the influence of his court to create a syncretistic new religion, the Din-i-Ilahi, rather than simply to foster a climate of mutual understanding through dialogue. The envisioned Banaras meeting to follow up on the Parliament did not take place. There was instead a meeting in Boston in 1900 of the International Council of Unitarian and Other Liberal Religious Thinkers and Workers. It came to include a few Muslims, Jews, Catholics, and reformist Hindu Brahmo Samajis, and in subsequent years its international congresses addressed questions such as justice for women and the expansion of narrow patriotism to a wider human loyalty. Two world wars in the twentieth century impeded the progress of organized interreligious efforts such as this one and underlined their importance.

Interreligious dialogue was certainly not on the agenda of the churches during the first half of the twentieth century. The prevailing energy was for mission, not for dialogue. The real breakthrough came in the 1960s. At the Second Vatican Council, the Roman Catholic Church focused attention on interreligious relations, published *Nostra Aetate*, and established the Secretariat on Non-Christians, now called the Pontifical Council for Interreligious Dialogue. In 1968, the General Assembly of the World Council of Churches, meeting in Uppsala, for the first time addressed the question of other faiths in a section called "Seeking Community: The Common Search of People of Various Faiths, Cultures, and Ideologies."

In 1970, the Central Committee of the WCC, meeting at Addis Ababa, declared interreligious dialogue to be "the common pilgrimage of the churches" and the first major multilateral dialogue meeting took place at Ajaltoun in Lebanon. Since then, the WCC Sub-unit on Dialogue, now the Office on Interreligious Relations, has worked at building relations with people of other faiths and at addressing the fears and hesitancies of the member churches. The WCC's *Guidelines on Dialogue* provides encouragement for churches to enter into active dialogue with neighbors of other faiths. *Ecumenical Considerations on Jewish-Christian Dialogue* and *Ecumenical Considerations on Christian-Muslim Relations* articulate the special histories and sensitivities that will shape relations with Jews and Muslims respectively. The study guide called *My Neighbour's Faith and Mine*, published now in fourteen languages and in use all over the world, aims at enabling Christians to think afresh about the theological implications of their relations with neighbors of other faiths. While the study guide has raised controversy and has even been "banned" by one national church council, its publication, according to one observer, "would have been unthinkable in the hallowed halls of the Christian *oikoumene* twenty years ago."[20]

Today interreligious dialogue is on the agenda not only of the churches, but also of Jewish, Muslim, Hindu, and Buddhist organizations. The International Jewish Committee on Interreligious Consultation (IJCIC) brings representatives from a variety of Jewish organizations into a single instrument for interfaith relations. The World Muslim League, based in Riyadh, Saudi Arabia, has an office for interfaith relations and its leader has exchanged visits with the National Council of Churches in the United States. The World Buddhist Fellow-ship, based in Thailand, and the U.S.–based International Network of Engaged Buddhists bring the energy of Buddhists to bear on global issues. There is now what one interfaith consultation called "a new momentum in all faiths to strengthen and give clearer voice to those elements in their traditions which drive toward recognizing our need for one another."[21] At that meeting, which took place in Mauritius under the auspices of the World Council of Churches, Christians, Jews, Muslims and Buddhists, Hindus, Native Americans, and Af-rican traditionalists affirmed together, "The world is one of inescapable interde-pendence in all realms. The threat to human life and to the whole earth urges upon all a growing recognition that no one faith can go it alone."[22]

There is no question that religious traditions have been part of the problem as one surveys the divisions and conflicts of the present world; and there is no question that religious traditions will also have to be part of the solution. The very concerns to which people of the various religious traditions address them-selves—militarism and violence, the degradation of the environment, the viola-tion of human rights, the transnational networks of drugs and prostitution, the need for a new international economic order—are increasingly seen to be con-cerns that cannot be addressed in a meaningful way, let alone solved, by any one people or any one nation alone. These are issues that demand the creation of new ways of thinking, new blueprints for working together, and new styles of in-ternational leadership. On a very practical level, they require the creation of a workable worldwide infrastructure of relationships.

Given that we cannot go it alone, the question of how to "go it together" is both critical and urgent. There are now many organizational expressions of a growing interreligious movement—global, regional, and local. The oldest of the international interreligious organizations is the International Association for Religious Freedom (IARF), which began with that congress of "religious liberals" in Boston in 1900. In Britain, the World Congress of Faiths was launched in 1936 to bring people of various religions together and make dia-logue "a concern for the many rather than a dream of a few." The Temple of Un-derstanding, based in New York since the mid-1960s, has sponsored a series of "spiritual summit conferences" and has taken a further step to bring religious leaders together with government and parliamentary leaders under the auspices of the Global Forum of Spiritual and Parliamentary Leaders for Human Sur-vival. The World Conference on Religion and Peace (WCRP), formed in 1968, has worked explicitly on peace and disarmament issues as a non-governmental organization of the United Nations. It has regional chapters throughout the world and it construes its commitment to peace widely, focusing energy on such issues as the Vietnamese "boat people," the Cambodian refugees, and the UN Convention on the Rights of the Child.

Like many worldwide movements, the interreligious movement has force and energy, but no single center. At the local level, in the United States there has been a notable rise of interreligious councils as the religious landscape of cities and towns becomes more diverse. When the construction of the Buddhist Hsi Lai Temple in Hacienda Heights, California, was stalled in five years of zoning battles, it was the Interreligious Council of Southern California that came to the support of the Chinese Buddhist community. In Houston, when a mosque was firebombed in the wake of an airline hijacking in the Middle East in 1985, the association called the Houston Metropolitan Ministries was challenged to become a broader interfaith forum actively engaged with the Islamic Society of Greater Houston. In 1988, the Buddhist community of Boulder, Colorado, submitted an application to join the local Council of Churches and a serious discussion about the new religious landscape of Boulder ensued. All over the United States local councils of churches have become councils of churches and synagogues, and are now wrestling with what it means to become interreligious councils. In October of 1988, people representing various religious traditions and local interreligious councils came together in Wichita, Kansas, to create the North American Interfaith Network (NAIN) in order to coordinate and facilitate an interfaith movement that is already growing.

Interfaith services of prayer are on the rise, especially at times of community or international crisis. During the war in the Persian Gulf, for example, there was a burst of local bridge building as many Jews and Christians discovered for the first time the mosques in their own cities. There were many interfaith prayer services, including one at the Hsi Lai Temple in Hacienda Heights where people of all faiths gathered in the great hall dominated by Amida Buddha. For the most part such services follow a pattern of sequential readings or prayer, each participant contributing in the style and distinctive vocabulary of his or her own tradition. The most ambitious of such symbolic events was the Assisi World Day of Prayer called by Pope John Paul II in 1986, which brought together religious leaders from every tradition, including the elders and spiritual leaders of native peoples of the Americas and Africa. Even in the planning stages, the great public visibility of the Assisi event began to elicit a backlash. The Vatican received a number of critical responses from Christians who insisted that "praying together" went too far. The Vatican then clarified its intent by issuing a carefully worded statement that the religious leaders of various traditions would be coming together to pray, they would not be coming to pray together. To underline this nuance, the event was organized so that after an initial convocation the Buddhists, Hindus, Muslims, Christians, etc., went their separate ways to separate locations for their prayers and meditations.

The question of whether we all can pray together, whether we can only be together while we pray separately, or whether there should be any interfaith worship at all is one that is boiling on the front burner of many interreligious councils. In Britain, it has been raised by the Inter-Faith Consultative Group of the Church of England in a recent publication entitled *Multi-Faith Worship?* Prayer quite aside, even the ritual implications of interfaith encounters raise questions. The Inter-Faith Consultative Group poses a number of cases. For example:

> The Sikhs have opened a community welfare centre next to their gurudwara, with the encouragement of some local clergy. Wanting to build on this link, they decide to invite the Bishop to visit the gurudwara at *Baisakhi*, the next major festival. This is the first time the Sikhs have issued such an invitation to a local church leader. *How can the Bishop discover what will be expected of him in the temple? He will have to cover his head and remove his shoes, but will he acknowledge the presence of the Sikh scriptures with a reverent bow, and if so, will he be endorsing their validity?*

Such situations and questions have unleashed a storm of controversy in England and have been debated in newspaper columns and radio programs. Should the imam speak in the Remembrance Day services for those who lost their lives in war? Should there be a commonly agreed upon order of service or should it be a Christian service in which Muslims and Hindus participate as guests? May the new Sikh mayor have a service in the parish church marking his first year of office? In the United States such matters have not become public issues. That time may be coming, however. On state occasions such as the inauguration of a president, Protestant, Catholic, and Jewish clergy have offered invocations, prayers, and benedictions. Given the growing number of Muslims in the United States, soon to be equal to the number of Jews, one can well anticipate that before long a Muslim imam will be asked to participate in such a state event, just as imams have already participated in opening daily sessions of the U.S. Congress and various state legislatures. These shifts in the public iconic expression of American religious pluralism will make visible a reality for which many Christian Americans are as yet unprepared.

Both the global village and the urban cosmopolis make clear that interreligious dialogue can no longer be regarded as the arcane speculative interest of a few liberal thinkers in the various religious traditions. It is at the very heart of a workable society. Dialogue begins with the questions that arise from the common context of our lives together. Education, good government, health, families, AIDS, violence, and the response to violence—these are the subjects of interreligious dialogue. What about humanity's relation to nature? What is an ethical issue? What is the meaning of justice? What criteria should we bring to the making of just decisions? These are the questions of interreligious dialogue. The nascent interreligious movement will need to gain strength and visibility in the coming years in order to become part of the essential infrastructure of an interdependent world. And it will need to deepen and mature far beyond general expressions of fellowship and common vision.

Keeping One Another's Image

Among the implications of religious interdependence is that we each depend upon the "other" to know us as we would like to be known. We are therefore the keepers of one another's image. In the village of a thousand people, there is no way we can avoid facing up to the need for basic education about our neighbors. Yet as most of us look down the roster of religious communities in this village, we note how little, even now, we understand one another. What are the five pillars of Islam and what do they mean to a Muslim? Who was the Buddha—a man or a god? What does it mean for the Jewish people to speak of being "chosen"? Why do Christians speak of eating the body and drinking the blood of Christ? We can scarcely address the problems that beset the world without first tackling the basic ignorance, the fear, and the misunderstanding that separate us from one another.

Remember the claim of John Henry Barrows that the Parliament of Religions would be "the first school of comparative religions, wherein devout men of all faiths may speak for themselves without hindrance, without criticism, and without compromise, and tell what they believe and why they believe it."[23] That event in 1893 did indeed give impetus to the academic study of religion in American colleges and universities, but the public schools in the United States still lag far behind in being able to teach basic world religions as part of the social studies and history curriculum; other countries do better and do worse, but nowhere is our basic religious knowledge up to the level of our basic knowledge of mathematics or biology. Gandhi called the sympathetic study of the world's religions a "sacred duty": "I hold that it is the duty of every cultured man or woman to read sympathetically the scriptures of the world. If we are to respect others' religions as we would have them to respect our own, a friendly study of the world's religions is a sacred duty."[24]

The knowledge of one another's traditions is not simply to inform our curiosity about the beliefs or customs of our neighbors. People of every religious tradition depend upon one another to interpret one another fairly and accurately. We are the keepers of one another's image. This is one of the most critical aspects of our interdependence and it is a sacred trust. We all depend upon one another not to tell lies, not to spread hatred, not to purvey a sensational or distorted image of one another. We all depend upon one another to correct those lies and distortions when they are made. There is no community that can do this entirely for itself. There is no amount of public vigilance and no amount of propaganda that can enable Christians, Muslims, or Buddhists to portray themselves as they would like to be understood.

In 1966, the Jewish philosopher Abraham Joshua Heschel delivered an address entitled "No Religion Is an Island," in which he outlined the implications of our religious interdependence: "The religions of the world are no more self-sufficient, no more independent, no more isolated than individuals or nations. Energies, experiences and ideas that come to life outside the boundaries of a particular religion or all religions continue to challenge and to affect every religion. Horizons are wider, dangers are greater. . . . No religion is an island. We are all involved with one another. Spiritual betrayal on the part of one of us affects the faith of all of us."[25] Spiritual betrayal may take many forms, but perhaps the most common is simply an inattention to hurt and defamation when it affects the image and well-being of another community. Such common daily betrayals have enabled the purveyors of hatred to ignite the fires of the pogrom, "ethnic cleansing," and the Holocaust.

Whether we like it or not, all of us bear witness to each other in an interdependent world. For those of us in the traditions of Moses, the commandment not to bear false witness against our neighbors is at stake every time we speak of our neighbors. We bear false witness against our neighbors because we do not know them. Or we bear false witness because we think it puts us in a better light to do so. We are tempted to compare the most refined aspects of our own tradition with the most crude aspects of the other. But the problem is that our testimonies about one another are reciprocal. If Muslims are dependent upon Christians for a faithful image of their tradition, Christians are also dependent upon Muslims for the kind of image of Christianity that is presented in Muslim schools and mosque-based education programs.

Not only are we all keepers of one another's image, we are also guardians of one another's rights. In one critical sense the village of a thousand people is misleading. No village is quite like it. No religious tradition is a majority everywhere, and no tradition a minority everywhere. We are all minorities somewhere, with the vulnerabilities and defensiveness that minority status might entail. And we are majorities somewhere, with the insensitivities, the presumption, and the power that goes with it. There are Muslim minorities in Europe and North America concerned about the rights of Muslims in public schools, city councils, and penal institutions; there are Christian minorities in the Sudan, Bangladesh, and Pakistan concerned about the consequences for them if the governments establish Islamic *shari'a* as the normative law of the land. There are Hindu minorities in Fiji and Malaysia, Buddhist minorities in Russia and France. Human rights and religious liberty cannot be guarded in one place and disregarded in another.

An important step in recognizing this kind of interdependence is being able to speak out when a religious tradition not one's own has been attacked or distorted. Taking offense when one's own rights have been attacked is expected. Groups like the Anti-Defamation League of the B'nai B'rith are formed explicitly to guard the well-being of the community in the public arena. But what is the context in which people and communities speak out for the rights of peoples of other faiths when there is a violation or offense? Why should it be the burden of Jews alone to speak out if a Roman Catholic convent is built right on the border of Auschwitz or if the Nation of Islam publishes an accusatory tract on Jewish complicity in black oppression? Why should Muslims have to be the first to speak out if a mosque is threatened or attacked with arson or if a newspaper publishes an article portraying Muslims as fanatical? Why should we think it primarily the Hindu community that is hurt if a temple is desecrated or its divine images broken? Being able to feel the hurt of one another and to speak out on behalf of one another is one of the great spiritual challenges of an interdependent world.

At a 1987 WCC consultation in New Delhi on "Religious Identity in a Multi-

religious Society," people of three religious traditions spoke of the urgent need
for this kind of mutual guardianship in the South Asian situation. It goes without saying that communities will try to protect their own civil, religious, and human rights. On this they agreed. But Sri Lankan theologian Wesley Ariarajah
asks, "He can we have solidarity *across* religious barriers? It is sad that there has
been no Buddhist group fighting for the rights of Tamils in Sri Lanka, and no
Tamils speaking out for the Sinhalese." Veena Das, a Hindu professor at Delhi
University, made a similar point. "In the riots of November 1984, after Mrs.
Gandhi's assassination, the violence and killing unleashed upon Sikhs was not
simply an offense to the Sikhs, but an offense to us all." Mohinder Singh, a Sikh,
said it too: "When we look in the paper and see, as we do daily, that 20 or 25 people were killed today in violence in the Punjab, we must not say that they were
Sikhs or they were Hindus. We must not simply scan the list of victims and
breathe a sigh of relief that our relatives or friends are not among them. All of
these victims of violence are our relatives, our kin."[26]

Being keepers of one another's image and guardians of one another's rights
are not roles that we as religious communities can either accept or reject. They
are assigned by the very nature of our world and we perform them, either well or
badly, either with neglect or vigilance.

Criteria and Criticism

Any real engagement with people of another faith will bring into play our
deepest criteria of truth and value. If people of different traditions engage energetically in dialogue, what criteria are there, finally, for truth? The pluralist is
often accused of being unable to answer that question, but that is precisely the
point. It is a question without an a priori universal answer. Whatever answer
there might be must emerge from the very process of dialogue that the askers of
the question usually want to challenge. People of every religious tradition and
people of none have irreducible criteria which they employ to navigate the waters of decision making, and deep values that provide a rudder and sense of direction. In each tradition these are articulated in different ways, and they may indeed be different values. That is not the real problem. Deepest values do not have
to be modified until they all converge; all the bumps in the road do not have to
be flattened. What we must be able to do, however, is to recognize and clearly articulate our deep guiding values, our criteria, and place them in clear, critical
conversation with others. At its deepest level, the dialogue that will undergird a

pluralist society is the encounter of commitments as well as the encounter of criteria.

Gandhi had one clear guiding value, one foundational criterion—*ahimsa*, or nonviolence. It was not a doctrine or a belief; it was not something he held to because he felt it was divinely revealed. It was the irreducible basis of his life, founded on his deepest conviction that Truth is both within and beyond all religious traditions and all human knowing. One can hold it openly and invite the allegiance of others, even unto death, but one cannot hold it tight-fistedly and kill in its name.

There was no wishy-washy relativism in Gandhi, but a very clear criterion for discerning Truth as best he could and acting accordingly. Not everyone would agree with Gandhi. What about Auschwitz and Bergen Belsen? What about apartheid, racism, and the systemic violence that it perpetrates? What about the power of sixty to control the wealth of the village of one thousand? Will the criterion of *ahimsa* prove adequate as we grapple together with any of these issues? We need to ask these questions and struggle together to answer them. Others bring their own irreducible criteria. The plumb line of justice from the Hebrew prophets. The criterion of love from the Gospels. The twin criteria of compassion and wisdom from the Buddha's teachings. We cannot begin by insisting upon common criteria. And yet we cannot avoid serious dialogue about the issues of race, oppression, injustice, and violence simply because we do not have common criteria. If foundational criteria for a common ethic emerge, it will be because people of all religious traditions have risked this encounter.

I remember a moment of dawning consciousness at a week-long interreligious meeting of women activists on "Women, Religion, and Social Change" held at Harvard in June of 1983. There were Muslim, Christian, and Jewish women, Hindus, Buddhists, and Native Americans. During one long day, women from South Africa, Central America, and the Middle East spoke of the issue of justice in their own contexts. The two women from Japan seemed more and more frustrated with the discussion and were whispering to one another. Finally one of them raised her hand. "What really do you mean by 'justice'? Why does everything come back again to 'justice'?" I was dumbfounded. What do you mean, What do we mean by 'justice'? I and most of the women there presupposed the importance of justice as a basic criterion of value. "How do you say 'justice' in Japanese?" I asked, as if that were a response. They conferred and said there was no such term. I remember my feeling, somewhere between disbelief and disapproval. No "justice" in Japanese? I said, "But if you had to tell your families at home what we have been talking about—the racism and violence in South Africa, for example, and the need for 'justice,' or fairness, what would you say? What would right relations be called?" They conferred again and said, "The word in Japanese would be something like what you mean by 'harmony.'" That was the beginning of a very revealing discussion. Is justice harmony? Is harmony justice? What do we mean by these words? What might the Japanese mean? What if justice produces no harmony? And what if harmony produces no justice? Our very criteria of value are at stake here.

Criticism is, so far, terra incognita on the map of interreligious dialogue. And yet the way forward on the most difficult issues in the village of one thousand people will not be found simply by settling for what we can all agree upon. A sense of ethics must be won through the difficult process of dialogue, built from ongoing relationship. Both within and between religious communities, criticism must finally be safe and accepted if there is to be relationship and if knowledge of one another is to be more than superficial. It is well known that absolutism cannot abide criticism, which is one reason that absolutists and exclusivists will not place themselves in the interchange of dialogue. But if even the pluralists and inclusivists within each tradition do not welcome criticism in dialogue, then the dialogue becomes merely another form of dogmatism. Dialogue is not a debate, but a search for a wider understanding of Truth.

Self-criticism within any religious tradition is sensitive and often difficult. Absolutism and fanaticism fan the flames of these sensitivities. Gandhi once defined communalism as the nurturing of a sense of concern and loyalty that stops short at the borders of one's own community. The term *communalism* is used mostly in India, but the phenomenon of religious chauvinism it names is readily visible throughout the world today. The communalist consciousness does not welcome criticism from within, and the linking of communalism to violence makes internal criticism all the more dangerous. Sikhs who have opposed Sikh extremism or communalism have been killed by other Sikhs, just as Gandhi, who opposed Hindu communalism, was killed by another Hindu. Communalism flourishes only by effectively halting self-criticism. Extremists often gain power not by intimidation of the people of other communities, but by the intimidation and silencing of the moderate voices within their own communities.

It is a challenge to every community of faith to benefit from the dynamic of internal self-criticism. As a historian of religion, I think it is safe to say that there is no religious tradition in which there is only one view and one voice. One of the

reasons that interreligious dialogue among women has been so successful is that
women know that they do not speak in the name of some invisible authority or
magisterium. Women are quite aware that as women they do not speak with the
imprimatur of "the tradition."[27] Meeting at the boundaries comes naturally for
those who have long felt marginalized. And in some traditions today those who
are working toward a truly pluralist society are among the marginalized. As one
of the participants in a dialogue meeting in New Delhi put it, "It is easier for me
to talk of interreligious dialogue outside the community than to speak of honest
dialogue within the community." Many have indeed found a strong sense of
we that crosses religious lines and engages a sense of common purpose that is
sometimes even stronger than the sense of the *we* within their own religious
community.

Beyond this difficult question of intra-community dialogue and self-
criticism there is the further question of the critique of one another's traditions.
Having come to understand the caste system, at least as best I can, may I express
my critique of it? Can I really understand the Jewish critique that Christian
anti-Semitism is rooted right in the Gospels? Sometimes even if we can accept
self-criticism we cannot abide the criticism of another. The history of conflict
and of stereotype is often too painful. But the question is nonetheless legitimate.
Is there also a role in dialogue for the criticism of one another? Or are we simply
too thin-skinned to speak words of mutual criticism across the sensitive lines
of religious traditions? Can we call another to accountability, at least in terms
of that person's own criteria of value? Can we challenge one another's criteria?
Can we say no harmony without justice? Can we say no justice without harmony?

Arun Shourie is an Indian journalist whose book *Religion in Politics* reflects
on the complexities of this issue in the recent history of communal conflict in India. In a chapter entitled "On Taking Offence," he documents the readiness to
take offense and the slowness to forget it in contemporary India: "How very
often it is that when someone of our faith criticizes some aspect of our religion,
the criticism seems to us to be perfectly in order, even scholarly, but how the identical criticism, if it has been made by someone who happens to have been born
into a different religion, sends us up the wall. We must grow up. We must discard
this defensive militancy."[28] Criticism is difficult, however, if people do not have
the ongoing responsibility and opportunity for relationship and reparation that
makes criticism a form of growth and not a form of violence. If interreligious dialogue is to move beyond occasional meetings and congresses to become what

Wesley Ariarajah calls "a culture of dialogue," it must create a context of ongoing relatedness and trust in which self-criticism and mutual criticism are acceptable and valuable parts of the interreligious exchange.

Mutual criticism and self-criticism also involve apology, reparation, what Jews call *tikkun olam*, "the mending of the world." Forgetting and leaving it behind will not do. There must be some mending. In 1987, the Christian bishops and church officials of the Pacific Northwest wrote a remarkable joint letter that I wish the prophet Seattle himself could have seen. It is addressed "To the Tribal Councils and Traditional Spiritual Leaders of the Indian and Eskimo Peoples of the Pacific Northwest." It is an example of one kind of mending:

> Dear Brothers and Sisters,
> This is a formal apology on behalf of our churches for their long-standing participation in the destruction of traditional Native American spiritual practices. We call upon our people for recognition and respect for your traditional ways of life and for protection of your sacred places and ceremonial objects. We have frequently been unconscious and insensitive and have not come to your aid when you have been victimized by unjust Federal policies and practices. In many other circumstances we reflected the rampant racism and prejudice of the dominant culture with which we too willingly identified. During the 200th Anniversary year of the United States Constitution we, as leaders of our churches in the Pacific Northwest, extend our apology. We ask your forgiveness and blessing. . . . We offer our commitment to support you in the righting of previous wrongs: To protect your peoples' efforts to enhance native spiritual teachings; to encourage the members of our churches to stand in solidarity with you on these important religious issues; to provide advocacy and mediation, when appropriate, for ongoing negotiations with State agencies and Federal officials regarding these matters. . . . May the God of Abraham and Sarah, and the Spirit who lives in both the cedar and the Salmon People be honored and celebrated.[29]

The speech of dialogue must come to include not only words of faith and witness, but words of self-criticism and apology, and words of forgiveness and mutuality. One of the things I have always liked about Gandhi was his criticism of Christianity. It no doubt annoyed many Christians in his day and others might have thought it in bad taste. Though I would like to respond to his critique, I see his willingness to offer it as a gesture of truthful love. Essentially, he criticized

Christianity not by his own yardstick, but by using the very criteria of love and service that he saw in Jesus. There was nothing self-serving or angry about it. Just honest. Gandhi pointed out the inconsistencies between Jesus' concern for the poor and the neglect of the poor in Christian countries, between Jesus' non-violence and the aggression of Christian countries. Gandhi did not reserve his critique for Christianity alone; he was equally hard on the rigidity of the caste system, and of the empty ritualism and excessive concern for ritual purity in the Hindu tradition.

Gandhi was clearly a man who could criticize and still love. He was also critical of himself, which is no doubt why one of his foremost interpreters, Erik Erikson, was able to step out of his scholarly role right in the middle of his book *Gandhi's Truth* to do one of the most unconventional things a biographer has ever done—write a critical letter to his subject. Erikson had to get some things off his chest before he could leave Gandhi's formative years in South Africa and follow him into his prophetic and even saintly years in India. Erikson wanted to see more of a search for *inner* truth in Gandhi, more awareness of the ambivalence of love and anger. He was upset by Gandhi's dissembling over his treatment of his wife, Kasturba, as he opened up his family and home in South Africa to a motley community of strangers. Gandhi had forced Kasturba to help with emptying the chamberpots. He had shown her the door when she revolted at his new open-house universalism. Erikson, the psychoanalyst, writes, "Non-violence, inward and outward, can become a true force only where ethics replaces moralism. And ethics, to me, is marked by an insightful assent to human values, whereas moralism is blind obedience; and ethics is transmitted with informed persuasion, rather than enforced with absolute interdicts. Whether the increasing multitudes of men can ever develop and transmit such an ethical attitude I do not know; but I do know that we are committed to it, and that the young are waiting for our support in attempting it."[30]

Imagining Communities

Benedict Anderson, in *Imagined Communities*, investigates the process through which nations imagine themselves and imagine others. Indeed it is through this imaginative process that nations come into being. Imagination is key, for we must take note that "the members of even the smallest nation will never know most of their fellow-members, meet them, or even hear of them, yet in the minds of each lives the image of their communion."[31] The images by which we imag-

ine ourselves to be American, Estonian, Czech, or Chinese are very powerful. America was the "melting pot," China was the "Middle Kingdom." These
imagined communities can be invested with a great deal of content for a time,
and they can also disintegrate, as is clear now in the 1990s, when we are recon-
figuring the world without the Soviet Union and all it was imagined to be.

Thinking about "imagined communities" in the context of our interdependent world raises many fascinating and important questions. It is clear that the
most powerful mapping of the world and its boundaries is done not by armies,
but by the power of the imagination which creates and bears for us a sense of
we—national, religious, cultural, multicultural. As imagined communities, religious traditions are more ancient and more tenacious than modern nation-
states. Hindus and Jews in different ways link their imagined communities to a
powerful sense of land. Hindus also posit the image of a four-petaled world lotus, with India being the southern petal. Muslims have a strong sense of center,
spiritual but not "ecclesiastical," anchoring a worldwide community of faith. In
a very different way, the Catholic church has a strong sense of center, so much so
that "Rome" and "the Vatican" convey a whole ecclesial order and authority.
The Buddhist tradition is highly de-centered, with its imagined communities
more ethnic than universal. The Oglala of the Great Plains think of themselves
as one people among the "Seven Fireplaces" of the Sioux. The Aboriginals of
Australia link their imagined community to the land and time they call The
Dreaming.

The body is a common image of the interrelatedness of the imagined community. For both Christians and Hindus, the body is the image of the interdependent whole. In the Christian tradition, the "body of Christ" is the church,
one body with many members. The eye cannot say to the hand, nor the head to
the feet, "I have no need of you" (1 Cor. 12). In the celebrated Vedic hymn called
the Purusha Sukta (Rig Veda X.90), the whole created order—temporal,
moral, and social—is seen to be the body of the cosmic person, Purusha, divided up in the beginning, at the time of creation. While the body is a holistic
image for community and in that sense is positive, it is also a hierarchical image.
There is a head and there are feet; no matter how valuable the feet are made to
feel, there is a hierarchy. An image inherently hierarchical will not be adequate
to imagine our interrelations as communities of faith in an interdependent
world.

In developing a sense of *we* that is wider than the *we* of culture, religion, or
clan, it will be important to have an image of what kind of human relatedness we

wish to bring into being. People of each religious tradition have dreams of what the world should ideally be and how we should all be related to one another even though we are not all the same. Glimpsing one another's dreams is an important step in beginning to reimagine the *we*. Do we imagine ourselves to be separate but equal communities, concerned primarily with guarding one another's rights in a purely civic construction of relatedness? Do we imagine ourselves to be related as parts of an extended family, or as many families of faith? Do we imagine ourselves to be religious communities competing in goodness and in righteousness, as the Qur'an puts it? Imaging a wider *we* does not mean leaving our separate communities behind, but finding increasingly generative ways of living together as a community of communities. To do this, we all must imagine together who *we* are.

Both Gandhi and Martin Luther King, Jr., are among the many for whom the image of the household suggests our close relatedness. King introduced his talk "The World House" with these words:

> Some years ago a famous novelist died. Among his papers was found a list of suggested plots for future stories, the most prominently underscored being this one: 'A widely separated family inherits a house in which they have to live together.' This is the great new problem of mankind. We have inherited a large house, a great 'world house' in which we have to live together—black and white, Easterner and Westerner, Gentile and Jew, Catholic and Protestant, Moslem and Hindu—a family unduly separated in ideas, culture and interest, who, because we can never again live apart, must learn somehow to live with each other in peace.[32]

A household gathers together a large and usually complex extended family, with all the diversity of temperament and personality that human beings have. The imagined community of the household includes both hospitality and mutuality. A household may also have its hierarchies, but they are not the built-in hierarchies of the body. They will be open to challenge and negotiation. There is no household without its arguments, but its foundation is undergirding love and its language the two-way language of dialogue. Can we imagine the world, locally and globally, as such a household? Can we imagine the diversity of religious faith and tradition as such a household?

The household as an imagined community makes even more proximate the inequalities of the village of one thousand people. The rich will see the suffering and hunger of the poor in the very rooms of our common habitation. The household elicits from us the true recognition that, as King put it, "in a real sense, all life is interrelated. The agony of the poor impoverishes the rich; the betterment of the poor enriches the rich. We are inevitably our brother's keeper because we are our brother's brother. Whatever affects one directly affects all indirectly."[33] To imagine such a household will require what King called a "revolution of values." "A genuine revolution of values means in the final analysis that our loyalties must become ecumenical rather than sectional. Every nation must now develop an overriding loyalty to mankind as a whole in order to preserve the best in their individual societies."[34]

Part of the revolution of values is a revolution of attitudes, a revolution of theological attitudes being foremost among them. A household cannot function on the underlying premise of exclusivity, though each community within the household may be exclusive in some things, such as its central rituals. A household cannot finally function on the underlying foundation of inclusivism either, for it will have to be *our* household as human beings, not ours as Christians, Muslims, or Buddhists, to which everyone else is welcome. No one community can set the terms for the whole. The underlying foundation of the world household will finally have to be pluralism.

In a household, people meet and live with one another at close range. The Hindu and the Christian know the Muslim and the Buddhist, who rise before dawn for prayer or meditation. Each community hears and overhears the prayers and sermons, the songs and silences of the others. Their privacy is respected. Occasionally there are invitations to join in. There are some joint celebrations. Each community also hears and overhears the hypocrisy of the others. As in any household, we come to know one another at our best and at our worst. We cannot sustain our pretenses to perfection.

Whether globally or locally, the household provides the context for understanding one another, not as strangers, but as neighbors. Mutual understanding may well lead to mutual transformation, as each of us begins to catch a glimpse of the glory as seen by the other. And above all, it provides the context in which the commitments of our faith can enable us to join with one another to solve the problems of our interdependent world.

Many religious traditions have their own distinctive visions of the imagined community of diverse peoples. In the Christian tradition, the dominant image of the community coming into being is the Kingdom of God—the world that God intends, the world of which we must be co-creators. The New Testament is filled with images of the Kingdom. This "imagined community" is not finally the Christian community, but the community of the whole inhabited earth. In Jesus' time, as in ours, the term *kingdom* was intended somewhat paradoxically. Jesus overturned the regal understanding and expectation of "kingdom," for what was envisioned by Jesus was not like any earthly kingdom. This imagined community would not be imposed from above and ruled from on high, but would grow from the smallest seeds, like big bushes from tiny mustard seeds. It would be a kingdom inherited not by the rich and powerful, but by the poor, the widows, the homeless, and the strangers. This community would not secure its identity by dominion or exclusion, but was imagined to be an open house for all the peoples of the earth, coming from the East and West, North and South, to eat at table together. This imagined community is not off in the future in some heavenly place and time, but among us in community in this very world and within us. It is not some other place, but this place transformed by justice and filled to the brim with peace. The Kingdom of God is much wider than the church. It is the Kingdom of God, not of the Christian church. The role of the immediate followers of Christ in bringing this to be is not imagined in grandiose language, but in the most humble of domestic language. We are to be like yeast in the bread dough, like salt in the food, like a light to the path.

At the end of the final book of the Bible, the book of Revelation, is another imaginative vision. At the center of this vision is a holy city where it is forever daytime. The gates of the city stand open in every direction and are never shut. Through them come people from throughout the world, bringing into the city the "glory and the honor of the nations" (Rev. 21–22). Saint John's vision draws upon the earlier imaginative vision of the prophet Ezekiel, who also saw the city and the temple. In Ezekiel's vision, from underneath the main door of the sanctum of the temple, facing east, a stream is flowing. At first it is ankle deep, then knee deep. Gradually it becomes a great river. Its waters are the waters of life, pouring forth from the temple and bringing life, abundance, and healing wherever they flow. Saint John, too, saw that river, flowing with living waters, though in the city John saw there was no temple at all, but God alone. "Then the angel showed me the river of the water of life, bright as crystal, flowing from the throne of God and of the Lamb through the middle of the street of the city. On either side of the river is the tree of life . . . and the leaves of the tree are for the healing of the nations." And the water of life is free. "Let anyone who wishes take the water of life as a gift."

It is a beautiful image. There is no temple, only the river of the water of life and healing flowing from the very presence of God. Having journeyed from

Bozeman to Banaras, I know that this image of the river c
alone. I cannot read the final chapters of Saint John's imagin.
seeing the Ganges in my mind's eye. For Hindus it is the Rive
ing from the foot of Vishnu, falling to the head of Shiva, touc
top of its highest mountain, Mount Meru, and then generously s
channels to flow in four directions, watering the whole of the eart
of blessing. The stream of the River of Heaven I know best flows so.   ᴵa
and even today skirts the sacred city of Banaras where pilgrims com. to bathe at
dawn. But surely the Jordan is one of those streams of the River of Heaven—and
the Gallatin as well.

Notes

1. Bozeman to Banaras

1. John A. T. Robinson, *Honest to God* (Philadelphia: Westminster Press, 1962), p. 28.
2. Quoted in Esther C. Niebel, ed., *A Century of Service: History of the First Methodist Church, Bozeman, Montana, 1866–1966* (Bozeman: First Methodist Church, 1966).
3. Robert W. Lind, *Brother Van: Montana Pioneer Circuit Rider* (Helena: Falcon Press, 1992), pp. 153–55.
4. Dorothy Eck, "Methodism and the Early History of Bozeman" (manuscript), p. 10. Cited in Niebel, *A Century of Service*, p. 7.
5. Rene Foure, *Krishnamurti: The Man and His Teaching* (Bombay: Chetana, 1964), pp. 8–9.
6. Ibid.
7. D. G. Moses in W. Paton, ed., *The Authority of the Faith* (London: Oxford University Press, 1939), p. 64.
8. John B. Cobb, Jr., *Beyond Dialogue: Toward a Mutual Transformation of Christianity and Buddhism* (Philadelphia: Fortress Press, 1982).
9. A. G. Hogg in Paton, *The Authority of the Faith*, pp. 94–95.

2. Frontiers of Encounter

1. John F. Kennedy, *A Nation of Immigrants* (New York: Harper Torchbooks, 1964), p. 3.
2. John Henry Barrows, ed., *The World's Parliament of Religions* (Chicago: Parliament Publishing Company, 1893), vol. 1, p. 73. For an understanding of the currents and undercurrents of the Parliament, I am indebted to my colleague Richard Seager, who has edited a volume of Parliament speeches, *The Dawn of Religious*

Pluralism (Chicago: Open Court, 1992), and written an interpretive work on the Parliament, "The World's Parliament of Religions, Chicago, Illinois, 1893: America's Coming of Age" (Ph.D. diss., Harvard University, 1986).

3. Barrows, *The World's Parliament of Religions*, pp. 20–21.

4. Rick Fields, *How the Swans Came to the Lake* (Boston: Shambala, 1986), p. 113.

5. Barrows, *The World's Parliament of Religions*, vol. 1, pp. 67–72.

6. Ibid., pp. 72–79.

7. Ibid., vol. 2, p. 977.

8. Ibid., p. 1571.

9. Ibid., vol. 1, pp. 444–50.

10. Ibid., vol. 2, pp. 989–90.

11. Ibid., p. 843.

12. Ibid., vol. 1, p. 540.

13. Ibid., vol. 2, p. 1580.

14. Ibid., p. 1575.

15. Ibid., p. 1573.

16. Ibid., p. 1578.

17. Ibid., p. 1565.

18. Ibid., p. 1559.

19. Ibid., p. 1560.

20. Ibid., p. 973.

21. Ibid., p. 1304.

22. Cited by Seager, "The World's Parliament of Religions," p. 47.

23. Barrows, *The World's Parliament of Religions*, vol. 2, pp. 635–36.

24. Ibid., p. 1250.

25. Ibid., pp. 1235–36.

26. Ibid., p. 1150.

27. Frederick Jackson Turner, "The Significance of the Frontier in American History," in *The Frontier in American History* (Huntington, N.Y.: Robert E. Krieger, 1976), pp. 1–38.

28. Hilda Lavisa Olson Fritz's "A Family History" was written in the 1940s and was later typed by my aunt, Irene Fritz Conca. The manuscript is currently being edited by my mother, Dorothy Fritz Eck. All the material about Hilda Olson Fritz is from this manuscript.

29. Marian Taylor in Virgina Keeting, ed., *Dungeness: The Lure of a River* (Port Angeles, Wash.: Olympic Printers, 1976), p. 48.

30. Jack Chen, *The Chinese of America* (San Francisco: Harper and Row, 1980), p. 147.

31. Ibid., p. 148.

32. Robert R. Swartout, Jr., "From Kwangtung to the Big Sky: The Chinese Experience in Frontier Montana," in Robert R. Swartout, Jr., and Harry W. Fritz, eds.,

Montana Heritage: An Anthology of Historical Essays (Helena: Montana Historical Society, 1992), p. 75.

33. Ibid., p. 78.

34. Fields, *How the Swans Came to the Lake*, pp. 123–24.

35. Swartout, "From Kwangtung," p. 77.

36. Ibid., p. 79.

37. Joan M. Jensen, *Passage from India: Asian Indians in North America* (New Haven: Yale University Press, 1988), p. 46.

38. Ibid., p. 48.

39. Joan M. Jensen, "Apartheid: Pacific Coast Style," *Pacific Historical Review* 38 (August 1969), pp. 339–40.

40. *The Supreme Court Reporter*, October 1923, "United States v. Bhagat Singh Thind" (argued Jan. 11, 12, 1923; decided Feb. 19, 1923), pp. 338–42.

41. Ronald Takaki, *Strangers from a Different Shore: A History of Asian Americans* (New York: Viking Penguin, 1989), p. 418.

42. *"Multi-faith Worship"?: Questions and Suggestions from the Inter-faith Consultative Group* (London: Church House Publishing, 1992).

43. Edward Sachau, ed., *Alberuni's India* (Delhi: S. Chand & Co., 1964), p. 19.

44. Ibid., p. 246.

45. Barrows, *The World's Parliament of Religions*, vol. 2, p. 978.

3. The Names of God

1. W. C. Vanderwerth, ed., *Indian Oratory: Famous Speeches by Noted Indian Chieftains* (Norman: University of Oklahoma Press, 1971), pp. 118–22. This version was translated and written down by Dr. Henry Smith at the time of the speech. The version of Chief Seattle's speech most commonly circulated, however, is really an adaptation written for a 1971 film on ecology and later published under the title "Brother Eagle, Sister Sky" ("Chief's 1854 Lament Linked to Ecological Script of 1971," *New York Times*, April 21, 1992). See Robert Cooney and Helen Michalowski, eds., *The Power of the People* (Philadelphia: New Society Publishers, 1987), pp. 6–7.

2. Gordon D. Kaufman, *Theology for a Nuclear Age* (Philadelphia: Westminster Press, 1985), p. 20.

3. Wesley Ariarajah, *The Bible and People of Other Faiths* (Geneva: World Council of Churches, 1985), p. 1.

4. Ibid.

5. Rig Veda I.64.46. My translation.

6. Paul Tillich, *The Shaking of the Foundations* (New York, Scribners, 1948), p. 57.

7. Cited in Wilhelm Halbfass, *India and Europe: An Essay in Understanding* (Albany: State University of New York Press, 1988), p. 106.

8. Svetasvatara Upanishad 1.1. Unless otherwise noted, for the Upanishads I have followed the translation of Robert E. Hume, *The Thirteen Principal Upanishads*, 2d ed. (Oxford: Oxford University Press, 1931).

9. Norman Macleod, *Days in North India* (Philadelphia: J. B. Lippincott & Co., 1870), p. 20.

10. James Hillman, *Re-visioning Psychology* (New York: Harper & Row, 1975), pp. xiv–xv, 158–59.

11. Friedrich Nietzsche, "The Greatest Utility of Polytheism," in *Joyful Wisdom* (New York: Frederick Ungar Publishing, 1960), pp. 178–80.

12. Rig Veda I.64.45–46 (Ralph T. H. Griffith, trans., *The Hymns of the Rigveda* [1896–97; reprint, Delhi: Motilal Banarsidass, 1973]).

13. Rig Veda X.90 (R. C. Zaehner, trans. and ed., *Hindu Scriptures* [London: Everyman's Library, 1966]).

14. Maitri Upanishad 5.1.

15. Cited in S. Radhakrishnan, *The Hindu View of Life* (New York: Macmillan, 1975), p. 35.

16. Ibid., pp. 21, 23.

17. Max Müller, *India: What Can It Teach Us?* (New York: John W. Lovell, 1883), p. 154.

18. Ibid., pp. 156–57.

19. Ibid., pp. 268, 285–86.

20. Ibid., pp. 285–86.

21. Krister Stendahl, "We Are All Minorities in God's Eyes," talk at the Center for the Study of World Religions, Harvard University, 27 February 1992.

22. Harivamsha, line 10660 ff., cited in M. Dhavmony, *Classical Hinduism* (Rome: Universita Gregoriana Editrice, 1982), p. 67. Dhavmony also cites other Epic sources which express just this sentiment.

23. G. V. Tagare, trans., *The Narada Purana*, Ancient Indian Tradition and Mythology Series, vol. 15 (Delhi: Motilal Banarsidass, 1980), 1.2.52–53.

24. Anand Swarup Gupta, ed., *The Kurma Purana*, with English translation (Ramnagar: All-India Kashi Raj Trust, 1972), II.1–11.

25. The myth of Shiva's appearance to Brahma and Vishnu as a *linga* of light is found in many places in the Puranas. See Shiva Purana I (Vidyesvara Samhita), 5–12; Shiva Purana II (Rudra Samhita), section I.6–9; Linga Purana I.17–21; Narada Purana 26; Kurma Purana 1.25, 31. The Shiva, Linga, and Narada Puranas are published separately in the Ancient Indian Tradition and Mythology Series (Delhi: Motilal Banarsidass).

26. J. L. Shastri, ed., *The Linga Purana*, translated by a board of scholars, Ancient Indian Tradition and Mythology Series, vol. 5 (Delhi: Motilal Banarsidass, 1973). The

first section of the Linga Purana tells the story of Shiva's appearance to Brahma and Vishnu twice. In I.17, the two of them fight; in I.20, in an earlier *kalpa*, or age, the two of them enter into each other.

27. Linga Purana I.3.10; I.19.12

28. Kalidasa, *Kumarasambhava* VII.44. This is a famous *trimurti* verse, translated here by C. B. Papali and cited by Kurian Mathothu in *The Development of the Concept of Trimurti in Hinduism* (Palai, Kerala, India: St. Paul's Press, 1974).

29. Swami Vijnanananda, trans., *The Srimad Devi Bhagavatam* (Delhi: Munshiram Manoharlal, 1977), pp. 129–30.

30. Ibid., p. 131.

31. *Ishvaragita*, Kurma Purana II.11.112–14.

32. This reference can be found in the *Mahimnastava* (19), W. N. Brown, ed. (Poona: 1965). This and other sources relevant to our topic are cited and discussed in a general way in J. Gonda, *Visnuism and Sivaism* (London: Athlone Press, 1970), chapter 5, "Mutual Relations of the Two Religions."

33. Cited in S. Radhakrishnan, *The Hindu View of Life* (New York: Macmillan Publishing Co., 1975), p. 34.

34. Swami Chidananda, contribution to the discussion of World Council of Churches pre-assembly dialogue, Hong Kong, August 1990.

35. David Broome, contribution to the discussion of World Council of Churches pre-assembly dialogue, Hong Kong, August 1990.

36. Djiniyini Gondarra, *Father You Gave Us the Dreaming* (Darwin: United Church in Australia, 1988).

4. The Faces of God

1. M. K. Gandhi, *The Message of Jesus* (Bombay: Bharatiya Vidya Bhavan, 1964), p. 13.

2. W. H. Auden, "For the Time Being: A Christmas Oratorio," in *Collected Longer Poems* (New York: Random House, 1934), p. 159.

3. Pauline Webb, sermon preached at the opening worship of the World Council of Churches General Assembly, Vancouver, B.C., August 1983.

4. Lesslie Newbigin, "Religious Pluralism and the Uniqueness of Jesus Christ," *International Bulletin of Missionary Research*, 13, no. 2 (April 1989), p. 52.

5. Quoted in Paul Knitter, *No Other Name?* (Maryknoll, N.Y.: Orbis Books, 1985), p. 96.

6. Roger Nicole, "One Door and Only One?" *Wherever* 2 (1979), p. 3. Cited in John Sanders, *No Other Name* (Grand Rapids: Wm. B. Eerdman, 1992), p. 38.

7. Quoted in Gerald H. Anderson, "The Truth of Christian Uniqueness," *International Bulletin of Missionary Research*, 13, no. 2 (April 1989), p. 49.

8. Stanley J. Samartha, "The Cross and the Rainbow, Christ in a Multireligious Culture," in J. Hick and P. Knitter, eds., *The Myth of Christian Uniqueness: Toward a Pluralistic Theology of Religions* (Maryknoll, N.Y.: Orbis Books, 1988), p. 69.

9. Paul Tillich, *Christianity and the Encounter of the World Religions* (New York: Columbia University Press, 1963), p. 81.

10. Wesley Ariarajah, *The Bible and People of Other Faiths*, p. 24.

11. Cited in Henry Chadwick, *The Early Church* (London: Penguin Books, 1967), p. 124.

12. W. H. Auden, "For The Time Being," pp. 183–84.

13. Karl Barth, "The Humanity of God," in Clifford Green, ed., *Karl Barth, Theologian of Freedom* (Minneapolis: Fortress Press, 1991), p. 64.

14. Stanley Samartha, *One Christ—Many Religions: Toward a Revised Christology* (Maryknoll, N.Y.: Orbis Books, 1991), p. 116.

15. Robert Ellsberg, ed., *Gandhi on Christianity* (Maryknoll, N.Y.: Orbis Books, 1991), p. 28.

16. Rabindranath Tagore, *The Complete Poems and Plays of Rabindranath Tagore* (London: Macmillan and Co., Ltd., 1962).

17. See Wilfred Cantwell Smith, *Faith and Belief* (Princeton: Princeton University Press, 1979).

18. Lesslie Newbigin, *The Gospel in a Pluralistic Society* (Grand Rapids: W. B. Eerdman, 1989), p. 101.

19. W. B. Yeats, "The Magi," in *The Collected Poems of W. B. Yeats* (New York: Macmillan, 1933), p. 124.

20. Holgar Kersten, *Jesus Lived in India* (Longmead, England: Element Books Ltd., 1986).

21. Barbara Stoler Miller, trans., *The Bhagavad Gita* (New York: Bantam Books, 1986).

5. The Breath of God

1. Herman Keyserling, *Indian Travel Diary of a Philosopher* (Bombay: Bharatiya Vidya Bhavan, 1969), p. 118.

2. George Khodr, presentation at the World Council of Churches consultation, "Theological Perspectives on Plurality," Baar, Switzerland, January 1991.

3. John V. Taylor, *The Go-Between God* (New York: Oxford University Press, 1979).

4. Donald L. Gelpi, *The Divine Mother: A Trinitarian Theology of the Holy Spirit* (Lanham, Md.: University Press of America, 1984), pp. 7–16.

5. *We Believe in the Holy Spirit: A Report by the Doctrine Commission of the General Synod of the Church of England* (London: Church House Publishing, 1991), pp. 5–6.

6. Brihadaranyaka Upanishad 4.1.

7. Cited in Timothy Ware, ed., *The Art of Prayer: An Orthodox Anthology* (London: Faber and Faber, 1966), p. 198.

8. Cited in E. Kadloubovsky and G. E. H. Palmer, trans., *Writings from the Philokalia on Prayer of the Heart* (London: Faber and Faber, 1962), p. 75.

9. Kallistos Ware, *The Power of the Name* (Oxford: SLG Press, 1974), p. 23.

10. Ibid.

11. I have taken this translation from R. Panikkar, ed., *The Vedic Experience, Mantramanjari* (Berkeley: University of California Press, 1977), p. 36. This anthology, compiled by Panikkar and his associates in Banaras, is something of a Vedic prayer book, compiled for contemporary celebration.

12. See Frits Staal, *Agni: The Vedic Ritual of Fire*, 2 vols. (Berkeley: Asian Humanities Press, 1983). The film *Altar of Fire* (Robert Gardner, Harvard University Film Archives) shows a modern performance of this particular ritual in Kerala.

13. See Victor Turner, *The Ritual Process* (Chicago: Aldine Publishing Company, 1969), chapter 4.

14. For the full text of the two addresses, see Michael Kinnamon, ed., *Signs of the Spirit: Official Report of the Seventh Assembly* (Grand Rapids: Wm. B. Eerdman, 1991).

15. "She Comes Sailing on the Wind," text and music by Gordon Light, Canada, cited in *In Spirit and in Truth: A Worship Book* (Geneva: World Council of Churches, 1991).

16. Patriarch Ignatios IV of the Greek Orthodox Patriarchate of Antioch and All the East, in a sermon at the WCC central committee meeting, Moscow, 16–27 July 1989.

17. Metropolitan George Khodr, in a presentation to the WCC "Theological Consultation on Religious Plurality," in Baar, Switzerland, January 1990.

18. Metropolitan Daniel of Moldavia and Bukovina, responding to questions following his address to the Section II meeting of the Seventh Assembly of the WCC, Canberra, Australia, February 1991.

19. Kinnamon, *Signs of the Spirit*, p. 104.

20. Ibid., p. 116.

21. Krister Stendahl, *Energy for Life* (Geneva: World Council of Churches, 1990).

22. V. K. Subramanian, *Saundaryalahari (Ocean of Divine Beauty of Sankaracarya)* (Delhi: Motilal Banarsidass, 1977), p. 1. I have only roughly followed Subramanian's translation.

23. Rabindranath Tagore, *Collected Poems and Plays of Rabindranath Tagore* (London: Macmillan and Co. Ltd., 1962), p. 33.

24. Ramprasad Sen, *Grace and Mercy in Her Wild Hair*, Leonard Nathan and Clinton Seely, trans. (Boulder, Colo.: Great Eastern, 1982), p. 21.

6. Attention to God

1. Kadloubovsky and Palmer, *Writings from the Philokalia*, p. 75.

2. Bishop Ignatii, in Ware, *The Art of Prayer,* p. 104.

3. Thomas Merton, *Thoughts in Solitude* (New York: Image Books, 1968), p. 47.

4. Anguttara Nikaya 3.38–39.

5. See Barbara Stoler Miller, trans., *The Bhagavad-Gita* (New York: Bantam Books, 1986), 4.18.

6. See Thomas Merton, *Contemplation in a World of Action* (New York: Image Books, 1973), especially chapter 9, "Contemplation in a World of Action."

7. In William H. Shannon, ed., *The Hidden Ground of Love: The Letters of Thomas Merton on Religious Experience and Social Concerns* (New York: Farrar, Straus, and Giroux, 1985), p. 115.

8. Naomi Burton, Brother Patrick, Hart, and James Laughlin, eds., *The Asian Journals of Thomas Merton* (New York: New Directions Books, 1973), p. 313.

9. See Bernard McGinn et. al., eds., *Christian Spirituality: Origins to the Twelfth Century*, The World Spirituality Series, vol. 16 (New York: Crossroads, 1985), p. xiii. The *World Spirituality* Series is edited by Ewert Cousins and will finally include twenty-five volumes.

10. Heinrich Zimmer, *The Philosophies of India* (Princeton: Princeton University Press, 1951), p. 1.

11. Swami Vivekananda, *The Complete Works of Swami Vivekananda* (Calcutta: Advaita Ashrama, 1960), vol. 3, p. 277.

12. Swami Vivekananda, *The Vedanta Philosophy* (Cambridge: Graduate Philosophical Society, 1896).

13. Evelyn Underhill, "God Is the Interesting Thing," in *Christian Century*, 31 October 1990, p. 998.

14. Anguttara Nikaya 1.18, found in Walpola Rahula, *What the Buddha Taught* (New York: Grove Press, 1974).

15. *The Cloud of Unknowing* (Baltimore: Penguin Books, 1973), p. 61.

16. Ibid., p. 92.

17. *The Way of a Pilgrim and The Pilgrim Continues His Way*, Helen Bacovcin, trans., (New York: Doubleday Image Books, 1978), p. 19.

18. Robinson, *Honest to God*, p. 93.

19. William Johnston, *The Still Point: Reflections on Zen and Christian Mysticism* (New York: Fordham University Press, 1970), p. xiv.

20. Anthony de Mello, *Sadhana: A Way to God* (St. Louis: Institute of Jesuit Sources, 1979).

21. John Main, *The Present Christ: Further Steps in Meditation* (London: Darton, Longman, and Todd, 1985). These simple instructions are at the very beginning of his book, before the first chapter begins.

22. Most of the formal talks are contained in Tosh Arai and Wesley Ariarajah, eds., *Spirituality in Interfaith Dialogue* (Geneva: World Council of Churches, 1989). In what follows, where a reference is not given, the citation is from the taped transcript of the discussion.

23. Michael Como, "Listening to the Silence, Through Zen and Taize," in *Spirituality in Interfaith Dialogue*, pp. 4–5.

24. The *Bulletin of the North American Board for East-West Dialogue* is now published from the Abbey of Gethsemani, 3642 Monks Road, Trappist, Kentucky 40051-6102.

25. C. Murray Rogers, "On the Pilgrim Path," in *Spirituality in Interfaith Dialogue*, p. 14.

26. Ibid., pp. 14–15.

27. Yves Raguin, "Deepening our Understanding of Spirituality," in *Spirituality in Interfaith Dialogue*, p. 83.

28. Ibid., pp. 83–84.

29. Bettina Bäumer, "A Journey with the Unknown," in *Spirituality in Interfaith Dialogue*, p. 37.

30. Ibid., p. 38.

31. Ibid., p. 38.

32. Ibid., p. 39.

7. "Is Our God Listening?"

1. Chaim Potok, *The Book of Lights* (New York: Ballantine Books, 1981), pp. 261–62.

2. Harvey Cox, *The Secular City* (New York: Macmillan, 1966), p. 1.

3. Knitter, *No Other Name?*, pp. 78–79.

4. *Report of the Naramata Consultation on Interfaith Dialogue: Faithfulness in a Pluralistic World* (Division of World Outreach, United Church of Canada, May, 1985), p. 2.

5. Knitter, *No Other Name?*

6. John Sanders, *No Other Name.*

7. Knitter, *No Other Name?*, p. 122.

8. "The Bull *Unam Sanctam*, 1302," in J. F. Clarkson et al., eds., *The Church Teaches* (St. Louis: B. Herder Book Co., 1955), pp. 73–75.

9. See "Letter of the Holy Office to Archbishop Cushing of Boston, 1949," in Clarkson et al., *The Church Teaches*, pp. 118–21. A treatment of the controversy may be found in George B. Pepper, *The Boston Heresy Case in View of the Secularization of Religion* (Lewiston, Me.: Edwin Mellen Press, 1988).

10. Quoted and translated from Luther's collected works by Kenneth Cracknell, *Towards a New Relationship: Christians and People of Other Faiths* (London: Epworth Press, 1986), p. 11.

11. Karl Barth, *Church Dogmatics* (Edinburgh: T.&T. Clark, 1956), vol. 1, part 2, pp.

299–300. The entirety of section 17, "The Revelation of God as the Abolition of Religion," concerns this matter.

12. Gerald H. Anderson, "Religion as a Problem for the Christian Mission," in D. G. Dawe and J. B. Carman, eds., *Christian Faith in a Religiously Plural World* (Maryknoll, N.Y.: Orbis Books, 1980), p. 114.

13. Hendrik Kraemer, *The Christian Message in a Non-Christian World* (London: Edinburgh House Press, 1938), p. 135.

14. Hendrik Kraemer, "Continuity or Discontinuity," in Paton, *The Authority of the Faith*, pp. 13–14.

15. Ibid., p. 21.

16. Bruce Lawrence argues effectively that "because modernity is global, so is fundamentalism," in the introduction to his book *Defenders of God* (San Francisco: Harper and Row, 1989).

17. Cited in William Kittredge and Annick Smith, eds., *The Last Best Place: A Montana Anthology* (Helena: Montana Historical Society, 1991), p. 26.

18. W. H. Lewis, ed., *The Letters of C. S. Lewis* (New York: Harcourt Brace Jovanovich, 1966), p. 247.

19. John Wesley, "On Living without God," in *The Works of John Wesley*, 3rd edition (Peabody, Mass.: Hendrickson, 1986), vol. 7, 353.

20. *New Catholic Encyclopedia* (Washington, D.C.: Catholic University of America Press, 1967), vol. 5, p. 768.

21. *Nostra Aetate*, in Austin P. Flannery, ed., *Documents of Vatican II* (Grand Rapids: Eerdman Publishing Co., 1975), pp. 738–42.

22. Gerald A. McCool, ed., *A Rahner Reader* (New York: Seabury Press, 1975), p. 218. See especially his selections in chapter 10 on "Anonymous Christians" and "Christianity and Non-Christian Religions." For discussion see also Paul Knitter in *No Other Name?*, Alan Race in *Christians and Religious Pluralism*, and Gavin D'Costa in *Theology and Religious Pluralism*, all of whom examine Rahner's position as an exemplar of the inclusivist position.

23. Knitter, *No Other Name?*, p. 128.

24. In David Gill, ed., *Gathered for Life: Official Report of the VI Assembly of the WCC* (Geneva: World Council of Churches, 1983), p. 40.

25. The "Baar Statement" is printed in full in S. Wesley Ariarajah, "Theological Perspectives on Plurality," *Current Dialogue*, June 1990, pp. 2–7.

26. The report of the consultation, edited by Allan R. Brockway, is published as *The Meaning of Life: A Multifaith Consultation in Preparation for the Sixth Assembly of the World Council of Churches* (Geneva: World Council of Churches, 1983).

27. John Hick, *God Has Many Names* (Philadelphia: Westminister Press, 1980), p. 71.

28. M. K. Gandhi, *All Religions are True*, ed. Anand T. Hingorani (Bombay: Bharatiya Vidya Bhavan, 1962), p. 25.

29. Dean Kleiman, "Immigrants Encountering Choice Between Friendship and Isolation," in the *New York Times*, 24 December 1982, cited by E. Allen Richardson at the outset of his superb book *Strangers in this Land* (New York: Pilgrim Press, 1988).

30. Elizabeth Spelman, *Inessential Woman: Problems of Exclusion in Feminist Thought* (Boston: Beacon Press, 1988), p. 182.

31. Ibid., p. 184.

32. Abraham Joshua Heschel, "No Religion is an Island," in F. E. Talmadge, ed., *Disputation and Dialogue: Readings in Jewish-Christian Encounters* (New York: KTAV Publishing, 1975), p. 345.

33. Wilfred Cantwell Smith, *The Faith of Other Men* (New York: New American Library, 1965), p. 92.

8. The Imagined Community

1. Barrows, *The World's Parliament of Religions*, vol. 2, p. 1560.

2. S. Radhakrishnan, *Eastern Religions and Western Thought* (New York: Oxford University Press, 1959), p. 2.

3. Ibid., pp. vii–viii.

4. World Development Forum, cited in *Encyclopedia Britannica Book of the Year, 1990*.

5. W. C. Smith, "Objectivity and the Humane Sciences," in *Religious Diversity: Essays by Wilfred Cantwell Smith*, ed. W. G. Oxtoby (New York: Harper & Row, 1976), p. 178.

6. Ibid.

7. M. K. Gandhi, *Hind Swaraj*, new edition (Ahmedabad, India: Navjivan Publishing House, 1938), p. 38.

8. M. K. Gandhi, *The Message of Jesus Christ* (Bombay: Bharatiya Vidya Bhavan, 1964), p. 24.

9. M. K. Gandhi, *Ashram Observances in Action* (Ahmedabad, India: Navjivan Publishing House, 1955), p. 8.

10. Ibid., p. 24.

11. Quoted in Louis Fischer, *The Life of Mahatma Gandhi* (New York: Harper and Brothers Collier Books, 1950), pp. 270–71.

12. E. Stanley Jones, *Mahatma Gandhi: An Interpretation*, quoted in I. Jesudasan, *A Gandhian Theology of Liberation* (Maryknoll, N.Y.: Orbis Books, 1984), p. 133.

13. Sudarshan Kapur, *Raising Up a Prophet* (Boston: Beacon Press, 1992). Kapur documents the coverage of Gandhi in the African-American press from the 1920s on.

14. Martin Luther King, Jr., *Stride Toward Freedom* (New York: Harper and Brothers, 1958), p. 85.

15. See W. C. Smith, "Participation: The Changing Christian Role in Other Cultures," in *Religious Diversity*, pp. 118–37.

16. Murray Rogers, "On the Pilgrim Path" in *Spirituality in Interfaith Dialogue*, p. 15.

17. See *The Faith of Other Men*, p. 92.

18. Abraham Joshua Heschel, "No Religion is an Island," in Harold Kasimow and Byron L. Sherwin, eds., *No Religion is an Island: Abraham Joshua Heschel and Interreligious Dialogue* (Maryknoll, N.Y.: Orbis Books, 1991), p. 11.

19. Rev. Jenkin Lloyd Jones, quoted in Marcus Braybrooke, *Pilgrimage of Hope: One Hundred Years of Global Interfaith Dialogue* (London: SCM Press, 1992), p. 25. I am indebted to the comprehensive work of Marcus Braybrook on the early history of the various interreligious movements.

20. Samartha, *One Christ—Mary Religions*, p. 3.

21. *The Meaning of Life: A Multifaith Consultation* (Geneva: World Council of Churches, 1983), pp. 2–3.

22. Ibid.

23. Barrows, *The World's Parliament of Religions*, vol. 1, pp. 72–79.

24. M. K. Gandhi, *Young India*, 2 September 1926.

25. Heschel, "No Religion is an Island," p. 6.

26. Kenneth Cracknell, ed., *Religious Identities in a Multi-Faith World*. Report of a multi-faith dialogue organized by the dialogue subunit of the WCC, New Delhi, November 1987 (Geneva: WCC, 1988). The citations are from the conference discussion.

27. See Diana L. Eck and Devaki Jain, eds., *Speaking of Faith: Global Perspectives on Women, Religion, and Social Change* (Philadelphia: New Society, 1985) for the proceedings of such a women's dialogue at Harvard; the Women in Interfaith Dialogue meeting called by the World Council of Churches in Toronto (1988) was made into a series of eight hour-long television programs, called *Faithful Women*, by the National Film Board of Canada.

28. Arun Shourie, *Religion in Politics* (New Delhi: Roli Books International, 1987), p. 21.

29. "A Public Declaration To the Tribal Councils and Traditional Spiritual Leaders of the Indian and Eskimo Peoples of the Pacific Northwest," *The NARF Legal Review*, Winter 1988.

30. Erik Erikson, *Gandhi's Truth* (New York: W.W. Norton, 1969), p. 251.

31. Benedict Anderson, *Imagined Communities* (London: Verso, 1983), p. 6.

32. Martin Luther King, Jr., *Where Do We Go from Here: Chaos or Community?* (Boston: Beacon Press, 1967), p. 167.

33. Ibid., p. 181.

34. Ibid., p. 190.

Selected Readings

Abhishiktananda, Swami [Dom Henri Le Saux]. *Hindu-Christian Meeting Point*. Bangalore: Christian Institute for the Study of Religion and Society, 1969.

Anderson, Benedict. *Imagined Communities*. London: Verso, 1983.

Arai, Tosh, and Wesley Ariarajah, eds. *Spirituality in Interfaith Dialogue*. Geneva: WCC, 1989.

Ariarajah, Wesley. *The Bible and People of Other Faiths*. Geneva: WCC, 1985.

———. *Hindus and Christians: A Century of Protestant Ecumenical Thought*. Grand Rapids, Mich.: William B. Eerdman, 1991.

Auden, W. H. *Collected Longer Poems*. New York: Random House, 1934.

Bacovin, Helen, trans. *The Way of a Pilgrim and The Pilgrim Continues His Way*. Garden City: Image Books, 1978.

Barrows, John Henry, ed. *The World's Parliament of Religions*. 2 vols. Chicago: Parliament Publishing Company, 1893.

Barth, Karl. *Church Dogmatics*. Edinburgh: T. & T. Clark, 1956.

Berger, Peter. *The Heretical Imperative*. Garden City: Doubleday, 1979.

Braybrooke, Marcus. *Pilgrimage of Hope: One Hundred Years of Global Interfaith Dialogue*. London: SCM Press, 1992.

Brockway, Allan R., and J. Paul Rajashekar. *New Religious Movements and the Churches*. Geneva: WCC, 1987.

Buber, Martin. *I and Thou*. New York: Charles Scribner's Sons, 1958.

Burlingame, Merrill G. *Gallatin County's Heritage: A Report of Progress, 1805–1976*. Bozeman, Mont.: Gallatin County Bicentennial Committee, 1976.

Burton, Naomi, Patrick Hart, and James Laughlin, eds. *The Asian Journal of Thomas Merton*. New York: New Directions, 1973.

Camps, Arnulf. *Partners in Dialogue: Christianity and Other World Religions*. Maryknoll, N.Y.: Orbis, 1983.

Carman, John B. *The Theology of Ramanuja*. New Haven: Yale University Press, 1974.

Castro, Emilio, ed. *To the Wind of God's Spirit: Reflections on the Canberra Theme*. Geneva: WCC, 1990.

Chadwick, Henry. *The Early Church*. London: Penguin Books, 1967.

Chen, Jack. *The Chinese of America*. San Francisco: Harper and Row, 1980.

Clarkson, J. F., ed. *The Church Teaches*. St. Louis: B. Herder Book Co., 1955.

The Cloud of Unknowing. Baltimore: Penguin Books, 1973.

Cobb, John B., Jr. *Beyond Dialogue: Toward a Mutual Transformation of Buddhism and Christianity*. Philadelphia: Fortress Press, 1982.

———. *Christ in a Pluralistic Age*. Philadelphia: Westminister, 1975.

Cox, Harvey. *Many Mansions*. Boston: Beacon Press, 1988.

———. *The Secular City*. New York: Macmillan, 1966.

Cracknell, Kenneth. *Towards a New Relationship: Christians and People of Other Faith*. London: Epworth Press, 1986.

Cracknell, Kenneth, and Christopher Lamb. *Theology on Full Alert*. London: British Council of Churches, 1986.

Cragg, Kenneth. *The Christ and the Faiths*. Philadelphia: Westminster, 1986.

Dawe, D. G., and J. B. Carman, eds. *Christian Faith in a Religiously Plural World*. Maryknoll, N.Y.: Orbis, 1978.

D'Costa, Gavin. *Theology and Religious Pluralism*. Oxford: Basil Blackwell, 1986.

———, ed. *Christian Uniqueness Reconsidered*. Maryknoll, N.Y.: Orbis, 1990.

de Mello, Anthony. *Sadhana: A Way to God*. St. Louis: Institute of Jesuit Sources, 1979.

Doctrine Commission of the General Synod of the Church of England. *We Believe in the Holy Spirit*. London: Church House Publishing, 1991.

Dupuis, Jacques. *Jesus Christ at the Encounter of World Religions*. Maryknoll, N.Y.: Orbis, 1989.

Eck, Diana L. "Darsana: Hinduism and Incarnational Theology." *Harvard Divinity Bulletin* 17, no. 2 (1986).

———. *Darsan: Seeing the Divine Image in India*. Chambersberg, Penn.: Anima Press, 1981.

———. "Dialogue in the Oikoumene." *The Ecumenical Review*, 1984.

———. "Interreligious Dialogue as a Christian Ecumenical Concern." *The Ecumenical Review* 37, no. 4 (1984).

———. "J. Krishnamurti: The Pathless Way." *Forum for Correspondence and Contact* 1, no. 2 (1968).

———. "The Manyness of God." Kathryn Fraser Mackay Lecture. St. Lawrence University, Canton, New York, 1985.

————. "Moderator's Report." Working Group on Dialogue: Themes from New Delhi, "Religious Identity in a Multi-Religious Society," and Kyoto, "Spirituality in Interfaith Dialogue." *Current Dialogue* 14 (1988).

————. "Multi-traditional Faith: A Personal View of Christians in Dialogue with People of Other Religious Traditions." Report from WCC Theological Consultation in Chiang Mai, Thailand. *Bulletin of the Center for the Study of World Religions*, Winter 1978 and Spring 1978.

————. "Oikoumene in the Eighties." *Harvard Divinity Bulletin* 14, no. 1 (1983).

————. "On the Field of Dharma: A Christian Understanding of the Bhagavad Gita." In *Dialogue in Community: Essays in Inter-Religious Relationship*. Edited by C. D. Jathanna. Mangalore: Karnataka Theological Research Institute, 1982.

————. "The Perspective of Pluralism in Theological Education." In *Ministerial Formation in a Multi-Faith Milieu: Implications of Interfaith Dialogue for Theological Education*. Edited by S. Amirtham and S. Wesley Ariarajah. Geneva: World Council of Churches, 1986.

————. "The Religions and Tambaram: 1938 and 1988." *International Review of Mission* 78, no. 307 (1988).

————. "What Do We Mean by 'Dialogue'?" *Current Dialogue* 11 (1986).

Eck, Diana L., and Devaki Jain, eds. *Speaking of Faith: Global Perspectives of Women, Religion, and Social Change*. Philadelphia: New Society, 1985.

————. "What Do We Mean by 'Dialogue'?" *Current Dialogue* 11 (1986).

Ellsberg, Robert, ed. *Gandhi on Christianity*. Maryknoll, N.Y.: Orbis, 1991.

Erikson, Erik H. *Gandhi's Truth*. New York: W. W. Norton, 1969.

Farquhar, J. N. *The Crown of Hinduism*. London: Oxford University Press, 1913.

Fields, Rick. *How the Swans Came to the Lake*. Boston: Shambhala Press, 1986.

Fischer, Louis. *The Life of Mahatma Gandhi*. New York: Harper and Brothers Collier Books, 1950.

Flannery, Austin P., ed. *Documents of Vatican II*. Grand Rapids, Mich.: William B. Eerdman, 1975.

Gandhi, M. K. *Ashram Observances in Action*. Ahmedabad, India: Navjivan Publishing House, 1955.

————. *Hind Swaraj*. Ahmedabad, India: Navjivan Publishing House, 1938.

————. *The Message of Jesus*. Bombay: Bharatiya Vidya Bhavan, 1964.

Gelpi, Donald L. *The Divine Mother: A Trinitarian Theology of the Holy Spirit*. Lanham, Md.: University Press of America.

Gill, David, ed. *Gathered for Life: Official Report of the Sixth Assembly of the World Council of Churches*. Geneva: WCC, 1983.

Goldstein, Joseph. *The Experience of Insight*. Boston: Shambhala Press, 1987.

Goldstein, Joseph, and Jack Kornfield. *Seeking the Heart of Wisdom*. Boston: Shambhala Press, 1987.

Green, Clifford, ed. *Karl Barth, Theologian of Freedom*. Minneapolis: Fortress Press, 1991.

Halbfass, Wilhelm. *India and Europe: An Essay in Understanding*. Albany: State University of New York Press, 1988.

Heschel, Abraham Joshua. "No Religion Is an Island." In *No Religion Is an Island*. Edited by Harold Kasimow and Byron L. Sherwin. Maryknoll, N.Y.: Orbis, 1991.

Hick, John, and Paul F. Knitter, eds. *The Myth of Christian Uniqueness*. Maryknoll, N.Y.: Orbis, 1987.

Hick, John. *An Interpretation of Religion*. New Haven: Yale University Press, 1989.

————. *God and the Universe of Faiths*. New York: St. Martin's Press, 1973.

————. *God Has Many Names*. London: Macmillan, 1980.

Hocking, W. E. *The Coming World Civilization*. New York: Harper and Row, 1956.

————. *Re-Thinking Mission: A Layman's Inquiry After 100 Years*. New York: Harper and Row, 1932.

Hume, Robert E. *The Thirteen Principal Upanishads*. Oxford: Oxford University Press, 1931.

Interfaith Consultative Group, Church of England. *Multi-Faith Worship?* London: Church House Publishing, 1992.

International Missionary Council. *The Authority of the Faith*. New York: IMC, 1939.

————. *Jerusalem Meeting Report*. Oxford: Oxford University Press, 1928.

Jathanna, C. D., ed. *Dialogue in Community: Essays in Honour of S. J. Samartha*. Mangalore: Karnataka Theological Research Institute, 1982.

Jenson, Joan. *Passage from India: Asian Indians in North America*. Ann Arbor: University of Michigan Press, 1988.

Johnston, William. *The Still Point: Reflections on Zen and Christian Mysticism*. New York: Fordham University Press, 1970.

Kadloubovsky, E., and G. E. H. Palmer, trans. *Writings from the Philokalia on Prayer of the Heart*. London: Faber and Faber, 1962.

Kapur, Sudarshan. *Raising Up a Prophet*. Boston: Beacon Press, 1992.

Kaufman, Gordon D. *An Essay on Theological Method*. Missoula, Mont.: Scholars Press, 1975.

————. *The Theological Imagination: Constructing the Concept of God*. Philadelphia: Westminister Press, 1981.

Keeting, Virginia, ed. *Dungeness: The Lure of a River*. Port Angeles, Wash.: Olympic Printers, 1976.

Kennedy, John F. *A Nation of Immigrants*. New York: Harper and Row, 1964.

Keyserling, Herman. *Indian Travel Diary of a Philosopher*. Bombay: Bharatiya Vidya Bhavan, 1969.

Kimball, Charles. *Striving Together: A Way Forward in Christian-Muslim Relations*. Maryknoll, N.Y.: Orbis, 1991.

King, Martin Luther, Jr. *Stride toward Freedom*. New York: Harper and Brothers, 1958.

―――. *Where Do We Go From Here? Chaos or Community*. Boston: Beacon Press, 1967.

Kinnamon, Michael, ed. *Signs of the Spirit: Official Report of the Seventh Assembly of the World Council of Churches*. Grand Rapids, Mich.: William B. Eerdman, 1991.

Kittredge, William, and Annick Smith, eds. *The Last Best Place: A Montana Anthology*. Helena: Montana Historical Society, 1991.

Knitter, Paul. *No Other Name?: A Critical Survey of Christian Attitudes Toward the World Religions*. Maryknoll, N.Y.: Orbis, 1985.

Kraemer, Hendrick. *The Christian Message in a Non-Christian World*. London: Edinburgh House Press, 1938.

Krishnamurti, J. *The First and Last Freedom*. New York: Harper and Row, 1954.

―――. *Krishnamurti's Journal*. New York: Harper and Row, 1982.

―――. *Talks and Dialogues*. New York: Avon Books, 1970.

Kung, Hans. *Christianity and the World's Religions*. New York: Doubleday, 1986.

―――. "The World Religions in God's Plan of Salvation." In *Christian Revelation and World Religions*. Edited by Joseph Neuner. London: Burns & Oates, 1967.

Lawrence, Bruce. *Defenders of God*. San Francisco: Harper and Row, 1989.

Lind, Robert W. *Brother Van: Montana Pioneer Circuit Rider*. Helena: Falcon Press, 1992.

Lochhead, David. *The Dialogical Imperative: A Christian Reflection on Interfaith Encounter*. Maryknoll, N.Y.: Orbis, 1988.

Lossky, Nicholas et at., eds. *Dictionary of the Ecumenical Movement*. Geneva: WCC, 1991.

Main, John. *The Present Christ: Further Steps in Meditation*. London: Darton, Longman, and Todd, 1985.

McCool, Gerald A., ed. *A Rahner Reader*. New York: Seabury Press, 1975.

Mehta, J. L. *India and the West: The Problem of Understanding*. Chico, Calif.: Scholars Press, 1985.

―――. *Philosophy and Religion: Essays in Interpretation*. New Delhi: Munshiram Manoharlal, 1990.

Merton, Thomas. *Contemplation in a World of Action*. New York: Image Books, 1973.

―――. *Mystics and Zen Masters*. New York: Farrar, Straus, and Giroux, 1967.

―――. *Thoughts in Solitude*. New York: Image Books, 1968.

―――. *Zen and the Birds of Appetite*. New York: New Directions, 1969.

Miller, Barbara Stoler, trans. *The Bhagavad Gita*. New York: Bantam Books, 1986.

Newbigin, Lesslie. *The Gospel in a Pluralistic Society*. Grand Rapids, Mich.: William B. Eerdman, 1989.

Niebel, Esther C. *A Century of Service: History of the First Methodist Church*. Bozeman, Mont.: First Methodist Church, 1966.

Oxtoby, Willard G., ed. *Religious Diversity: Essays by Wilfred Cantwell Smith*. New York: Harper and Row, 1976.

Panikkar, Raimundo. *The Intra-religious Dialogue*. New York: Paulist Press, 1978.

————. *The Unknown Christ of Hinduism*. Maryknoll, N.Y.: Orbis, 1981.

————. *The Vedic Experience, Mantramanjari*. Berkeley: University of California Press, 1977.

Race, Alan. *Christians and Religious Pluralism: Patterns in the Christian Theology of Religions*. Maryknoll, N.Y.: Orbis, 1982.

Radhakrishnan, S. *Eastern Religions and Western Thought*. New York: Oxford University Press, 1959.

————. *The Hindu View of Life*. New York: Macmillan Publishing Co., Inc., 1975.

Rahner, Karl. "Anonymous Christianity and the Missionary Task of the Church." In *Theological Investigations* 12, New York: Seabury, 1966.

————. "Christianity and the Non-Christian Religions." In *Theological Investigations* 5.

————. "Observations on the Problem of the 'Anonymous Christian.'" In *Theological Investigations* 14, 1976.

————. "Reflections on Dialogue within a Pluralistic Society." In *Theological Investigations* 6, 1969.

Robinson, John A. T. *Honest to God*. Philadelphia: Westminster Press, 1963.

————. *Truth Is Two-Eyed*. Philadelphia: Westminster Press, 1980.

Samartha, Stanley. *The Courage for Dialogue*. Maryknoll, N.Y.: Orbis, 1981.

————, ed. *Faith in the Midst of Faiths*. Geneva: World Council of Churches, 1977.

————. *The Hindu Response to the Unbound Christ: Toward a Christology in India*. Bangalore: Christian Institute for the Study of Religion and Society, 1974.

————. *One Christ — Many Religions*. Maryknoll, N.Y.: Orbis, 1991.

Seager, Richard Hughes, ed. *The Dawn of Religious Pluralism*. Chicago: Open Court, 1993.

Seager, Richard Hughes. "The World's Parliament of Religions, Chicago, Illinois, 1893: America's Coming of Age." Harvard University, doctoral dissertation, 1986.

Sen, Ramprasad. *Grace and Mercy in Her Wild Hair*. Translated by Leonard Nathan and Clinton Seely. Boulder, Colo.: Great Eastern, 1982.

Shannon, William H., ed. *The Hidden Ground of Love: The Letters of Thomas Merton on Religious Experience and Social Concerns*. New York: Farrar, Straus, and Giroux, 1985.

Smith, W. C. *Faith and Belief*. Princeton, N.J.: Princeton University Press, 1979.

————. *The Faith of Other Men*. New York: Mentor Books, 1962.

————. *The Meaning and End of Religion*. New York: Harper and Row, 1962.

————. *Towards a World Theology: Faith and the Comparative History of Religion*. Philadelphia: Westminister Press, 1981.

Spelman, Elizabeth. *Inessential Woman: Problems of Exclusion in Feminist Thought*. Boston: Beacon Press, 1988.

Stendahl, Krister. *Energy for Life*. Geneva: WCC Risk Series, 1990.

Swartout, Robert R., Jr., and Harry W. Fritz, eds. *Montana Heritage: An Anthology of Historical Essays*. Helena, Mont.: Montana Historical Society, 1992.

Swearer, Donald. *Dialogue: The Key to Understanding Other Religions*. Philadelphia: Westminster Press, 1977.

Tagore, Rabindranath. *The Complete Poems and Plays of Rabindranath Tagore*. London: Macmillan and Co., Ltd., 1962.

Takaki, Ronald. *Strangers from a Different Shore: A History of Asian Americans*. New York: Viking Penguin, 1989.

Taylor, John V. *The Go-Between God*. New York: Oxford University Press, 1979.

Tillich, Paul. *Christianity and the Encounter of the World Religions*. New York: Columbia University, 1963.

————. *The Shaking of the Foundations*. New York: Charles Scribner's Sons, 1948.

Toynbee, Arnold. *An Historian's Approach to Religion*. London: Oxford University Press, 1959.

Troeltsch, Ernst. *The Absoluteness of Christianity and the History of Religions*. Richmond, Va.: John Knox, 1971.

Tulpule, Shakar Gopal. *The Divine Name in the Indian Tradition*. New Delhi: Indus Publishing Company, 1991.

Turner, Frederick Jackson. *The Frontier in American History*. Huntington, N.Y.: Robert E. Frieger, 1976.

Vivekananda, Swami. *The Complete Works of Swami Vivekananda*. Calcutta: Advaita Ashrama, 1960.

————. *The Vedanta Philosophy*. Cambridge: Graduate Philosophical Society, 1896.

Ware, Timothy, ed. *The Art of Prayer: An Orthodox Anthology*. London: Faber and Faber, 1966.

WCC. *Guidelines on Dialogue with People of Living Faiths and Ideologies*. 4th printing, revised. Geneva: WCC, 1990.

————. *The Meaning of Life: A Multifaith Consultation*. Geneva: WCC, 1983. (Excerpts from the Mauritius Consultation in 1983.)

————. *My Neighbour's Faith—and Mine: Theological Discoveries through Interfaith Dialogue*. Geneva: WCC, 1986.

Wilson, Frederick R., ed. *The San Antonio Report: Your Will Be Done, Mission in Christ's Way*. Geneva: WCC, 1990.

Zaehner, R. C., trans. *Hindu Scriptures*. London: Everyman's Library, 1966.

Zimmer, Heinrich. *The Philosophies of India*. Princeton, N.J.: Princeton University Press, 1951.

Index